D0194548

A Practical Guide to

Information Systems
Strategic Planning

A Practical Guide to

Information Systems
Strategic Planning

By

Anita Cassidy

S^t_L

St. Lucie Press
Boca Raton   Boston   London   New York   Washington, D.C.

Library of Congress Cataloging-in-Publication Data

Cassidy, Anita
   A practical guide to information systems strategic planning / by
Anita Cassidy.
         p. cm.
   Includes bibliographical references and index.
   ISBN 1-57444-133-7 (alk. paper)
     1. Information technology – Management – Planning. 2. Strategic
planning. I. Title.
   HD30.2.C395 1998
   658.4′ 038 — dc21

                                      98-13359
                                       CIP

No claim to original U.S. Government works
International Standard Book Number 1-57444-133-7
Library of Congress Card Number   98-13359
Printed in the United States of America   2 3 4 5 6 7 8 9 0
Printed on acid-free paper

About the Author

Anita Cassidy has over 20 years of experience in Information Systems. She is Vice President and Chief Information Officer at a worldwide manufacturing company. She has been President and founder of a consulting practice, Strategic Computing Directions Incorporated, in Minneapolis, Minnesota, which specialized in assisting companies through the information systems strategic planning process. She has also been Director of Information Systems at a medical device manufacturing company and several divisions of a Fortune 100 instrument engineering and manufacturing company, and has completed the information systems strategic planning process many times in a variety of organizations and divisions. She has assisted complex worldwide organizations in examining their information systems direction, and in selecting and implementing new state-of-the-art directions for their business applications systems.

Ms. Cassidy received a business degree from St. Cloud State University, as well as a Bachelor of Science degree from the University of Minnesota.

About the Author

Acknowledgments

Foremost, I would like to thank my husband, Dan, for his encouragement, advice, and support while I was writing this book. I would also like to thank my sons, Mike and Ryan, for their patience while the book was in progress. Without the support of my family and friends, this book would not have been possible.

I would also like to thank all those with whom I have worked over the years, from both the business and information systems areas. They have given me continuous support and ideas as I have developed the strategic planning process presented in this book.

Contents

Preface   xiii

1   Getting Started 1
- Purpose of Information Systems Strategic Planning   1
  - Effective Management of an Expensive and Critical
    Asset to the Organization   3
  - Improving Communication Between the Business and
    Information Systems Organizations   4
  - Linking the Information Systems Direction to the
    Business Direction   4
  - Planning the Flow of Information and Processes   6
  - Efficiently and Effectively Allocating Information
    Systems Resources   7
  - Reducing the Time and Expense of the Information
    Systems Life Cycle   7
- Involvement of the Organization   9
  - Information Systems Steering Committee   11
  - Executive Management   14
  - Information Systems Organization   15
  - Vendor Review and Implementation Team   15
- Conclusion   16

2   The Planning Process 17
- Planning Components   17
- Planning Process   19

- Phase 1: Conceptual Business Level   21
- Phase 2: Detailed Business Analysis   22
- Phase 3: Conceptual Information Systems Plan and Vision   23
- Phase 4: Detailed Information Systems Recommendation   24
- Plan Contents   25
- Phase 1 of the Planning Process: Conceptual Business Level   27
  - Purpose   29
  - Process   30
  - Scope   30
- Conclusion   32

3   Understanding the Business Direction..33
- Document High-Level Business Direction   34
- Executive Management Interviews   36
- Summarize and Present the Business Direction   39
- Environmental Requirements   41
- External Requirements   41
- Operating Vision   44
- Phase 2 of the Planning Process: Detailed Business Analysis   46
  - Information Needs   47
  - Business Processes   52
  - Business Requirements   57
- Conclusion   59

4   Understanding and Communicating the Current Information Systems Situation..61
- Phase 3 of the Planning Process: Conceptual IS Plan and Vision   61
- Current Situation   63
- Information Systems Environment   63
  - Business Application Environment   65
  - PC and Local Area Network (LAN) Environment   68
  - Network   70
- Organizational Structure   72
- Expenditures   79
- Backlog   81
- Other Locations   86
- Document Current IS Situation   86
- Industry Trends   87

■ Competitor Profiles   90
■ Conclusion   94

**5 Determining the High-Level Direction
of Information Systems** 95
■ Mission   97
■ Vision   98
■ Strategic Objectives   100
■ Strategies   102
   • Custom versus Packaged Business Applications   103
■ Information Systems and Business Goals   110
■ Computing Architecture   120
■ Information Architecture   126
■ Policies and Responsibilities   130
■ Annual Objectives   132
■ Information Systems Service Architecture   135
■ Conclusion   140

**6 Determining the Gap Between Your Current Situation
and Where You Want to Be in the Future** 143
■ Phase 4 of the Planning Process: Option Analysis
   and Action Plan   143
■ Business Operating Vision Assessment   143
■ Environmental Requirements Assessment   144
■ Information Needs Assessment   146
■ External Requirements Assessment   146
■ Business Application Assessment   146
■ Business Requirements Assessment   150
■ Technical Computing Architecture Assessment   151
■ Service Architecture Assessment   152
■ Summary of the Gap   153
■ Conclusion   157

7 Determining How to Get to Where You Want to Be 159
■ Option Identification   160
■ Information Gathering, Request for Quote   162
■ RFQ Response Review   166
■ Option Analysis   171
■ Recommendation   177
■ ROI Analysis   178

■ Conclusion   181

8 Selling the Recommendation 183
   ■ Management Overview   183
   ■ Plan Document   187
   ■ Executive Committee Presentation   187

9 What to Do Next 197
   ■ Vendor Review and Implementation Team   197
   ■ Project Plan   198
   ■ Project Kick-Off Meeting   203
   ■ Vendor Review   204
     • Script   204
     • Data Package   205
     • Key Requirements   205
     • Rating Methodology   205
     • Demonstration Guidelines for the Vendor   205
     • Demonstration Guidelines for Team Participants   205
     • Vendor Introduction to Company   207
   ■ Vendor Selection   208
   ■ Recommendation   208
   ■ Risk Management   209

Appendix 213
   1. Business Application Description   215
   2. Technology Description   227
   3. Stages of Team Development   231
   4. Detailed Script   239
   5. Key Requirements   271

Index 277

Preface

Many organizations today are experiencing continually increasing information systems costs. In addition to increasing costs, organizations are finding their information systems to be a bottleneck to business improvements and growth. These organizations are taking a close look at their information systems and asking basic yet tough questions, such as:

- Are we obtaining true value from the investments made in information systems?
- How well are our current information systems applications meeting our business needs today?
- Are we working on the right information systems projects to provide the most value to the business?
- Will our current information systems applications meet business requirements in the future?
- What information systems mission, objectives, strategies, and computing architectures are necessary to meet the business challenges of the future?

With major improvements in technology over the past several years, many organizations are finding their old business application software unable to easily take advantage of the new technology. Many organizations are ready to invest in new technology to gain a competitive edge in the marketplace, or may even find it necessary just to stay in business. Industry statistics show more organizations will invest in new information systems hardware and software in the next three years than ever in the past. There are also more options, packages, and directions available to choose from than in the past. Many industry examples show that organizations investing and executing information systems projects properly are gaining a competitive edge. However, there are also many examples of organizations investing poorly, losing a significant amount of money, and in some cases jeopardizing the existence of their entire organization. The information systems planning process is a crucial step for any organization and when done properly, will improve your odds of success.

By following the information systems planning process described in this book, the process will facilitate communication between business management and the Information Systems function. Often, business management does not have a good understanding of the Information Systems function and might have questions such as:

- What is our current information systems environment? What computers and software do we use to manage the business? What is the condition of our information systems environment? What are the strengths, weaknesses, and areas of vulnerability of our information systems environment? Are our information systems and associated processes structured to help us facilitate the delivery of services and products to our customers in the most cost-efficient and effective manner?

- How can we make the best decisions about our information systems investments? What should be our investment priorities for information systems?

- What are our information systems resources working on currently? How do the Information Systems resources spend their time? How does the size of our Information Systems organization compare with others in the industry?

- How much money is the company spending on information systems? How does our IS spending compare to the industry? How much has spending grown over the past few years? We've been doing well without substantially increasing spending, so why do we need to spend more now?

- What are the industry technology trends, and how do the industry trends affect us?

- What is the status of our competitors' information systems? Is our company behind or ahead of our competitors?

- Do we have the internal skills necessary to take the environment where it needs to be? How much can we do, and how much should we utilize external resources?

At the same time, Information Systems management may not have a thorough understanding of the business direction, and might have questions such as:

- What are the business mission, objectives, and strategies?
- What type of business will the company be in during the next few years?
- How does the business want to function in the future?
- What are the true business requirements?
- What are the key information needs?
- What are our customers and suppliers demanding of us?

The information systems strategic planning process can answer all these questions and provide a communication vehicle between the Information Systems function and business management.

The foundation of the process is that the business direction and requirements must drive the information systems direction and computing architecture. Although this sounds like a basic concept, many organizations will actually reverse the concept and let the attractive new technology drive their direction. In actuality, these organizations end up looking for a business problem to solve with the technology they want to utilize. This book will outline a step-by-step approach to guide you through the process of developing a solid information systems plan which is linked to the business plan.

While information systems planning is critical, many organizations either spend too much time and money in the planning process, complete the plan in isolation, or skip the planning process altogether. This can result in over-analysis, inability to obtain approval of the plan, or spending millions of dollars solving the wrong problem. Many companies mistake a proper information systems strategic planning process as something that must take many months (or even years) and thousands (or even millions) of dollars. However, with a solid process in place, you can complete the planning process with your own internal resources in a matter of weeks or a few months.

This book will outline a quick and easy approach to completing a thorough plan. It will also provide a set of concepts, techniques, and templates for analyzing, organizing, and communicating the information in the Information Systems Strategic Plan. The process described will assist the organization in coming to a solid decision that has the support of the entire organization. Through the process, you will have a plan that will sell itself to management and others who need to approve the necessary investment.

This book is intended for both Information Systems executives as well as business executives interested in improving their information systems environment and utilizing information systems as a competitive business advantage. If your Information Systems function is an integral part of the business and well connected with the business plans and direction, portions of this planning process will go quickly. However, it has been my experience that many organizations may not have a solid business plan, or Information Systems may not be tightly integrated with the business direction. For these organizations, the process will outline a step-by-step approach to determining and documenting that business direction, because it will be the foundation for the information systems direction.

This book references Information Systems as the name of the function which provides computer-based business applications and technology for the organization. In some companies, this function may be referred to as Information Technology, Information Services, Information Resources, or many other names.

I sincerely hope this book helps you in your journey to world-class information systems. Good luck on your planning process!

1 Getting Started

"He who is outside his door already has a hard part of his journey behind him."

Dutch Proverb

Purpose of Information Systems Strategic Planning

Why do we need to complete strategic planning for the Information Systems function? What is the purpose of the plan and the planning process?

I have seen an information systems strategic planning process initiated in organizations for a variety of reasons. Some of these include:

- A company had business application systems that were not capable of handling the year 2000. Information Systems estimated the cost of converting the current systems to handle the year 2000. Rather than changing the company's current systems, management decided to take the opportunity to complete a strategic plan and review their existing systems to determine if they would meet the company's needs for the future before investing a significant amount of money in them.
- A company was recently acquired and initiated the planning process to determine how to meld the systems and processes of two previously separate organizations. Business management viewed the application systems and processes as critical vehicles for providing customers with a common face of the new organization. In addition, Executive Management wanted to obtain consistent information to manage the newly merged company as one organization. The new business also saw an opportunity to leverage and reduce the overhead costs of the previously separate organizations.

- A small and growing company was experiencing severe quality problems and found that the company was losing its competitive edge in the marketplace. In the past, the company had very favorable statistics and key indicators (such as inventory turns, days sales outstanding, profits) relative to the competition. The company was gradually falling behind the industry as sales and profits were on a downward trend. Management viewed information systems applications as a major roadblock to improving the quality, processes, and key measurements. Executive Management initiated the planning process to review the systems available on the market to determine the best direction for the business applications.

- A new Vice President was hired to lead Information Systems for an organization. The strategic planning process was initiated to assess the current information systems situation, and have the new leader provide input with a vision of information systems for the future.

- The business departments were frustrated with the response of Information Systems in another company. The users did not feel that Information Systems was connected to the business. Response to requests for any changes by the business was extremely slow. The business applications simply could not keep pace with the changes in the business. Management initiated the strategic planning process to determine the cause of the problems, link Information Systems more closely to the business direction, and determine the proper solution.

- A manufacturing division of a large worldwide organization was getting pressure to implement a particular vendor-supplied application package that was chosen by the corporate division of the company. Since the manufacturing division was not directly involved in the selection of the software, the division felt the package would probably not be the best fit for the unique business requirements of the division. Divisional Executive Management initiated the information systems strategic planning process to look objectively for the best solution rather than simply following the corporate mandate.

- One company faced the common problem of a growing and endless backlog of information systems projects. This company began the information systems strategic planning process to prioritize the projects and align information systems priorities with business priorities. Information Systems also wanted to determine if they should continue to build upon and invest in the current systems, or start over with a new set of business applications.

- Another company faced the unpleasant task of downsizing. Executive Management initiated the information systems strategic planning process to determine ways to reduce costs and gain efficiencies. Management wanted to evaluate the possibility of leveraging or consolidating multiple data centers and differing business applications to reduce costs while still meeting business needs.
- A high-growth company restructured the business to operate on a worldwide basis. Previously, the company functioned on a geographic basis from both a business accountability standpoint as well as having unique information systems in each geographic area. Here, management began the information systems planning process to determine how to bring the information together so that they could manage the new worldwide business.
- Another business had completed a business planning process to determine and document their business vision, mission, and objectives. Management began the information systems strategic planning process to develop an information systems strategy and direction that was aligned with its newly stated business direction.

Although the reasons driving the formulation of an information systems strategic plan may be different, the **purpose of a plan** is basically the same. The purpose or end result of an information systems strategic plan that is discussed below includes:

- Effective management of an expensive and critical asset of the organization
- Improving communication between the business and Information Systems organization
- Linking the information systems direction to the business direction
- Planning the flow of information and processes
- Efficiently and effectively allocating Information Systems resources
- Reducing the time and expense of the information systems life cycle

Effective Management of an Expensive and Critical Asset to the Organization

Business management may view Information Systems as a necessary evil rather than as a critical business function. Many times this is because business management does not understand the function and there is a lack of communication. It may even be difficult for Information Systems to get time with Executive Management for a presentation. Why should management take the time to understand Information Systems?

For any company, information systems is an expensive asset. If the company invested the same amount of money in a building, each member of management would know the location, age, and purpose of the building. Many companies spend more money on their information systems, yet business management may not know as much about their systems as they do about their building! Does management know how much they are spending on this critical asset of information systems? What is the company really getting for the investment, and will it meet the company's needs in the future? Management must have a clear understanding of their information systems environment to manage this asset as effectively as they would any other business asset.

Improving Communication Between the Business and Information Systems Organizations

The planning process will significantly improve the communication between business management and Information Systems. Business management will obtain an excellent understanding of their current systems, as well as identify any risks and opportunities. Information Systems will understand the business direction and how technology can help business management achieve the company's objectives. This mutual understanding will help establish a solid direction, and it will also assist in the approval process necessary to get the new direction sold through the organization. The communication resulting from the planning process can drastically change the environment so that the business will perceive Information Systems as a critical component to achieving company objectives.

Linking the Information Systems Direction to the Business Direction

A plan is a key component to the success of any Information Systems function and is also an important factor in assisting a company with meeting its business objectives, as shown in Figure 1.1.

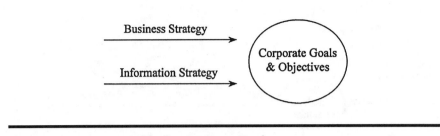

Figure 1.1   Keys to Achieving Business Goals

You need to proactively manage the direction of information systems rather than continually building upon your current information systems investment in a reactionary mode. As a result, Information Systems will be in the position to support the growing requirements and strategic direction of the business.

The information systems direction must be aligned with business drivers and must also conform to boundary conditions imposed by the business environment. As shown in Figure 1.2:

- Business drivers identify what to do.
- Boundary conditions may limit what can be done.
- The resulting plan describes how to do what can be done.

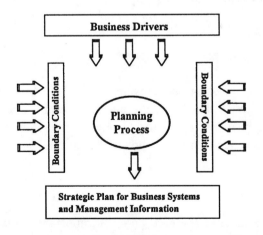

Figure 1.2   Business Drivers and Boundaries

Strategic Plan Linkage

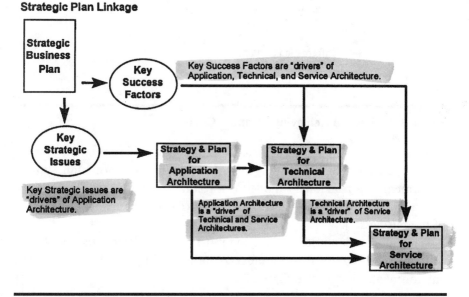

Figure 1.3   Drivers of Information Systems Plan

One company looked at three components in the strategic planning process:

- Application architecture: business systems and business requirements
- Technical architecture: client and server hardware, network, operating software
- Service architecture: management information people and processes

All three of these components were driven from the business strategic plan. Business drivers that affect the business systems and the supporting architectures were identified in the business strategic plan as key success factors and key strategic issues as shown in Figure 1.3.

Planning the Flow of Information and Processes

Information is a valuable resource, and it is important to maximize its value for the corporation. Planning and managing the flow of information throughout the organization can minimize labor, data redundancy, and inconsistency, in addition to increasing the quality and accuracy of the information.

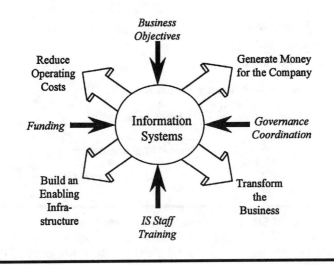

Figure 1.4   Expectations of Information Systems

Efficiently and Effectively Allocating Information Systems Resources

Developing systems that provide the business with a competitive advantage must be the focus rather than simply satisfying the wheel that squeaks the loudest (or the Vice President who complains the most). Planning will direct the effective allocation of Information Systems resources and minimize the costs of redesign, rework, or correction of errors.

Information Systems must manage both tangible and intangible resources, design flexibility and sourcing skills into the plans, and become business-focused consultants who help the company optimize human resources in addition to computing resources. Information Systems must utilize both computing and human resources to obtain the most value for the corporation. Figure 1.4 outlines the expectations of Information Systems.

Reducing the Time and Expense of the Information Systems Life Cycle

When a company feels that it needs improvement in the area of information systems, it may jump right into a vendor review of business application packages. Typically, these organizations will follow the steps outlined in Figure 1.5.

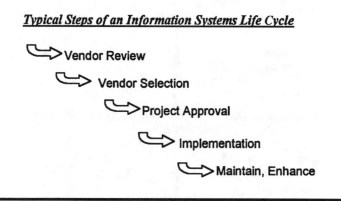

Typical Steps of an Information Systems Life Cycle

⤸Vendor Review

⤸ Vendor Selection

⤸Project Approval

⤸ Implementation

⤸Maintain, Enhance

Figure 1.5   Typical Steps in Information Systems Life Cycle

Without proper planning, several steps of the traditional life cycle are inefficient and waste significant time and money. The vendor review and selection process takes a long time because it may be unclear exactly what the company is looking for, what is important, or what problems the company is trying to solve. The company may utilize manual methods of developing requirements and reviewing vendor packages on the market. The approval step also consumes a large amount of time, because costs are generally more than management anticipates. Management starts asking questions like: "Do we really need it?" "Are there less expensive alternatives?" "What are the real benefits to be gained?" Implementation takes longer than anticipated because it is an inefficiently planned execution, or priorities are not clear. Trying to make an incorrectly chosen package fit the business means more effort expended in the maintenance years. Figure 1.6 shows the time and effort expended in the typical life cycle.

Figure 1.7 outlines a more efficient process including additional steps for strategic planning, implementation planning, post-implementation audit, and planning.

Adding time to the beginning of the process for strategic planning will significantly reduce the amount of time spent in vendor review, selection, and project approval. An automated vendor review process to identify the business objectives and issues will save a considerable amount of time and effort. The strategic planning step will also obtain management support throughout all levels of the organization so that the project sells itself. Carefully planning and prioritizing the implementation can reduce the implementation time. A post-implementation audit and check against the strategic plan will align priorities for critical enhancements. Overall time expended on the process is significantly less, as depicted by Figure 1.8.

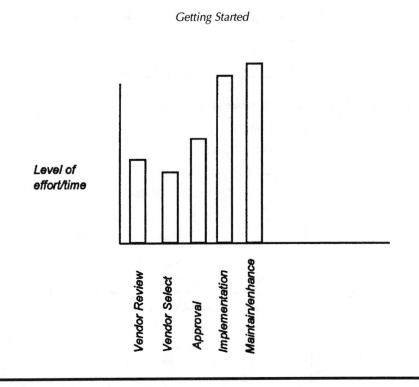

Figure 1.6   Time Spent on Typical Life Cycle

Involvement of the Organization

Once you complete the plan, how do you ensure commitment to it? Some Information Systems organizations are very efficient in developing a strategic plan by taking their top computer technicians and outlining the technical architecture of the future. When these technicians complete their planning, they end up with a terrific technical plan, but one which business management hardly understands, let alone approves. These plans tend to accumulate dust on someone's bookshelf and never really affect the direction of information systems or the business.

Where do these technical computing architecture plans go wrong? These organizations fail **to involve the business** and management throughout the entire process. It is critical to let the business direction drive the information systems direction. To be effective, information systems planning must be an ongoing visionary process integrated with the business planning process. It is critical to have business management participation and ownership of the plan, because it will establish the future direction. The plan must reflect management ideas, styles, and objectives. To be successful, the entire organization must support the information systems objectives. The single largest

Improved Information Systems Life Cycle

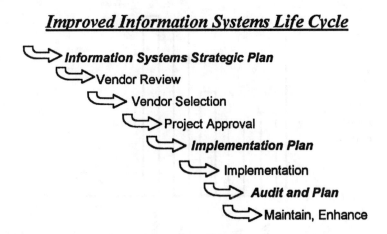

➥Information Systems Strategic Plan
➥Vendor Review
➥ Vendor Selection
➥Project Approval
➥ Implementation Plan
➥ Implementation
➥ Audit and Plan
➥Maintain, Enhance

Figure 1.7   Improved Information Systems Life Cycle

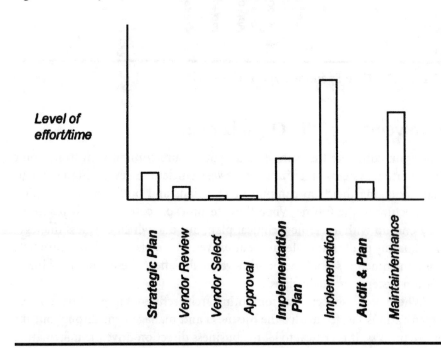

Figure 1.8   Time Spent on Improved Life Cycle

factor between a successful strategic plan that impacts the organization and a plan that simply sits on the shelf is the **involvement of the organization**. Communication and involvement are key aspects of the planning process. The planning process consists of 80% communication and obtaining input, and 20% planning.

So, how do you start developing a strategic plan? How do you get this involvement and commitment, even if it is difficult to get management's attention? You start by involving all levels of the business organization in the planning process.

You need to form several different planning groups to involve the various levels of the organization. The involvement of four different groups is necessary in a typical organization:

1. Information Systems Steering Committee
2. Executive Committee
3. Information Systems Organization
4. Vendor Review and Implementation Team

Begin your process with the executives of the organization. In short one-on-one sessions or in a group meeting, you can explain the planning process and what Executive Management can hope to gain through the process. This is a good time to ask for their key issues and concerns, and ask them to identify someone in their organization to participate on the Information Systems Steering Committee. In small organizations, the Information Systems Steering Committee could be the same as the Executive Committee.

Information Systems Steering Committee

The **Information Systems Steering Committee** is the most important group involved and is instrumental in the success of the planning process. The Steering Committee provides the Information Systems organization with a voice from all areas of the business. This group will formulate recommendations regarding project priorities and resources that will, in turn, be approved by Executive Management. This group will also provide input to the strategic direction of information systems.

The committee typically consists of Directors, or individuals one level below Executive Management. Typically, the next level below Executive Management has a strong interest in information systems and is burning with desire for changes.

Many companies have already formed Information Systems Steering Committees. You will want to review the composition of its members to ensure it is the correct group of individuals to participate in the strategic planning process. Have Executive Management select their own representatives on the committee. It is in the best interests of Executive Management to ensure that they have the best person representing their interests and concerns.

If an Information Systems Steering Committee has not been previously formed, look at the organizational structure to see if there is already a business team functioning one level below Executive Management. To help integrate information systems with the business, it would be best to have the Information Systems executive become a part of this business committee and dedicate a portion of the meetings to information systems activities and plans. One company referred to this critical group of management as the Shadow Strategy Committee, while the Executive Management team was referred to as the Business Unit Strategy Group. Another company referred to this group of management as the Operating Committee, while Executive Management was referred to as the Policy Committee. Whatever this group of management is called, Information Systems should be an integral part and responsibility of the group. Although this book refers to the group as the Information Systems Steering Committee, it would be best to integrate with your business team and refer to the group as it has been previously defined.

Include management from all the company's business areas, as well as the various geographic areas on the Information Systems Steering Committee. The members must understand the strategic business direction as well as the business issues. Although it is critical to have the major business areas represented, it is difficult to manage a group larger than twelve individuals. You need to keep the group small enough to efficiently conduct meetings and make decisions. Consider using video or teleconferencing for individuals located around the world. At a minimum, send out-of-town members material and notes from the meetings and have them attend critical meetings. Also post the minutes and presentations in an electronic mail bulletin board for all employees to see. You want to get as much visibility for the information as possible.

Do not formally include individuals from the Information Systems organization as voting members of the group. The top individual from Information Systems (typically the Vice President or Director) schedules, organizes, documents, and chairs the meetings. Have additional members from Information Systems attend meetings as required to provide information or give presentations. The business representatives must see and feel they provide the direction for the committee, which is not the case if the committee includes too many Information Systems individuals.

The responsibilities of the Information Systems Steering Committee are:

- To provide recommendations and input to the information systems strategic direction and plans. The group will ensure the plans are in alignment with the business plans and direction, and will also communicate business issues and plans affecting information systems activities or direction in technology.
- To provide input and assist in developing the vision for the deployment of technology to meet the business requirements of the future.
- To approve, sponsor, and support business-requested project efforts and tactical project plans. This group will be the vehicle for users to propose and recommend information systems projects.
- To prioritize all project efforts and tactical project plans. The group will provide recommendations in the allocation of resources and monitor project progress against the approved plan. Projects are efforts that meet one or more of the following criteria:
  - Estimated hours to complete the project are in excess of some predetermined number of hours
  - Cross departmental boundaries
  - Have a capital expenditure or non-recurring costs exceeding some predetermined amount
  - Have recurring costs in excess of a predetermined amount per year

Prioritize all requests smaller than the above project definition through the normal information systems work-order process. Determine the hours and cost limits above for your specific environment. You want to be careful to establish the approval level for projects so the committee is not reviewing every single request, but rather just the major ones. In other words, following the 80/20 rule, 20% of the projects will use 80% of your resources.

- To provide communication to other members within the organization regarding information systems activities.
- To sponsor and initiate business process re-engineering projects.
- To communicate and discuss functional business issues arising from information systems activities. For example, the manufacturing department wants to structure the bill-of-material or product number one way and the engineering department wants it another way, and the groups cannot come to agreement.
- To review information systems standards and procedures that have an impact on other business functions.

The Information Systems Steering Committee meets on a regular basis, typically monthly. The top Information Systems executive (Director, Vice President, CIO) can schedule, organize, and document the meetings.

Executive Management

As you can see, the Information Systems Steering Committee has a key role in the process. However, it is also crucial to involve **Executive Management**. Ultimately, it is the Executive Management team that will approve the expenditure of funds. Their involvement at the beginning and throughout the process will make the approval process significantly easier.

The role of the Executive Committee in the planning process is to provide Information Systems with strategic business direction and priorities. It is important to develop and maintain the systems in accordance with the business objectives and direction. The Executive Committee addresses information systems issues on an as-needed basis rather than having regularly scheduled meetings. Although the top Information Systems executive initiates the presentations, it is extremely helpful to have a business person from the Information Systems Steering Committee make the majority of the presentations to the Executive Committee. This demonstrates business management's ownership, support, and commitment to the recommendations.

The responsibilities of Executive Management relative to the information systems planning process are:

- To provide input and approve the information systems strategic direction and plans. The group will ensure the information systems plans are in agreement with the strategic business plans of the organization.

- To approve all large project efforts and provide the final authority in the allocation of resources.
- To provide direction relative to high-level business issues that affect the information systems.

Information Systems Organization

It is also important to involve the **Information Systems organization** in the planning process, because any changes in direction will significantly affect them. The Information Systems organization is more of a technical reference and takes more of a back-seat or behind-the-scenes role in the process so that the business can lead the process. If possible, involve the entire Information Systems organization in the process to some extent, and at a minimum communicate with them at each step in the process. The top Information Systems individual in the organization leads the involvement from the Information Systems organization.

After obtaining a thorough understanding of the business direction in the planning process, communicate the business direction to the entire Information Systems organization. The Information Systems organization can then be effective in brainstorming potential information systems goals and objectives. These objectives and information systems directions would only be a "starting kit" or rough draft for the Steering Committee to actually update and approve.

Vendor Review and Implementation Team

In the event the planning process leads to the conclusion that major changes are necessary, it is often necessary to form an additional group to look at the various options in detail. Often this is a time-consuming task, and the Steering Committee does not have the time or the detailed knowledge to provide a thorough evaluation. The Vendor Review or Implementation Team must include representatives from various areas of the business, as well as one or two individuals from Information Systems. Have the Information Systems Steering Committee appoint or select the individuals, because this group will be providing recommendations to the Steering Committee. The members of the Information Systems Steering Committee need to feel their area of the business is represented. Involve these individuals in preparing the detailed requirements, or in reviewing vendor packages. The top Information Systems person leads the team to provide a connection to the Steering Committee.

The Vendor Review or Implementation Team is also typically the group of individuals you would select to implement the new system. Whenever possible, it is best to have the group that selects the new system also be the group that implements the system. It is critical that these people have an excellent understanding of the business and business processes, and that they be open to changing the business processes. These individuals will be responsible for doing the business process re-engineering, establishing the parameters and procedures on how the company will use the system, testing the system, and training the users.

Conclusion

Congratulations! You have accomplished the most difficult step — starting your journey. Recognizing the need for an information systems strategic plan, involving the entire organization, and beginning the process are the most difficult steps in the journey.

2 | The Planning Process

"Behold the turtle. He makes progress only when he sticks his neck out."

James Bryant Conant (1893–1978)
U.S. university administrator, diplomat

Through the planning process, Information Systems can be a part of the solution to business challenges and can significantly assist the business. Information Systems can be in partnership with the business, with the business having ownership in the direction of information systems. With the proper infrastructure, tools, and technology in place, Information Systems can be not only responsive, but proactive to the changing business requirements.

Planning Components

What are the basic components of a strategic plan?

The information systems planning process has the same basic components as a business planning process:

- Identification of where we are today: Assess the environment to answer the question, "Where are we now?" This includes looking internally and externally at the business as well as information systems. An external view will answer the questions, "What is possible?" and "What are the best practices?" Since the business must drive information systems, you must thoroughly understand the business objectives and challenges in addition to where information systems are currently.

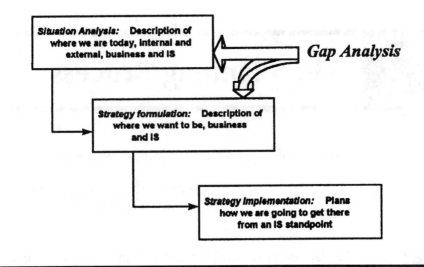

Figure 2.1   Plan Components

- Identification of where we want to be in the future: Develop the vision and strategy to answer the question, "Where do we want to be?" This is from a business perspective as well as an information systems perspective. The future business direction must be the main determinant in the information systems direction.
- Identification of the information systems gap between where we are and where we want to be in the future.
- Identification of how to get information systems to where we want to be in the future. Develop a plan to answer the question, "How will we get there?"

These components are depicted in Figure 2.1.

The plan begins with understanding the future business operating vision. The business operating vision then becomes the basis for the information systems mission, objectives, strategies, and technical computing architecture. Assess the current systems by comparing them to the future business operating vision and the desired information systems computing architecture. This is depicted in Figure 2.2.

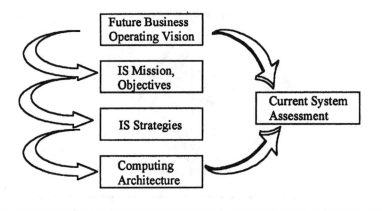

Figure 2.2   Plan Development

Planning Process

So, how do you actually develop an Information Systems Strategic Plan?

As stated earlier, the foundation of this strategic planning process is that the business direction and business requirements drive the information systems direction and computing architecture. Although this sounds like a basic concept, it is amazing how many strategic plans do not have the business direction as the foundation for the information systems direction.

Does this mean you cannot develop an Information Systems Strategic Plan if your organization does not have a formal business plan in place? Absolutely not! It means a little more work and possibly a little more time, but it is possible and is more necessary than ever. If a formal business plan does not exist, this process will outline how to develop the key components of a business plan that are necessary to effectively establish an information systems plan.

In one case, this process actually caused the business to begin a formal business planning process as management realized the lack of a clear and concise business direction. A very detailed financial plan had been developed each year, but a formal business plan was never developed identifying how the business would actually achieve its financial forecasts. The President of the division claimed that the whole executive team had a shared vision of the future. The President was verbally questioning why this step of the process was even necessary at all. However, when asked specific questions about the

Conceptual Level

Detailed Level

Figure 2.3   Phases of the Planning Process

business direction, each Vice President provided a slightly different perspective or set of priorities. When I summarized the findings and highlighted the inconsistencies, the President realized that Executive Management had never really formally agreed upon the business mission and goals. A formal business planning process was subsequently initiated.

There are four phases to the planning process as depicted in Figure 2.3.

It is critical to start the planning process by looking initially at the business. At a high conceptual level (phase 1), understand the long-term strategic direction and goals of the company by working with upper management. Then, at a more detailed level (phase 2), understand the specific business goals, objectives, and requirements for the next few years.

Once a clear, detailed business understanding is in place, you can begin to look at the information systems direction. Again, on the information systems side, you start at a high conceptual level (phase 3), outlining the direction of information systems before getting into the specific goals and objectives (phase 4).

As mentioned in Chapter 1, this process does not need to be time consuming. To be most effective, the process should proceed as quickly as possible. Although the length of time varies drastically with the size, complexity, and commitment of the organization, the following is a guideline for each phase of the plan:

1. Conceptual Business Level   2–4 weeks
2. Detailed Business Analysis   3–6 weeks
3. Conceptual IS Plan and Vision   2–4 weeks
4. Detailed IS Recommendation   6–12 weeks

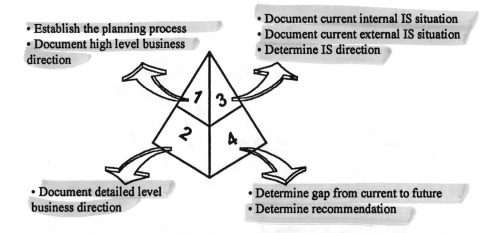

Figure 2.4   Planning Phases Definition

At the end of the planning timeframe, you will have:

- A well-documented information systems strategic plan
- A business and information systems situation that is understood by the entire organization
- A direction that is supported throughout the organization

Next, we will look at the four phases of the planning process in more detail. Figure 2.4 outlines the next level of detail for each of the four phases.

Phase 1: Conceptual Business Level

In the first phase, the **Conceptual Business Level,** you need to establish the planning process. This means establishing the purpose of why the organization is beginning the strategic planning process and what management hopes to accomplish from it. You also need to establish the process that you will be using to develop the plan. You may want to tailor the planning process utilized in this book for your specific environment. Communicate the process and establish expectations so that the organization knows what to expect from the plan and the planning process.

Also in the first phase, you need to document the high-level business direction. This includes documenting the business mission, vision, values, goals, objectives, and business priorities. You can obtain much of this information directly from a business plan, if one exists. Executive interviews are

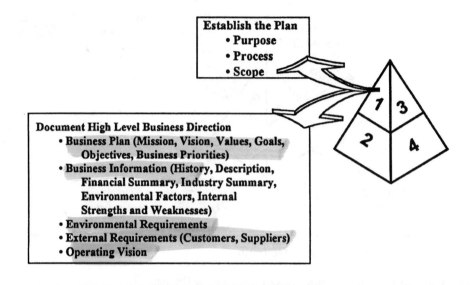

Figure 2.5   Phase 1, Conceptual Business Level

also a way to obtain or clarify this information. In this phase, you will also document information about the business. This includes a brief history of the company, a description of the business, a financial summary, and a summary of the industry. Through interviews, you will assess the environmental factors, as well as the strengths and weaknesses of the business. You will determine the environmental requirements, which are the basic categories of requirements resulting from your business or product. It is important to look externally and determine what customers, suppliers, or other external entities (for example, government, the Food and Drug Administration, International Standards Organization) are requiring from your company. Finally, the business operating vision will be statements or a vision of how management wants the business to function in the future.

Figure 2.5 outlines the details of the Conceptual Business Level, or phase 1.

Phase 2: Detailed Business Analysis

In the second phase, the **Detailed Business Analysis**, you will document the business direction at a more detailed level. Many times, this is where information that is lacking in the business comes to light. This includes developing key information needs. This will not be every single piece of information or

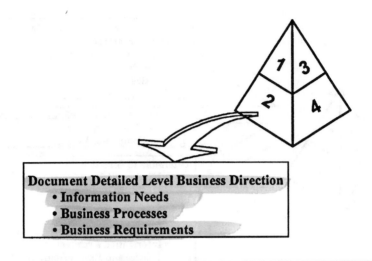

Figure 2.6   Phase 2, Detailed Business Analysis

data that is captured, but rather the key pieces of information that management requires to run the business. Typically, this information measures the pulse of the company to determine its overall health or trends. You will identify and document the business processes and initiate the business process improvement efforts. Finally, you will define detailed business requirements for the business in the future. Figure 2.6 outlines the second phase of the planning process.

Phase 3: Conceptual Information Systems Plan and Vision

Until now, you have focused on the business. The third phase, **Conceptual Information Systems Plan and Vision**, is where you begin turning your attention to the information systems. During this phase, you will document the current information systems environment, identify the Information Systems organization and the individual roles, responsibilities, and skills by group. You will review information systems expenditures, trends, and compare spending to that of the industry. You will identify the backlog or all the various projects that have been requested. You will also look at the external information systems situation. This includes looking at information systems industry trends and how the industry trends affect your environment and future. An interesting part of the planning process is to look at your competitors and determine how they utilize information systems.

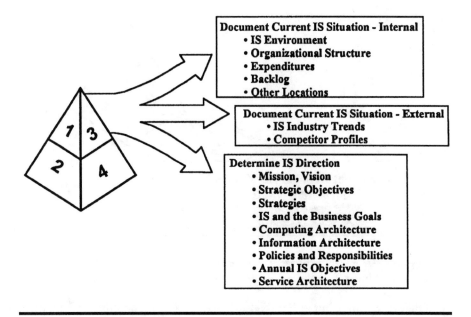

Figure 2.7   Phase 3, Conceptual Information Systems Plan and Vision

It is in this Conceptual Information Systems Plan and Vision phase where you review the business information and direction to determine the most appropriate mission and vision for Information Systems. You will also formulate the strategic objectives that are necessary to assist the business in achieving its objectives. Another key portion of the plan is to review each business goal and determine ways in which Information Systems can help the business achieve the goal. You will also determine the technical computing architecture that is necessary to reach your objectives. You will document specific policies and responsibilities as well as prioritizing specific information systems projects and objectives. You will prioritize the current information systems projects. You will also determine the information systems service architecture, which includes the people and processes necessary in information systems. Figure 2.7 shows the details of phase three.

Phase 4: Detailed Information Systems Recommendation

During the final phase, **Detailed Information Systems Recommendation,** you will determine the gap between the current situation and the desired environment of the future. This includes assessing the business operating

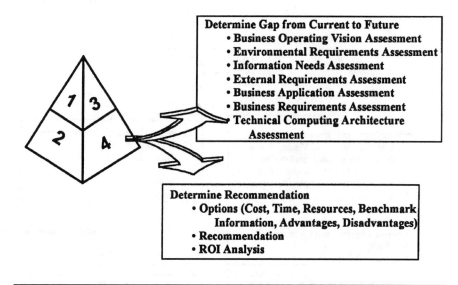

Figure 2.8   Phase 4, Detailed Information Systems Recommendation

vision, environmental requirements, information needs, external requirements, business applications, business requirements, and the technical computing architecture. Once you determine the gap, you will formulate the recommendation to close the gap. This includes identifying the various options available, including estimating the cost, time, and resources required. Benchmark data will also be helpful in validating the estimates. You will identify advantages and disadvantages for each option. Finally, you will determine the proper recommendation with a detailed return on investment analysis. Figure 2.8 identifies the components of the fourth phase.

Plan Contents

When completed, what will the plan look like? What can management expect to see and get from the plan document? Where is the process headed? Figure 2.9 depicts an outline of the **contents** in the completed strategic plan document. This will actually become the Table of Contents for the final document.

As you proceed through the steps, it is extremely helpful to build the plan document and distribute it periodically to the Information Systems Steering Committee and the Information Systems organization to obtain their input.

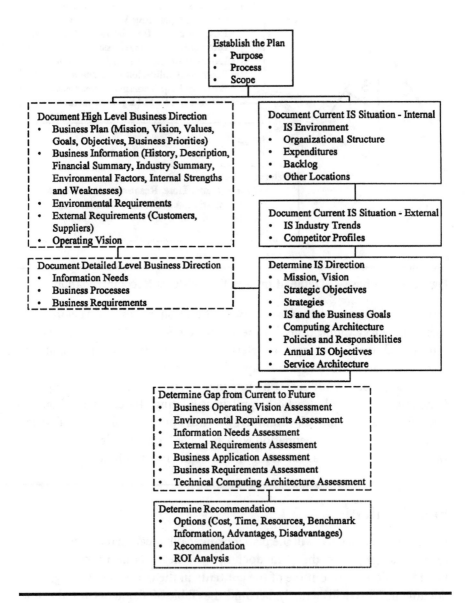

Figure 2.9   Plan Contents

To obtain involvement from all areas of the organization, the various planning groups outlined in Chapter 1 can develop and update the various sections of the plan document. The plan is a living document with many iterations. The business should gain a sense of ownership for the plan and recommendations. Specifically:

- Information Systems can initially draft the items enclosed with a solid line in Figure 2.9. You will do this after completing discussions and interviews. This is the information that the Information Systems organization is most familiar with. The Information Systems Steering Committee would then update the items that have been drafted, and Executive Management would finally review and approve the items. This updating process and communication typically involves several iterations.
- The items outlined with a dashed line are ideas generated by the Information Systems Steering Committee, drafted by Information Systems, updated again by the Information Systems Steering Committee, and reviewed by Executive Management. It is this business information that the Information Systems Steering Committee is most familiar with.
- Finally, the Vendor Review Team can prepare the items outlined with a dotted line. This is the detailed option analysis and review of packages or options. The Information Systems Steering Committee can then update the items, and Executive Management can review and approve them.

Modify the plan document and process for your own situation and requirements. Exhibit 2.1 shows an example of a Table of Contents for a complete plan document with the corresponding phase of the planning process in which you will complete the section.

Phase 1 of the Planning Process: Conceptual Business Level

Now that you know what the completed plan will look like and you have the involvement of the organization, you are ready to begin the process! We will begin with Phase 1 of the planning process, the Conceptual Business Level, as shown in Figure 2.10.

The planning process begins with understanding the business at a high conceptual level. However, before beginning, establish the purpose and boundaries to the planning process.

Exhibit 2.1   Table of Contents with Phases

Table of Contents

I.	Management Overview	Phase 1,2,3,4
II.	The Plan	Phase 1
	A. Purpose	Phase 1
	B. Process	Phase 1
	C. Scope	Phase 1
III.	High-Level Business Direction	Phase 1
	A. Business Plan (Mission, Vision, Values, Goals, Objectives, Business Priorities)	Phase 1
	B. Business Information (History, Description, Financial Summary, Industry Summary, Environmental Factors, Internal Strengths and Weaknesses)	Phase 1
	C. Environmental Requirements	Phase 1
	D. External Requirements	Phase 1
	E. Operating Vision	Phase 1
IV.	Detailed Business Direction	Phase 2
	A. Information Needs	Phase 2
	B. Business Processes	Phase 2
	C. Business Requirements	Phase 2
V.	Current Information Systems Situation — Internal	Phase 3
	A. Information Systems Environment	Phase 3
	B. Organizational Structure	Phase 3
	C. Expenditures	Phase 3
	D. Backlog	Phase 3
	E. Other Locations	Phase 3
VI.	Current Information Systems Situation — External	Phase 3
	A. Information Systems Industry Trends	Phase 3
	B. Competitor Profiles	Phase 3
VII.	Information Systems Direction	Phase 3
	A. Mission	Phase 3
	B. Vision	Phase 3
	C. Strategic Objectives	Phase 3
	D. Strategies	Phase 3
	E. Information Systems and the Business Goals	Phase 3
	F. Computing Architecture	Phase 3
	G. Information Architecture	Phase 3
	H. Policies and Responsibilities	Phase 3
	I. Annual Objectives	Phase 3
	J. Service Architecture	Phase 3

Exhibit 2.1   Table of Contents with Phases (continued)

Table of Contents	
VIII. Gap Analysis	Phase 4
IX. Recommendation	Phase 4
A. Options	Phase 4
B. Recommendations	Phase 4
C. Return On Investment Analysis	Phase 4
X. Appendix	
A. Planning Groups	Phase 1
B. Planning Process	Phase 1
C. Business Direction	Phase 1
D. Detailed Business Requirements	Phase 2
E. Roles and Responsibilities	Phase 3
F. Information Systems Backlog	Phase 3
G. Information Systems Industry Technologies	Phase 3
H. Competitor Profiles	Phase 3
I. Business Application Assessment	Phase 4

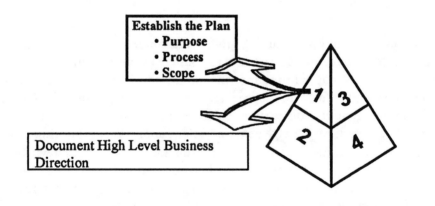

Figure 2.10   Conceptual Business Level

Purpose

In your initial meetings with Executive Management in which you are determining their representatives on the Information Systems Steering Committee, it is a good time to ask what they hope to accomplish from the strategic planning process. You may be surprised to find a few hidden agendas. You can be sure it is better to be aware of these before beginning the process! Document the purpose of the planning process in the plan and obtain agreement from Executive Management. Management may also communicate some constraints or boundaries that you must deal with in your planning. For example, Executive Management may have a constraint on the amount of expenditures or their timing. These constraints must be clear up-front before beginning the process or you may waste a lot of time looking at alternatives that are not realistic.

Process

Before beginning the planning, document the process you will use to develop the plan. Agree on the process with the Information Systems Steering Committee and the Executive Committee. You may need to make modifications to the process outlined in this book to fit your particular situation, environment, and planning needs.

Scope

After establishing your planning groups and communicating the planning process to be used, the next step is to establish the scope of your plan. Obtain agreement up-front with the Information Systems Steering Committee on the scope of the effort. The scope will frame the planning boundaries. Obtain this information from discussions (either meetings or individual discussions) with both Executive Management and Information Systems Steering Committee members. After obtaining the information, you can present what you think is the scope of the plan to obtain confirmation from both the Information Systems Steering Committee and Executive Management before proceeding with the remainder of the plan.

Following are some of the questions that your scope can address:

1. What geographic locations are included and excluded?
2. Does the scope include providing worldwide information? Do you have authority over the systems necessary to provide the information, or does it require interfaces?

3. What product lines or divisions are included and excluded?
4. What functional departments are included and excluded?
5. What business applications are included and excluded?
6. Are there phases or timed expectations?
7. Will the scope include business process re-engineering? If so, to what extent will you do business process re-engineering?
8. Will the scope include interfaces to external entities (for example, customers, suppliers, third parties)?
9. Will the scope include paper files and manual processes?
10. Will the scope include other hardware platforms (for example, Engineering environment)?

Many companies mistakenly think the scope of the planning process includes only the business application systems that are under the control of Information Systems. With the ease of developing applications with current PC software, there are typically a tremendous number of critical business applications hidden from Information Systems. These could be as simple as an Excel spreadsheet, an Access database, or even an Intranet application. If a department has a system they developed on a PC and it is critical to the operation of the business, include the system within the scope of the plan. Although it is not the intention to stifle the creativity of functional departments in solving their own business problems, it is necessary to maintain some form of control over the investment in information. It is the responsibility of Information Systems to protect, audit, and secure critical information and systems.

Use the following "acid tests" to determine the scope of business information that falls into the realm of Information Systems procedures and plans. If any of these tests proves true, it is a good idea to include the system within the scope of the plan:

1. Information that is highly critical to the operation of the company
2. Information that is used or accessed by more than one functional business department
3. Information that interfaces to any entity outside the company, whether a customer, supplier, representative, regulatory agency, or other related entity

Conclusion

You can now complete the following sections in your planning document which were included in phase 1:

II. The Plan
   A. Purpose
       Identify the purpose of developing the strategic plan.
   B. Process
       Identify the high-level steps and process you will use in developing the plan as discussed in this chapter. Identify the planning groups. Reference Appendix A and B in your plan document for detailed information.
   C. Scope
       Identify the specific scope of your plan, including locations, functional departments, business applications, and platforms.
X. Appendix
   A. Planning Groups
       As discussed in Chapter 1, include here the detail of the planning groups, including the names and titles of members, as well as the charter of each group.
   B. Planning Process
       As discussed in this chapter, include in the Appendix the detailed schedule and steps for developing the strategic plan.

Draft these sections in the plan document and present the information in overview form to the Executive Committee, Information Systems Steering Committee, and the Information Systems organization. These groups can review and update the information before you proceed with the next step. You have done it. You have stuck your neck out like the turtle for the sake of making progress!

3 Understanding the Business Direction

"If you don't know where you are going, you might wind up some-place else."

Yogi Berra (B. 1925)
American baseball player

The purpose of Information Systems, like any other organization in the company, is to add value. The purpose of the planning process is to help the Information Systems organization determine how best to add value to the organization. How an Information Systems organization would add value could be drastically different depending on the corporate or business unit strategies. The business unit strategy and corporate policy establishes the boundaries for the information systems direction, as shown in Figure 3.1.

In a complex or large organization, you will need to consider the business direction and policy of the corporation as well as the business unit strategy in your information systems planning. For example, the corporation may have a stated policy of synergy or a policy of portfolio management. In a corporate environment of synergy, an information systems planning process may be more closely aligned with other business unit directions. The business units may even choose to leverage common systems across business units, where possible. A corporate environment of portfolio management would tend to drive the information systems direction to be autonomous so that the business could be sold if necessary. Leverage and sharing information systems applications in a portfolio-managed company may not be easy or even encouraged.

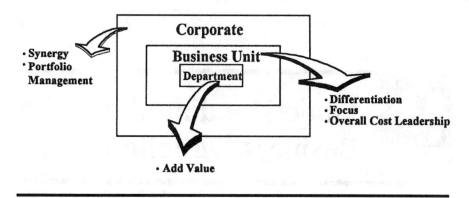

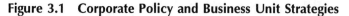

Figure 3.1   Corporate Policy and Business Unit Strategies

The business unit (division, company) strategy could be one of differentiation, focus, or overall cost leadership. Again, each of these business unit strategies has very different information systems approaches. If a business unit has a strategy of differentiation, it will be important to utilize information systems to provide the company with a competitive advantage. Utilizing new technologies to beat competitors to the market with added service or functionality will be important. This approach is drastically different than in an environment of overall cost leadership, where cost containment is your number-one goal.

Document High-Level Business Direction

Continuing with phase 1 of the planning process, the Conceptual Business Level, the next step is to **document the high-level business direction** as shown in Figure 3.2.

If your Information Systems organization is tightly integrated with the business, the business direction may be well known to the Information Systems organization, making this phase of the planning process go very quickly. However, it has been my experience that, typically, Information Systems management may not fully understand the business challenges and the future direction of the business. According to a 1996 survey by the research wing of the American Management Association, 600 senior executives reported that most functional areas in their company (for example, Human Resources, Information Systems, Marketing, Research and Development, Sales) understood

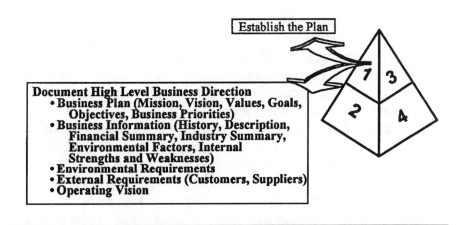

Figure 3.2   Document High-Level Business Direction

the company's mission, vision, and values "poorly or not at all." The survey ranked only 35% of Information Systems departments as having an understanding of the company direction. So, 65% of Information Systems organizations did not fully understand the business direction!

These statistics may seem alarming, but unfortunately I think they are accurate. If you don't believe it, try a test: ask several executives, including Information Systems management, to explain the top three objectives of the company. You are in an above-average company if all are able to accurately recite the objectives!

It is difficult, if not impossible, to accurately determine the proper direction of Information Systems without a complete and thorough understanding of the business direction. Since business application systems are expensive and time consuming to implement, organizations often utilize their systems for more than 8 to 10 years. With the frequent changes in the business environment, a company could often change products, customers or channels of distribution, type of manufacturing, or even industry during the same time period. You need to be aware of potential changes and account for them when planning your information systems strategic direction.

For example, one company selected and implemented a new manufacturing application system. At the time, the company was in the business of manufacturing reagents for blood testing, which is process manufacturing. Therefore, when reviewing systems, the company looked mainly at process manufacturing requirements. A few years after the system was installed, the company began manufacturing instruments to automate the blood tests in addition to the liquid reagents. The instrument manufacturing was discrete manufacturing and had totally different requirements than the process business. Had the review group known or asked executives about the direction of the company, the organization may have selected a totally different application system to meet its current and future requirements.

If the organization does a good job of strategic planning for the business as a whole, there may be a business strategic plan available. An existing business plan makes this phase of the process proceed very quickly. However, many companies do not have an updated strategic plan, or Executive Management think they have a plan, but it may be lacking many important components. Many businesses strategic plans focus mainly on the financial targets and do not really address the key business questions. Whether a plan exists or not, it is a good idea to meet with Executive Management to review the goals of the business to ensure you thoroughly understand the business direction and challenges.

Following are four steps you can follow:

1. Obtain a copy of the strategic plan or any information regarding business planning. Review this information carefully.
2. Meet with each member of the Executive Committee. Probing questions will be outlined below.
3. Assemble the information in a summary format.
4. Meet with Executive Management in a meeting to report what you have heard regarding the business direction in order to obtain confirmation of your information.

Executive Management Interviews

Following are some of the questions that you can ask in your **Executive Management interviews** to obtain a thorough understanding of the business direction:

1. Charter, Mission, Vision, Credo or Values, Goals, Objectives:
   - What is the mission and vision of the business? If you have a copy of the mission or vision, ask for confirmation to ensure it is current. If no formal mission exists, ask members of Executive Management to paraphrase what they feel would be the mission if one existed.

- Are there any other high-level business direction statements, such as values, credo, etc.?
- What are the goals and objectives of the company?
- What is the company's goal in terms of market position? Does it want to be number one in the industry for all markets or just for targeted markets?

2. Strategies, Business Priorities for the Year, Critical Issues for the Year:
   - What are the specific strategies or business priorities for this year, in priority order?
   - What are other prioritized business projects, issues, or objectives for this year?
   - What must the business accomplish this year to remain competitive?
   - What critical issues face the organization today?
   - What critical issues face the organization in the future?

3. Business Information (History, Description, Financial Summary):
   - What is a brief history of the company? When was it founded? Were there any acquisitions or change of ownership? Are any acquisitions or divestitures anticipated?
   - In what business markets does the company participate? Are there any changes in the business markets in the future? (For example, does the company design, manufacture, sell, distribute, service? Does the company plan to outsource service in the future? Is the company make-to-order, make-to-stock, engineer-to-order, process, discrete?)
   - Who are the customers? (For example, does the company sell and lease; does the company go through independent representatives; does it sell to the government?)
   - What is the company's niche? Why do customers buy from this company rather than from the competition?
   - Is the company global or local in nature? How is the company organized? Does management see this changing in the future?
   - Are there other divisions or related organizations? Do you need to bundle services or products with sister organizations, divisions, or buying groups?
   - What are the basic product lines?
   - What are the lead times?
   - What are the total sales for the past five years?
   - What has been the growth rate?

- How many employees does the organization have on both a global and geographic basis? What is the planned number of employees in three years and in five years? What was the number of employees three years ago?
- What is the capital budget?
- What is the operating profit?
- What are the inventory turns? How does it compare to the industry?
- What is the days sales outstanding? How does it compare to the industry?
- What is cost of goods sold? Direct labor? Indirect labor?

4. Industry:
   - How large is the total industry? What market share does the company have? How many competitors are in the industry and what is their size? Who are their main competitors? Obtain a list of the competitors and their size. (For example, is it a highly polar industry with the top five companies sharing 60% of the market, while the next 200 share the remaining 40%?)
   - Are there any industry associations or affiliations?
   - What trends, developments, or changes are taking place in the industry at this time or predicted in the next few years? Is it a fast or slowly changing industry?
   - What change in the industry, if it could be made, would totally change the way we do business or serve our customers?
   - What are your customers requesting of you? Why do customers buy from your company rather than your competitors?
   - What is your competitive advantage?
   - Do you plan on growth through acquisition?

5. External Environmental Factors:
   - What are the external environmental factors? What challenges does the company face in the marketplace? What are the external opportunities and threats?

6. Internal Strengths and Weaknesses:
   - What are the internal strengths of the organization?
   - What are the internal weaknesses of the organization?
   - What are the internal environmental factors? What internal challenges, opportunities, and threats does the company have?

7. Information Systems:
   - What is Information Systems doing well?

- What are the areas in which Information Systems must improve?
- Are you aware of the information systems of any competitors? What features or functionality can competitors offer with their systems that you cannot?
- What business decisions are difficult or impossible to make given existing information available in systems?
- How are decisions being made? Who needs the information?
- Are there any boundaries or management desires in implementing the recommendation?

Begin the meeting by explaining that it is critical for you to have a good understanding of the business direction. This is necessary to ensure that you map the direction of information systems in a direction consistent with the business. Ask the same questions of all the executives. Meetings should be no longer than two hours.

Summarize and Present the Business Direction

After the executive interviews, **summarize the information** in a 30- to 60-minute presentation and obtain confirmation of the information. If you heard conflicting information from several executives (which frequently happens), summarize what you think to be the most likely information. Highlight any conflicting information you have received, and come out of the meeting with consensus. Although a consensus on direction is desired at this meeting, if Executive Management has not gone through a strategic planning process, it could take several meetings to obtain consensus.

One company summarized the business strategic plan by identifying key success factors, key strategic issues, and boundary conditions that affect information systems as shown in Exhibit 3.1.

In an example mentioned earlier, Executive Management in one company thought they had a strategic business plan. After I talked to all the executives and obtained conflicting information on the company's mission and direction, Executive Management realized that their business plan was mainly financial targets and lacked key components. Executive Management from the various functions had slightly different approaches and opinions on how the company would achieve the agreed-upon financial targets. The business questions raised through the information systems strategic planning process actually initiated the process to develop a thorough business plan.

Exhibit 3.1   Summary of Business Drivers

The business plan identifies better operating effectiveness through the following key success factors:

- Creation of high performance customer-oriented organization
- Increased manufacturing efficiencies, consolidations, and outsourcing
- Enhanced sales and customer-support processes
- Redefined financial and administrative processes that reduce cost

The key success factors that apply to information systems are:

- Improved operating efficiency
- Improved operating effectiveness

The following key strategic issues may have a significant impact on business systems and support architectures:

- Divestitures, acquisitions, partnerships
- Investments in emerging markets
- Third-party distribution
- Automation of activities that connect the company with customers and suppliers
- Company initiatives

Following are the boundary conditions for information systems:

- Implement the plan in segments; define each segment as a project
- Balance costs with benefits for each project
- Minimize external customer disruption
- Adhere to predominant information technology industry standards
- Rely on proven information technology products and processes

---

Upon obtaining agreement from Executive Management on the direction of the company, it is then important to present the information to the Information Systems Steering Committee. Although the Steering Committee will not be changing the vision, mission, and other information for the company, you can obtain its confirmation of the information, as well as obtaining additional detailed information. The next level of management may have a slightly different perspective.

It is also critical to present the same information to the Information Systems group. This business information may be new to them, and they are typically eager to hear information about the company's direction as described by Executive Management.

In the Information Systems Strategic Plan, document the following items regarding the business direction:

- Business Plan
  - Mission, Charter
  - Vision
  - Values, Credo
  - Goals, Objectives
  - Strategies, Business Priorities for the Year
- Business Information
  - History
  - Description
  - Financial Summary
  - Industry Information
  - Environmental Factors: Internal and External
  - Internal Strengths and Weaknesses

Environmental Requirements

Environmental requirements are the high-level requirements the company has as a result of the product or type of business the company is in. Complete this section through group discussions with the Information Systems Steering Committee. It is valuable to have group discussions because different departments have varying types of business requirements.

For example, an organization may find a few of the environmental requirements included in Table 3.1.

External Requirements

It is also very important to determine what **external business requirements** are placed on the company. This includes requirements from customers, suppliers, and regulatory agencies, as well as competitive pressures. Typically, companies have customer and supplier surveys that provide valuable information. It can be helpful to visit or talk directly to a customer or supplier, but that may not be possible because companies typically like to control access to external entities. In that case, you can also assemble this information from discussions with the Information Systems Steering Committee.

Table 3.1   Environmental Requirements

- Make-to-order
- Make-to-stock
- Configure-to-order
- Process manufacturing
- Discrete manufacturing
- Repetitive manufacturing
- Job shop
- Discrete work orders
- Sell software
- Sell hardware
- Sell services
- Distributed processing
- Support of multiple divisions and locations
- Multiple plants, integrated
- Multiple locations in a warehouse
- Distribution
- Distribution network, multi-level
- Multiple currency: sell, invoice, buy, pay, report
- Purchase non-stock products for re-sale
- Configure products for sale
- Repair, recondition, or service our product
- Input to worldwide financial and sales reporting
- Blanket purchase orders
- Just-In-Time manufacturing capabilities
- Decimal inventory/Bill of Material quantities
- Back-flush inventory and resources
- Finite capacity loading
- Computer Aided Design and Computer Aided Manufacturing interface
- Electronic Data Interchange interface
- Interface to automated plant equipment
- Shelf life sensitive materials
- Use potency and grade materials
- FDA and government reporting requirements (EPA, NRC, etc.)
- Free-stock capabilities
- Forecast demand
- Standard and actual costing
- Subcontract production
- Hazardous use and toxic materials
- Lot control
- Serial number control
- Engineering change control

Table 3.2   Customer Requirements

- Electronic Data Interchange
- Electronic sales and compliance information
- Improved communication through the Internet (for example: home page)
- Worldwide corporate combined information for buying agreements
- Ability to interface with distributors and affiliates
- Bar coding
- Enhanced switchboard and telecommunications to more quickly get to the right person
- Credit card capabilities
- Improved lead times
- Easier order entry
- Improved order information, availability, advise on late orders
- Ability to handle special orders and requests
- Services subscriptions
- Better price and value
- High quality
- Easier to do business with
- Ability to provide electronic media and documentation (e.g., CD-ROM)
- Capabilities for providing data from bundling sales
- Warranty information

Table 3.3   Supplier Requirements

- Electronic Data Interchange
- Supplier certification, preferred vendor information
- Ability to link and integrate with outside services for materials and dependent services
- Supplier corrective action information
- Ability to interchange drawings and specifications electronically
- Conformance history
- Product development information

Table 3.2 includes examples of possible customer requirements.

Table 3.3 identifies examples of possible requirements from suppliers which the company utilizes.

Operating Vision

The next step of the process is to work with the Information Systems Steering Committee to translate the higher-level business direction to the next level of detail, the **business operating vision**. Executive Management has provided strategic direction for the company, but how is the company really going to look and function in the future? It is this business operating direction that directly impacts the information systems strategic direction and requirements. The next level of management, members of the Information Systems Steering Committee, are in the best position to answer this question.

Develop the business operating vision during several group meetings with the Information Systems Steering Committee. You can ask several high-level questions such as those stated below, obtain notes, meet again to report what you have heard, and take additional notes. Then, present the results to the Executive Committee to confirm and update the business operating vision.

When working with the Information Systems Steering Committee, tailor the following questions to your specific industry and business. Examples of questions or information to obtain include:

1. With the information obtained from Executive Management, read the mission and vision statements. Ask questions such as:
   - What businesses is the company involved in?
   - Is the company in any other markets? (For example, do we develop, manufacture, sell, market, distribute, install, service our product?)
   - Is the product just one item, or several? (For example, in addition to a product, do we sell service and software?)
   - Does the company need to be able to "bundle" services or products with sister organizations or divisions?
   - Do you see the company changing or expanding businesses? Often there can be other types of businesses found in certain corners of the organization. Although they are minor parts of the company initially, consider these other businesses, because the areas can expand significantly in the future.
   - Who are the customers? With whom do we need to interface?
   - What are the company goals in terms of market position? Do we want to be number one in the industry for all markets or only certain markets?
   - What are key industry trends? Is it a fast or slowly changing industry?
   - Are acquisitions or divestitures likely?

2. How will the company operate the business in the future?
   - Will it operate locally or worldwide?
   - What business functions will be done locally, and which worldwide?
   - How will distribution be handled? Does the company need the ability to accept an order anywhere in the world and fill it anywhere depending on availability, inventory, etc.?
   - Will project teams be worldwide?
   - Will procurement be worldwide?
   - Will customer support and service be worldwide?
   - Are multi-language and multi-currency skills required?
   - How does the company want the business processes to look in the future? How will the processes be different from today? (For example, electronic mail, paperless, ease of obtaining information, no manual or redundant efforts, etc.)
3. What are the key factors to our success in the marketplace? (For example, does the company need to be fast, flexible, and service oriented?) Can the factors be weighted or prioritized?
   - How does the company want to look from a customer's perspective? Does the company want to be doing business differently? (For example, Electronic Data Interchange, electronic access, electronic payments, ability to bundle orders with sister organizations or divisions, use of the Internet, etc.)

In the session, it is most important to listen and take notes. It may take several meetings to get a solid business operating vision. When complete, it is a list of items or high-level requirements on how the business wants to function in the future.

Executive Management may be reluctant to prioritize the key factors of success in the marketplace. However, it can be very helpful to have a clear understanding of what is important to the business. Different priorities may drive totally different information systems approaches. For example, one company identified the key factors in order of priority to be: limit customer risk, reduce cost to the customer, and increase speed of delivery. On a daily basis, as employees make decisions, having clear priorities can help guide their decisions. For example, if a change is requested in the company mentioned above (with the priorities of risk, cost, speed) that will reduce order time but will significantly increase costs to the customer, the change should be evaluated.

One critical piece of information to determine is whether the company has global or domestic objectives now as well as in the future. If the company has intentions in the future (or present) of a global presence, it has significant implications on your information systems strategic direction and scope. A company may make the mistake of determining the direction of information systems domestically without recognizing a global impact or potential. Half of the 146 executives responding to an American Management Association survey identified globalization as the issue with the greatest impact on business in the near future. Similarly, a study commissioned by A. T. Kearney, Louis Harris and Associates identified that more than half of the 800 U.S. and European companies surveyed expect to increase their international focus before the year 2000.

Although companies have been global for some time, a more recent requirement is to utilize technology to operate the worldwide business with the speed, efficiency, and information of one unified local company. For example, you may need to take an order anywhere in the world and fill it anywhere in the world depending on inventory, availability, and capacity. If the company truly operates on a global basis, Executive Management may choose to locate components of the business anywhere in the world. This means the design, development, procurement, and manufacturing functions can take place in different parts of the world. This single issue prompts entirely different requirements from your information systems strategy because your systems need to communicate, interface, share information, or even be the same system. Figure 3.3 shows an example of a business operating vision.

You have now completed phase 1 of the planning process, the Conceptual Business Level. In this phase, you established the plan, including the purpose, process, and scope. You also documented the high-level business direction, including the business plan, business information, environmental requirements, external requirements, and the operating vision. You are now ready to proceed to the second phase of the planning process, the Detailed Business Analysis, where you will develop the next level of detail to the business direction and requirements.

Phase 2 of the Planning Process: Detailed Business Analysis

You now have a good high-level understanding of the business direction and the general business requirements. You are ready to begin to document **the detailed level business direction** as shown in Figure 3.4.

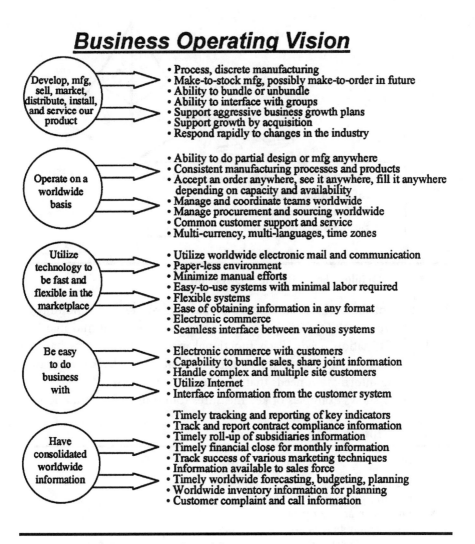

Business Operating Vision

Develop, mfg, sell, market, distribute, install, and service our product
- Process, discrete manufacturing
- Make-to-stock mfg, possibly make-to-order in future
- Ability to bundle or unbundle
- Ability to interface with groups
- Support aggressive business growth plans
- Support growth by acquisition
- Respond rapidly to changes in the industry

Operate on a worldwide basis
- Ability to do partial design or mfg anywhere
- Consistent manufacturing processes and products
- Accept an order anywhere, see it anywhere, fill it anywhere depending on capacity and availability
- Manage and coordinate teams worldwide
- Manage procurement and sourcing worldwide
- Common customer support and service
- Multi-currency, multi-languages, time zones

Utilize technology to be fast and flexible in the marketplace
- Utilize worldwide electronic mail and communication
- Paper-less environment
- Minimize manual efforts
- Easy-to-use systems with minimal labor required
- Flexible systems
- Ease of obtaining information in any format
- Electronic commerce
- Seamless interface between various systems

Be easy to do business with
- Electronic commerce with customers
- Capability to bundle sales, share joint information
- Handle complex and multiple site customers
- Utilize Internet
- Interface information from the customer system

Have consolidated worldwide information
- Timely tracking and reporting of key indicators
- Track and report contract compliance information
- Timely roll-up of subsidiaries information
- Timely financial close for monthly information
- Track success of various marketing techniques
- Information available to sales force
- Timely worldwide forecasting, budgeting, planning
- Worldwide inventory information for planning
- Customer complaint and call information

Figure 3.3 Business Operating Vision

Information Needs

It is critical to identify the **information needs,** or key measures, that indicate the general health and direction of your business. This is typically the information that Executive Management requests immediately after having been out of the office for several weeks or months. Often, it is also this information that is reported to other branches, divisions, or a corporate entity to indicate

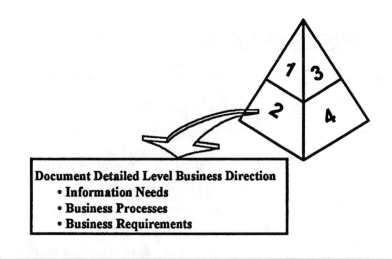

Figure 3.4   Detailed Level Business Direction

the welfare of the business on an ongoing basis. If you review a monthly or quarterly President's Operating Report or Summary, you will find many of the key information needs. Each functional area of the business has key measures. Rather than identifying all the information needs, it is critical to focus on the information needs that are key to the business.

Table 3.4 shows examples of key measures found in various functions.

Table 3.4   Information Needs

Financial:

- Sales (domestic, export, inter-company)
- Gross margin or profit (cost of sales), %
- Operating margin or profit
- Capital commitments and expenditures
- Days Sales Outstanding
- Cost reductions
- Incurred expenses
- Selling expenses, General & Administration
- Other income and expenses
- Interest expense
- Net income
- Balance sheet
- Cash flow
- Budget
- Forecast
- Operating expenses

Table 3.4 Information Needs (continued)

- Profits by customer or industry
- Backlog (units and dollars)
- Royalty income and expense

Human Resources:

- Employee information, including background, experience, demographic, personal
- Number of employees: Manufacturing, Product Support, Sales, Marketing, General & Administrative, R&D, by location
- Salary, increase, and pension data
- Training courses taken
- Employee survey data
- Turnover rate
- EEO measurements and government reporting
- Organizational reporting relationships
- Workers comp incidents, costs
- Healthcare costs
- Benefit information
- Salary market data by geography, type

Manufacturing Operations:

- Variances (overhead spending, volume, manufacturing, purchases, work order, purchase price, other)
- Scrap (product changes, expiration)
- Overdue
- Throughput time
- Rework (percentage, hours)
- Scrap (dollars, units)
- Reserve for potentially obsolete material
- Shrinkage and inventory adjustments
- Scrap and obsolescence % to standard receipts
- Labor hours by system and operations (tracking run average of actual versus standard, labor tracking by part number)
- Variances (rework, work order, scrap, obsolescence) by product
- Inventory (turns, dollars, Days Inventory On Hand)
- Allocation and backlog, average throughput time versus stated lead time by part number
- Direct material, direct labor cost, percent
- System cost roll-up
- Cost of revisions (Design Change Orders: scrap, rework, standard increase)
- DCO throughput and volume by distinction code
- Fixed costs
- Batch size costs
- SPC and work order activity

Table 3.4   Information Needs (continued)

- Corrective action status (internal and external)
- Simulation capability (what if)
- % on time, on quality of work orders
- Capacity levels (shop floor, facilities)
- Inventory accuracy
- Excess and slow moving inventory
- Facility and equipment utilization ratio
- Forecast versus actual units produced
- Pending changes — BOM, standard cost, routings
- Customer service level
- Standard receipts to inventory
- Summary of shipments (dollars, units by zone)
- First-pass yield by assembly
- Supplier cost, quality and delivery performance
- Reporting on vendor activity
- Conformance and acceptance (Incoming, In-process, Final testing)
- Volume produced by commodity

Field Service and Support:

- Total service costs per product (labor, travel, other field, in-house, parts)
- Number of installations completed (net, cumulative, average)
- Number of preventive maintenance calls
- Product support costs
- Number of repair service calls
- Service contracts
- Warranty obligations
- Cost and time to repair
- Reliability measurements

Quality:

- First-pass access yield
- Warranty cost
- Installation success
- Number of complaints
- Unscheduled service calls per product
- Calls per instrument for key accounts
- Mean time to repair
- Mean time between service calls
- Average number of calls per service rep
- Total scrap and obsolescence
- Volume produced
- Service level
- Corrective actions and recalls
- Total cost of recalls
- Customer survey results

Table 3.4   Information Needs (continued)

- Number of returns
- Mean time between failure
- Number of Design Change Orders

Regulatory:

- Shipment control
- ISO requirements and documentation
- Export commodity reporting
- EPA, NRC, hazardous waste info
- FDA information

Marketing:

- Customer placements
- Sales by zone, region, territory, representative, customer, product group and class, account, product
- Market share data: gains, losses by product and location
- Gross profit by account and product
- Competitive activity
- Customer membership data, including sales and administrative fees
- Placements by location
- Data won and lost
- Pricing, discount
- Commissions
- Forecast (units)
- Revenue by business segment, product class, etc.
- Integration of buying group data

Engineering and R&D:

- R&D expenses
- New product sales
- Time to market
- Number of releases
- Patents, awards
- Infringements costs

IS:

- IS costs as % of sales
- Backlog and completed hours (project, support maintenance)
- Average time for request completion
- Process elapsed time for completion
- Sales per employee
- System availability
- System response time
- Cost of processing a transaction
- Value-added ration per process

Business Processes

It is important to document the critical **business processes** within the organization. You will also determine which business processes require re-engineering and prioritize these improvements. How well your company's key business processes are identified, analyzed, and improved will determine your company's success in the future. These business process improvements result in information systems projects or changes, and are, therefore, important to identify in the strategic planning process. The amount of change necessary to a process may also have an impact on the overall fit of the information systems business application. If the business decides to complete major re-engineering of a process that utilizes an aging business application system, it may be a good opportunity to look at replacing the system, or it will be one more factor in the replacement decision.

Some excellent tools for looking at your business processes which are summarized here are provided by David Ames & Associates, Inc. (a company in Minneapolis, Minnesota, that teaches and consults in business process re-engineering). It is often helpful to bring in an external consultant to teach business process re-engineering to the users and Information Systems individuals participating in the project. Although this effort must be largely completed by the business users, it is helpful if the process is initiated as a result of the information systems strategic planning. Once the business users are trained in these methodologies, they typically make considerable process improvements and changes, many of which have no impact on the computer systems.

The first step in looking at the business processes is to develop a business process map to graphically depict the high-level, or macro, key business processes. This process map will also show the relationship between processes. This map will facilitate understanding between all departments and provide the basis for the detailed business process identification. Note that the business process map shows the processes, not the organizational departments. Many processes will cross organizational boundaries. The business process map contains only the macro processes. Include the detailed processes such as Order Entry, Shipping, in the next level of detail. Identify an owner within the business (usually a high-level executive with organizational responsibility over the majority of the process) for each macro process on the map. This owner will be a key individual to champion change within the business process. Figure 3.5 shows an example of a business process map from David Ames & Associates, Inc.

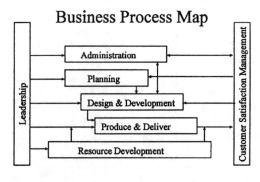

Figure 3.5   Business Process Map

Next, identify the detailed, or micro business processes within each of the macro business processes identified in the map. This may result in changes to your business process map as you identify new processes. The micro business processes that support the macro business processes each have a distinct beginning and an end. The micro business processes can be identified through tasks performed by various departments in the company and by measures or output from the department. The output could be sent externally (for example, an invoice), internally (for example, a Profit and Loss statement), or required by external entities (for example, ISO and FDA). Table 3.5 shows an example of micro business processes from David Ames & Associates, Inc.

Table 3.5   Micro Business Processes

Administration:

■ Accounts payable	■ Payroll
■ Accounts receivable	■ Billing
■ Credit & collections	■ Closing
■ Internal audits	■ Pricing
■ External audits	■ Tax
■ Shareholder	■ Legal
■ Term negotiation	■ Regulatory
■ Advertising	■ Sales
■ Revenue accounting	■ Invoicing

Table 3.5   Micro Business Processes (continued)

Customer Satisfaction Management:

- Customer interviews
- Development of surveys
- Market research
- Complaint handling
- Warranty & claims
- Information requests
- Focus groups
- Survey execution
- Gap analysis
- Post-sales service
- Inquiries

Design & Development:

- Feasibility studies
- Requirement definition
- Quality targets
- Approvals
- Full-scale development
- Supplier certification
- Life cycle development
- Preproduction build
- Reliability analysis
- Product release
- Deviation
- Tooling development
- Project planning
- Specifications
- Patent application
- Cost estimation
- Design review
- Testing
- Prototype
- Qualification
- Process design
- Engineering change
- Bills of materials
- Release

Leadership:

- Long-term vision
- Organizational goals
- Involvement
- Mission statement
- Organizational design
- Development

Planning:

- Competitive analysis
- Technological direction
- Market selection
- Business unit strategies
- Economic analysis
- Demographics
- Benchmarking

Produce & Deliver:

- Request for quote
- Order entry
- Schedule
- Purchasing
- Parts ordering
- Receiving
- Manufacturing
- Provide a service
- Test/check
- Warehousing/storing
- Shipping
- Forecasting
- Production control
- Material planning
- Materials management
- Consignment process
- Expediting
- Create
- Maintenance
- Packaging
- Transportation
- Installation

Resource Development:

- Hiring employees
- Employee involvement
- Performance reviews
- Well-being and satisfaction
- Employee records
- Medical programs
- Compensation
- Training and education
- Recognition and reward
- Health and safety
- Placement
- Suggestions
- Benefits

You can identify your business processes at a level of detail that makes sense for your company. Another company identified the following macro and micro business processes:

- Customer Interaction
  - Sales
  - Order management
  - Distribution
  - Credit and collections
  - Post-sales support
- Product Development and Manufacturing
  - Design
  - Development
  - Procurement
  - Receiving
  - Payables
  - Manufacturing
  - Engineering change
- Finance and Administrative Support
  - Finance
  - Human resources
  - Other support functions

Next, you will review the business processes to determine their level of efficiency. If a business process requires major restructuring or re-engineering, this often results in an information systems project. Again, these projects may not have been requested, but these hidden projects may have more impact on the company than any of the projects on the original backlog list. The following process outlines one way to prioritize the work needed by business process area:

1. Identify basic opportunities to impact business performance. These could be the business objectives, or generic business opportunities. For example, David Ames & Associates, Inc. identified the following potential business opportunities if processes improved:
   a. Impact on external customers or entities (for example, customers, subsidiaries, buying groups, government agencies, ISO). This could be the result from an internal process that at some point has an impact on the final customer or a process that has obvious external impact. Measure impact in terms of how (either positive or negative) the customer feels about the process.

b. Impact on quality of service or product. Measure this impact by the quality of product or the waste, defects, errors, and rework.
c. Reduction of business costs. This would be any effect on costs and resources.
d. Impact on internal customers. Measure this in terms of how much positive or negative feeling the internal customers have about the process.
e. Impact on the speed of the process. This would be the importance of speed in moving through the process, both internally as well as externally.

Your company may have slightly different performance impacts that management feels are important, but the ones identified above seem to fit a large number of organizations. You can confirm these performance impacts by looking closely at the business goals and mission for the organization. You will typically find many of the terms in the mission or goals identified in the measures above, such as satisfied customers, profitability, speed, and high quality.

2. Next, rank each of the macro business process areas identified in the business process map against the performance impacts identified above. A high number indicates that the process can have great impact on that performance area. For mathematical comparisons, use numbers 6 through 10 because this keeps a factor from being disproportionately large or small. For example, if I make a change in the Design to Deploy process, how much of an impact can I have on external customers, quality, business costs, etc.? Table 3.6 is an example of the ranking for one company.

Table 3.6   Rating Impact of Macro Business Processes

Performance Impact	Design to Deploy	Administration
Further impact external customers	8	6
Further reduce quality issues	9	8
Further impact business costs	6	9
Further impact internal customers	7	10
Further increase process speed	10	7

Next, take the micro business processes identified within each macro business process, and score the impact each micro business process can have on each performance impact on a scale of 0 to 10. Note a significant impact with a 10 and note "no impact" with a 0. For example, "If I make a positive change to the purchasing micro process within Procure to Pay, how much could I impact external customers?" Multiply that number times the performance impact identified for that process. Note reasons for the rating. For example, Table 3.7 shows an analysis done in one company.

3. By considering the total ratings for each micro process, you can determine which processes are in more need of changes. Through this process, the company in the example (Table 3.7) found that in the Procure to Pay macro process area, the micro processes that would have the largest impact if they were to improve would be the Receiving/Inspection, Supplier Quality/Certification, and Purchasing processes.

Use this mathematical model only as a general guideline. You need to review the chart and make sure it makes sense for your business. It can be useful in confirming known areas of waste and identifying areas of waste that are not as obvious.

Business Requirements

Many companies can get "hung-up" on this step of the planning process, determining the detailed **business requirements**, and spend many months identifying their requirements. There are several businesses you can utilize to complete this process in two days, and they are well worth the expense. For example, Expert Buying Systems (BuySmart software with a Choose-Smart process) or Gartner Group Decision Drivers are examples of companies with automated selection tools and processes. These companies have a software tool and a database with thousands of common requirements requested by businesses. You can assemble key users from all areas to go through the requirements in just a few days. It is critical during these sessions to involve individuals who are very familiar with the detailed business requirements. The individuals can simply answer "yes" or "no" if the requirement applies to their environment. Also identify key requirements. Complete

Table 3.7 Business Process Rating

Business Process — Procure to Pay   Owner: Date:

Organizational Processes	Further Impact: External Customers	Further Reduce: Quality Issues (6)	Further Impact: Business Costs (9)	Further Impact: Internal Customers (10)	Further Increase: Process Speed (8)	(7)	Total
		0 / 0	0 / 0	0 / 0	0 / 0	0 / 0	0
Purchasing	Transparent	Correct specifications — 2 / 12	Manual, high overhead — 5 / 45	Many approvals, not user friendly — 8 / 80	Takes too long — 7 / 56	8 / 56	249
Receiving	Transparent	No barcode — 2 / 12	Improve Efficiency — 2 / 18	Traveler, lots of paper — 5 / 50	< 24 hour cycle, no barcode — 7 / 56	8 / 56	192
Receiving Inspection	Transparent, if no change to quality	For instruments, high frequency, WIP Reject — 2 / 12	High lot freq, all direct materials inspected — 8 / 72	For instruments, high freq WIP Reject — 10 / 100	Two days Inspection — 8 / 64	9 / 63	311
Raw Material Whsing/ Storing/Material Hand	Transparent	Good but not integrated — 2 / 12	Excess Inventory unnecessary handling — 3 / 27	Increase efficiency high overhead — 9 / 90	No automation, bin management — 7 / 56	8 / 56	241
Accounts Payable	Transparent	Minimal — 0 / 0	Terms — 0 / 0	Manual system — 9 / 90	Slow, manual — 6 / 48	8 / 56	194
Cycle Counting	> 99% Customer Service	Minimal — 0 / 0	> 98% Accuracy — 1 / 9	Lumpy Demand — 3 / 30	Lumpy Demand, adequate — 7 / 56	4 / 28	123
Supplier Quality/ Certification/2nd source	Transparent	Under developed Program — 0 / 0	No Partners — 10 / 90	High WIP Rej requires SF intervention — 10 / 90	Cycle time, Inspection — 5 / 40	6 / 42	262
Corporate Purchasing	Transparent	No impact — 0 / 0	Cost Savings — 0 / 0	No impact — 10 / 100	No impact — 0 / 0	0 / 0	100
OEM/Contract Purchasing	Distributor B. O.'s	Number of Complaints — 5 / 30	Make/Buy Decisions — 7 / 63	No impact — 8 / 80	Number of days to process — 0 / 0	6 / 42	215
Inbound Logistics	Transparent	Minimal — 0 / 0	Reduce freight rates — 0 / 0	Minimal — 10 / 100	Reduce transit time — 0 / 0	5 / 35	135
Performance Measurements	Transparent	Preventative and Corrective Action — 1 / 6	Preventative and Corrective Action — 8 / 72	Valid Measurements — 8 / 80	Minimal Time — 8 / 64	3 / 21	243

this process through the use of the vendor-provided software tool, and at the end of the workshop you can generate a list of requirements for your business.

Since the generic requirements only cover the main requirements at other typical companies, you will need to add company-specific requirements at the end of the session. Add these company-specific requirements to a separate section of the generic requirements and these unique requirements can become key factors when evaluating packages or sending out a Request for Quote.

Conclusion

Congratulations! You have now completed phases 1 and 2 of the four planning phases, understanding the business. You are now ready to turn your attention to the information systems side of the process.

You can now complete the following sections in your strategic plan document from phase 1 and 2:

   III. High-Level Business Direction
       A. Business Plan (Mission, Vision, Values, Goals, Objectives, Business Priorities)
       B. Business Information (History, Description, Financial Summary, Industry Summary, Environmental Factors, Internal Strengths and Weaknesses)
       C. Environmental Requirements
       D. External Requirements
       E. Operating Vision
   IV. Detailed Business Direction
       A. Information Needs
       B. Business Processes
       C. Business Requirements
   X. Appendix
       C. Business Direction
       D. Detailed Business Requirements

Draft these sections in the plan document and present an overview to the Executive Committee, the Information Systems Steering Committee, and the Information Systems organization. These groups can then review and update the information before you proceed with the next phase of the planning process. You now know where you are going and have a much better chance of getting there!

4 Understanding and Communicating the Current Information Systems Situation

"What's the use of running if you're not on the right road?"

German Proverb

Phase 3 of the Planning Process: Conceptual IS Plan and Vision

Now you have a good understanding of the business and where it is heading in the future. Only now can you turn your attention to information systems. However, before discussing where you want information systems to go in the future, it is absolutely critical to understand where information systems is today, as shown in Figure 4.1.

It is extremely helpful to have one-on-one interviews with each member of Information Systems. These individuals work with the business departments on a daily basis and usually have a good understanding of issues and potential corrective actions. For very large Information Systems organizations, managers can complete the interviewing of their groups and report the results. An additional option with a large group would be to have a workshop approach where teams break out to answer questions and report

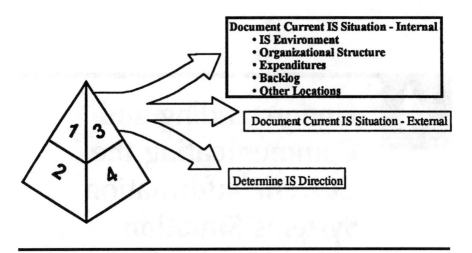

Figure 4.1   Document Current IS Situation — Internal

back to the group. When talking to Information Systems individuals, it is useful to understand or identify:

■ Any concerns or internal issues within Information Systems or where Information Systems is going. Internal problems are usually not just internal and can affect the end user or customer.

■ Suggestions on how to improve Information Systems and the service the organization provides.

■ What things do they like about their jobs and the Information Systems group? These are the things that you want to avoid disrupting or changing in the transformation process. The Information Systems organization is key to completing the execution of the strategic plan. Therefore, it is useful to try to improve the Information Systems environment. Treat your employees as you want them to treat the users.

■ Any particular career interests or direction. In mapping the future organization, it is extremely helpful to know where individuals want to direct their careers. Again, happy Information Systems employees are key to providing good service to the business community.

In addition to talking to the individuals included in the formal Information Systems organization, you may also find it useful to interview the informal Information Systems support organization. You may find several key users who are reporting to the business organization, but really function in an information systems capacity. This could include someone doing business analysis, report generation, or support of an engineering network or tools.

Current Situation

If management is not versed in the **current situation,** they will not be able to appreciate (or approve) the steps needed to get to the vision, as stated by the adage, "A journey begins on common ground." Establish this common ground before setting out toward the vision.

Many business managers are not able to answer basic questions about their current information systems environment, yet they do know the basics of other business functions such as marketing, engineering, or finance. Often, this lack of communication can be due to the Information Systems area not communicating in a language that the business understands. It is definitely a challenge (but not impossible) to explain a technical environment to a nontechnical professional. For an Information Systems professional who is extremely knowledgeable about the current environment, this step may seem too basic and not necessary. However, it is essential that all levels of business management understand the current environment, and the step is well worth the time. You need to ask yourself, "How would I describe our information systems environment to someone outside the company or to someone who is not from an information systems background?" It is extremely important when presenting the information to try to summarize it in pictures and be as brief as possible while still conveying the important points. This chapter will identify what information should be part of the Conceptual Information Systems Plan and provide suggestions for your presentation, since a clear and concise communication of the information is critical.

Information Systems Environment

Describe the **information systems environment** as having several major building blocks, or components:

- The business application systems
- Desktop computing
- Engineering environment
- All connected by the network in the background

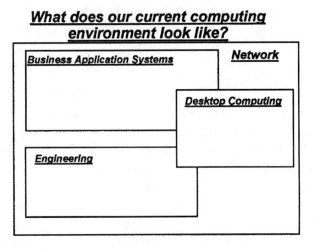

Figure 4.2   Communicating Current Environment

Figure 4.2 shows one example of how you can display this information. Another company looked at the following components in its environment:

■ Functional automation: automation of business activities and business transactions
■ Decision support: collection, retrieval, and presentation of business information
■ Documentation: preparation, storage, and retrieval of electronic documents
■ Office automation: electronic forms management and personal/ group productivity tools

When the same company looked at the technical architecture, it looked at the following four components:

■ Client: desktop computers, notebook computers
■ Network: Local Area Networks (LANs), Wide Area Network (WAN)
■ Server: file, print, and utility servers, remote communications servers, application servers, database servers
■ Operating software: operating systems, databases, system management tools, application development tools

However you break down the components, you can then go on to explain each in more detail.

Business Application Environment

Answer the following questions regarding the **business application environment:**

1. On what hardware do your business applications operate? What relative size is this hardware ... large, medium, small? When did you acquire the hardware?
2. How many business users utilize the applications by functional department? You can obtain this data from performance information on the computer.
3. What business application modules do you utilize? Are the applications tightly integrated or interfaced?
4. Are the applications vendor-supplied packages? Is the company on maintenance contract? Is the company on the current release? When did you implement the last release and how long does it typically take? Have the packaged applications been customized?
5. In what programming languages is the system written?
6. What is the size of the systems in terms of lines of code? How many reports do the systems generate? How many programs are in the systems? How many lines of code are in the systems?
7. What is the average response time for online transactions? How does it compare with the industry standard? What is the utilization of the hardware, and how does it compare to the industry standard? Obtain these statistics from hardware performance data. Request industry information from your hardware vendor (for example, IBM, HP, etc.). How does system utilization compare to historic utilization? Are there any known performance or sizing concerns?
8. How many workstations, terminals, and printers are connected? Are there any special devices necessary to support future requirements (for example, bar code readers, optical imaging, point of sale devices)?

Outline this information in detail in the plan document, and summarize in presentation format with a few charts. Going back to the basic building blocks described above, talk briefly about each environment or computing component in just a few slides. Figures 4.3 and 4.4 show examples.

You can diagram the business applications that are utilized and identify interfaces. Represent integrated modules with overlapping circles, and arrows for interfaces. This diagram should be at a very high level. Be sure

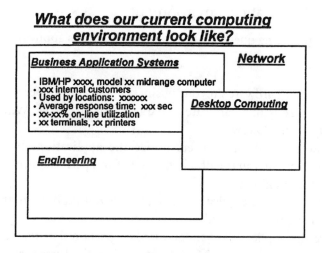

Figure 4.3   Business Applications Overview

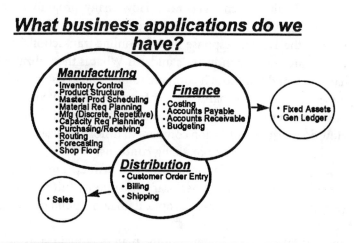

Figure 4.4   Business Applications Detail

to include external interfaces or connections, such as Electronic Da
change and Internet or Intranet applications. Also show interfa'
other environments, such as if the business applications have an '
the engineering environment or to a Computer Integrated M'
environment.

Following is a diagram of what departments use the AS/400 on an on-line basis:

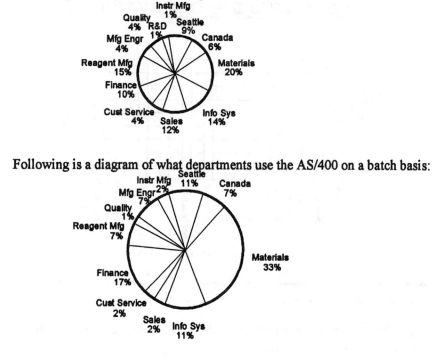

Following is a diagram of what departments use the AS/400 on a batch basis:

Figure 4.5   System Utilization

It will be helpful to display pie charts with the number of users at each location and each functional department that uses the business application systems. A particular Vice President may be surprised at how many people in his or her area utilize the systems. An example is shown in Figure 4.5.

It is helpful to relate the lines of code to things that are familiar to the average person to provide management with an understanding of the size of the systems the organization owns and maintains. For example, at one company, the lines of code were compared to the number of lines of code in Microsoft Excel or in a Lincoln Continental (which was the car the President owned). Compare the number of lines of code to the product that the company sells, if it involves software. The lines of code comparison can be especially helpful if you have custom systems requiring resources to maintain. You may surprise management with the size of the system the Information Systems organization must maintain, especially if you correlate to the number of programmers maintaining Microsoft Excel or other products that have hundreds of programmers. An example is shown in Figure 4.6.

How large are our systems?

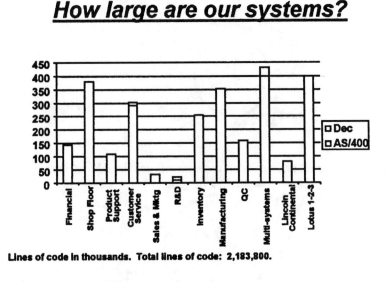

Lines of code in thousands. Total lines of code: 2,183,800.

Figure 4.6   Size of Systems

Bar charts can be very helpful in showing how utilization has changed over time, as shown in Figure 4.7.

Some business users and management may not be familiar with all of the business applications. Plan to distribute more detailed information about what each business application is used for. A simple, short explanation of each business application in your environment would be useful. Appendix 1 in the back of this book outlines one example of this type of supporting data.

PC and Local Area Network (LAN) Environment

Answer the following questions regarding the **PC** (including workstations) and **LAN** (including servers) **environment:**

1. How many PCs does the company have? How many PCs by location and functional department?
2. What is the breakdown by class of PCs? (For example, Pentium, 486, 386, Mac, etc.) What is the standard PC that is purchased? Are PCs purchased or leased? Is there any plan or program in place to replace older equipment?
3. What is the breakdown by brand of PCs? (For example, Compaq, IBM, Gateway, etc.) Is the environment standardized?

The following diagram shows how the AS/400 usage has changed since 1992:

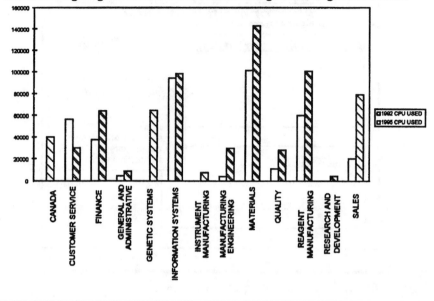

Figure 4.7   Historical System Usage

4. How much has the PC environment grown over the past five years?
5. What business applications have business departments developed utilizing PCs? Be sure to include all uses, such as critical spreadsheets, Access databases, EDI, Intranets, Internet access, customer bulletin boards, Lotus Notes applications.
6. What percentage of the PCs is connected to the network?
7. How many servers are there? Are the servers located in other locations?
8. How many printers are there?
9. What standard PC software does the company utilize? (For example, Word Processing, Spreadsheet, Presentation, Database, CAD/CAM, Desktop Publishing, etc.)
10. How many dial-up users are there? What dial-up capabilities does the company have?
11. What electronic mail system does the company utilize? How many people are connected? Do you use it for external entities such as customers and suppliers? How many are connected?
12. Are you connected to the Internet? How does the company use the Internet? Do you have a home page? How frequently do employees access the Internet? Are you connected to other companies?

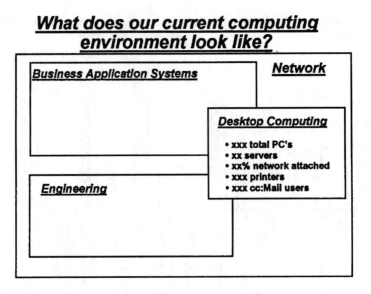

Figure 4.8   Desktop Computing Overview

Quickly and thoroughly convey the information in just a few slides when describing this information to management, as shown in Figures 4.8 and 4.9. You can have an additional chart with three pie charts representing the location, class, and make of the PCs, as shown in Figure 4.10. The fourth slide could be a bar chart representing the growth of the PC environment over the past years, as shown in Figure 4.11.

Network

Answer the following questions and obtain the information relative to the **network environment:**

1. What is the current network operating system? (For example, Novell Netware version XX.)
2. How many servers are there? What is the hardware platform?
3. What is the network topology? (For example, XX Mbps Token Ring, Ethernet.)
4. What type of cabling does the company use? (For example, Type X, category X.)
5. What is the network backbone? (For example, Fiber.)

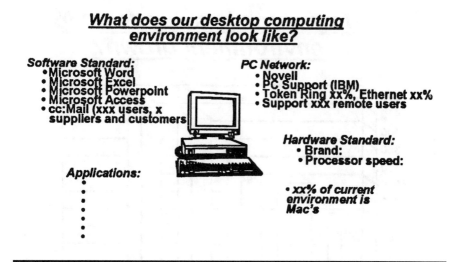

Figure 4.9   Desktop Computing Detail

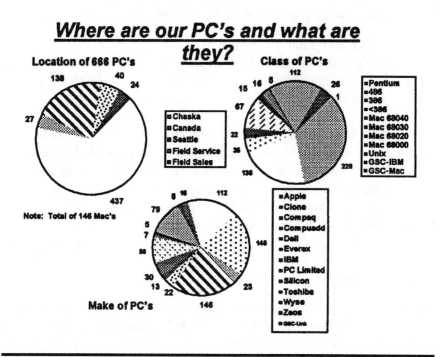

Figure 4.10   Summary of PC Environment

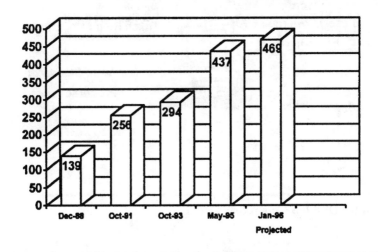

Figure 4.11   Summary of Growth of PC Environment

  6. Do you have routers or switches?
  7. Are there any known concerns or growth areas relative to the network?
  8. What is the reliability of the network?
  9. Obtain several levels of network diagrams.

Due to its technical nature, the network environment is more difficult to explain to management. A top-level diagram of the network, including the various locations connected, can be useful. The only additional information that it is important to communicate to management regarding the network includes any concerns or growth areas and cost trends. Examples of two diagrams are shown in Figures 4.12 and 4.13.

Organizational Structure

You will need to provide business management with a clear understanding of the responsibilities and activities of the **Information Systems organization**. Any changes in your environment may affect the size and responsibilities of the organization, and it is important to understand what is being done currently.

The following diagram depicts the network which connects the four different computing environments outlined above:

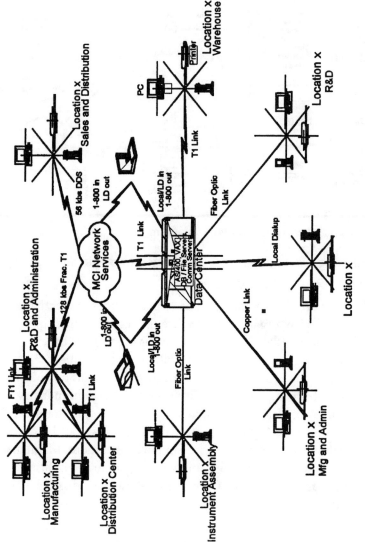

Figure 4.12   High Level Network Diagram

The following diagram depicts an example of the next level of detail for the network architecture:

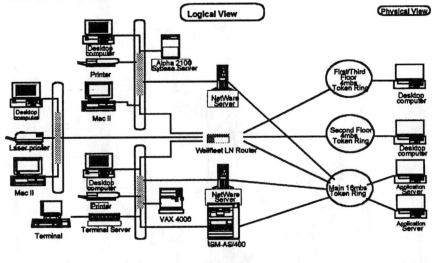

Figure 4.13   Next Level Network Diagram

Following are questions and information to obtain and address relative to Information Systems resources:

1. What are the general areas of responsibilities and activities, or how is the group organized? What are the responsibilities of each group? On what activities do the individuals spend their time?

2. Include an organization chart with names and titles.

3. How many people are in the Information Systems organization? How does this compare to industry standards? Obtain industry information from various research organizations (for example, Gartner Group, Giga, AMR, etc.). How does the break-out by function (for example, Administration, PC support, Operations, Maintenance and Development, Communications) compare to the industry? Can you draw any conclusions from the similarities or dissimilarities to the industry information?

For presentation purposes, summarize this information and present it as clearly as possible, without technical jargon. You can start with the organization of the group and then briefly explain the responsibilities of each segment. Provide a flavor of what the group does, without going into excruciating detail. Following are a few examples to explain a simple Information Systems organization (Figures 4.14, 4.15, 4.16, 4.17, and 4.18).

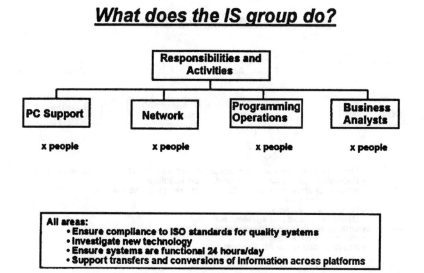

Figure 4.14   Information Systems Responsibilities Overview

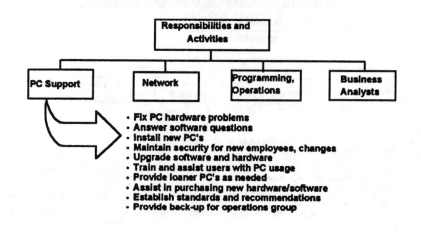

Figure 4.15   PC Support Responsibilities

When talking about each area, some additional support charts might be helpful. For example, when talking about the HELP desk, show a chart of how many calls the HELP desk gets. A line chart by month for the past year is a good way to depict this, as in Figure 4.19.

What does the Network group do?

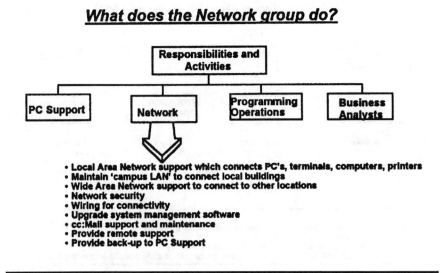

Figure 4.16   Network Responsibilities

What does the Programming/Operations group do?

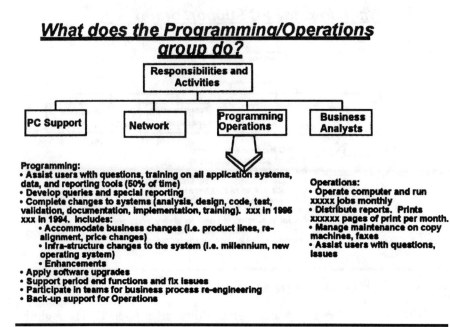

Figure 4.17   Programming, Operations Responsibilities

What do the Business Analysts do?

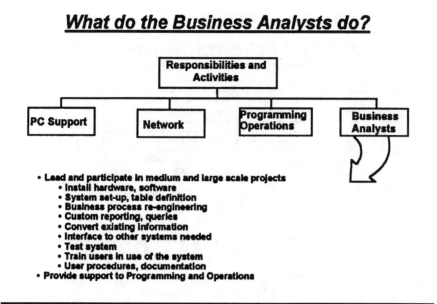

Figure 4.18   Business Analyst Responsibilities

How many calls does the HELP desk get?

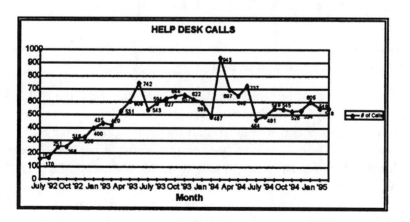

- **Calls are 83% software, 17% hardware**
- **Call volume is significantly higher than industry average**

Figure 4.19   Call Volume at the HELP Desk

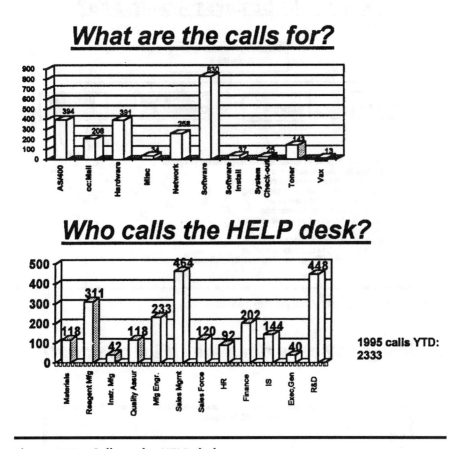

Figure 4.20   Calls at the HELP desk

Also show a chart on which functional departments call the HELP desk. Management may be surprised to see the number of times their organization calls the HELP desk. An additional chart on the type of calls the HELP desk resolves can also be enlightening (for example, software, hardware, electronic mail, network, printers, etc.). An example of this is shown in Figure 4.20.

Additional charts are helpful when talking about the Programming Group. A chart can explain how many enhancements, projects, or work orders the group receives and completes by month, as well as a chart showing the functional business areas for which projects are completed. An example is shown in Figure 4.21.

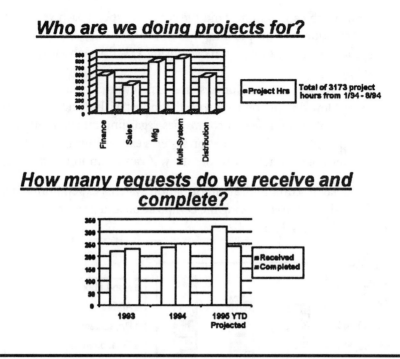

Who are we doing projects for?

How many requests do we receive and complete?

Figure 4.21   Programming Requests

Expenditures

Continuing on with describing the current environment, next address the following questions relative to **expenditures:**

1. What is the total information systems expenditure?
2. What is the breakdown by category, such as labor, nonlabor, outside services, equipment repairs and maintenance, telecommunications, depreciation, and amortization. Be sure to include the amount of money the entire organization is spending on either leasing or owning (depreciation, amortization) PCs, not just those charged to Information Systems.
3. How do the expenses by category compare to the past three years? What is the breakdown of expenses for the building blocks that were previously identified (for example, business applications, PC, network).

4. How much capital money did the company spend each year on total information systems purchases? How much money did the company spend for the past three years acquiring PCs throughout the organization?

5. What are the information systems expenditures as a percentage of sales? How does it compare with the industry? Industry information is available from research companies regarding information systems spending. Although information systems expenditures as a percentage of sales does not tell the whole story, it can be an important factor.

The best way to communicate information systems expenditures is with several bar and pie charts showing the composition and growth of spending, as shown in Figures 4.22 and 4.23.

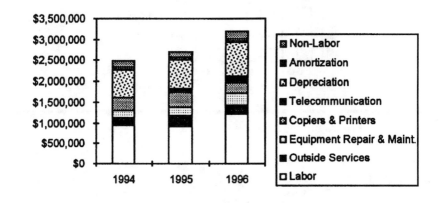

Figure 4.22   Growth of IS Spending by Category

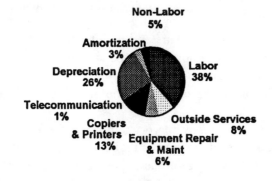

Figure 4.23   Spending Percent by Category

Exhibit 4.1   Project and Support Definition

Determine Type of Request
Definitions

Support	Projects (Major & Minor)
Problem Identification	New Service
Problem Resolution	Expanded Service
Consulting (General Q&A)	Improved Service
Routine Operations Activities:	
Purchasing	
Installation Hardware/Software	
Add Users	
Facilities Move	
Upgrades	
Report Changes Maintenance	
Back-up	
Ad Hoc Reporting	

Backlog

Assemble the entire **backlog of projects** requested by the various functional areas of the business. As stated earlier, the Information Systems Steering Committee cannot review every single user request. Focus attention on projects above a certain predetermined effort of work, projects that cross departmental boundaries, or projects that have capital or recurring costs above a certain level. Small requests, normal support, or efforts below the established criteria should be prioritized by Information Systems management. Exhibit 4.1 shows how one company categorized support and projects while Figure 4.24 shows how the company defined minor and major projects that would be reviewed by the Information Systems Steering Committee.

In addition to user-requested projects, there are also several "infrastructure" projects, or projects that are necessary from an information systems standpoint. Projects that are an example of infrastructure projects include: converting systems for the year 2000, improving the network, and PC software license management. Assemble these projects for each area of the Information Systems organization. For each project, capture the following information in a project spreadsheet:

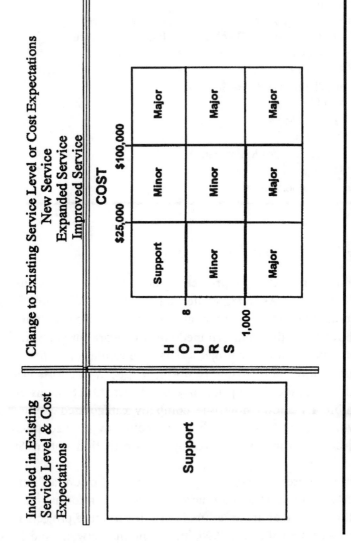

Figure 4.24   Support, Major and Minor Project Classification

1. Project name
2. Project description. This is an understandable description including why the project needs to be completed.
3. Priority. Prioritizing projects will be discussed further in Chapter 5. For our purposes here, it can be a simple High, Medium, and Low priority based on your understanding of the project or the urgency of the requesting user.
4. Status: Is the project in progress, on hold, in test, etc.?
5. What are the total estimated hours to complete the project?
6. How many hours have been completed to date?
7. What is the estimated completion date or elapsed time?
8. Who is assigned to the project from Information Systems?
9. What business objective does the project support? An infrastructure project does not support a particular business objective and can just be noted as infrastructure.
10. What are the total cost savings anticipated as a result of the project?
11. Who is the business person or area requesting the project? Again, an infrastructure project would not be requested by a business person, and can be noted as "Information Systems."
12. Who is the Information Systems Steering Committee member sponsoring the project?
13. What capital outlay or additional expenses are required for the project?
14. Going back to the building blocks previously identified in the current environment, in what platform is the project? (For example, business application, PC, network.)

It can be tempting to assemble a project backlog list for each area of the Information Systems organization. However, one word of caution in doing this: if projects require assistance from other branches of the organization, it can be confusing to have multiple lists. With one combined list, the priorities are clear if assistance is necessary from various areas of Information Systems. One list will reduce the chance of conflicting or unclear priorities.

Assemble all the backlog information and present a summary to management. You can do this with as few as two slides. The first can outline how many "project resources" are available. This is not the same as the number of your total resources. If you think about your total resource pool, a significantly smaller amount of resources actually apply to project hours due to administration, sick time, vacation, training, general support, and maintenance requests. A simple table can show the following:

- Number of resources for each functional area of Information Systems (for example, PC, network, operations, programming).
- The total hours available (number of resources times 2080 for a 40-hour week)
- The number of non-worked hours (number of resources times total sick and vacation time, etc.)
- The number of administration hours (number of resources times the number of hours typically spent in meetings and administrative duties)
- The number of support and maintenance hours (number of resources times the number of hours typically spent answering user questions, *ad hoc* queries, completing maintenance requests, etc.).
- The number of project hours available per year (total hours available minus non-worked minus administration minus support and maintenance).
- Project hours per week (project hours per year divided by 52).

An example is shown in Figure 4.25.

	# of Resources	Total Hours /Year	Non-work	Admin	Support	Project Hrs/Yr	Project Hrs/Wk
PC	4	8320	857	1248	4160	2055	40
Network	1	2080	200	312	1300	268	5
DEC Systems	3	6240	780	1080	2652	1728	33
AS/400 Systems	5	10400	1000	1560	5200	2640	51
Technical Support	1	2080	200	240	1220	420	8
Total	14	29120	3037	4440	14532	7111	137

- Time/tasks for management not included
- Open Network positions not included
- 24% of total resources for projects

Figure 4.25   Project Resource Hours Available

Through this process, you will find that only a small portion of resources actually goes toward project time. In the example above, the company found that only 24% of its total resources could be allocated to projects. This was one indicator of an aging and maintenance-intensive application portfolio. By ignoring this step in the process, many managers typically over-commit their resources. As mentioned in the example, this analysis can also identify potential problems with too much support and maintenance, indicating custom or aging systems that require replacement.

Now that you know how many resources you have, the second slide can show a summary of the backlog of projects. Again, a table showing the following can be useful:

- For each functional area of Information Systems (for example, network, PC, operations, programming), what is the total of outstanding project hours for each priority (high, medium, and low)?
- What is the total for all priority projects?
- What are the project resource hours available per year from the previous slide?
- What are the years of backlog for each functional group? (Project hours divided by project resource hours available.)

An example is shown in Figure 4.26.

	Priority "A" Hours	Priority "B" Hours	Priority "C" Hours	Total Project Hours	Project Resource Hrs / Yr	Years of Backlog
PC	1761	70	200	2031	2055	1.0
Network	368	250	173	791	268	3.0
Product Related (DEC)	872	360	340	1572	1728	.9
Business Application (AS/400)	3462	4764	11720	19946	2640	7.5
Technical Support/Op	1406	0	0	1406	420	3.3
Total	7869	5444	12433	25748	7111	3.6

- New projects are added throughout the year
- Size of AS/400 backlog indicates total application replacement may be necessary

Figure 4.26   Current Backlog

This analysis shows if an area is over-burdened with projects and where you need to shift resources. It also indicates if an area of Information Systems has aging systems or technology to address. In the example above, it appears there are not enough resources in the area of AS/400 applications. It also may indicate that those applications may be worth replacing because of the high backlog of requests.

Other Locations

When doing a strategic plan, you must be careful to look at the **entire worldwide picture**, not just your particular location or division. Are there other domestic or international locations, sister organizations, or divisions that have some impact on your future direction? Does the company have any business objectives to leverage, bundle products, or manage the business on a more global or broader basis? If so, it is critical that you obtain information on the information systems situation in the related locations.

It is critical to distinguish if the business requirement is just information sharing, or if true information consistency and exchange are necessary across the locations. This could mean the difference between a worldwide warehouse requirement, or a requirement for a total enterprise solution. These two solutions are drastically different and would have very different costs associated with them.

Assemble the following information regarding the other locations:

1. What is the size of their Information Systems organization? How are the resources organized? Are any functions outsourced?
2. What business application systems does the company utilize?
3. What computer hardware does the company utilize?
4. Does the company have any major initiatives or projects in progress in the next few years?
5. How much does the company spend on information systems a year?
6. How many PCs does the company have?
7. What interfaces are there between systems?

Summarize this information for management.

Document Current IS Situation — External

You now have a good understanding of the current internal information systems situation. It is now time to focus *externally*, as shown in Figure 4.27.

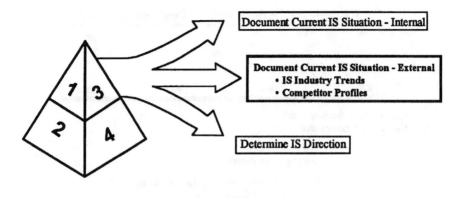

Figure 4.27   Document Current Information Systems Situation — External

Industry Trends

Technology and the **information systems industry** is continuously changing, which also affects your strategic direction. It is an industry with thousands of acronyms, and new ones appear every year. How do you provide management with an understandable overview of where technology has been in the past and where it is going in the future? Management needs to understand some of the basic trends and terminology, because these may be involved in your new direction. The following discussion identifies one way to expose management to the growth of technology in approximately four slides.

The information systems industry has experienced several phases of growth and expansion as depicted by the diagram in Figure 4.28. During each phase, various tools emerged.

- The first phase (1970–80) focused on automation of the business as a whole, with the emphasis on mainframes and improving the efficiency and information flow within the business. Information systems spending and use was largely controlled by the Information Systems department.
- The second phase (1980s) moved more toward mid-range computers with the advent of the IBM AS/400 and other computers. An organization's information systems spending was still largely focused within the Information Systems group.
- With the birth of the PC industry and Local Area Networks, the next phase (1980–90), focused more on the automation of individuals.

Phases of Information Systems Growth

Time

| 1970 | 1980 | 1990 | 2000 |

•Automating the business
•Mainframe computers

•Cost containment
•Midrange computers

•Automating the individual
•PC's, LAN's

•Flexibility
•Object orientation

•Connectivity
•Internet

Figure 4.28   Phases of Information Systems Growth

The number of PCs in the industry rose dramatically during this time as spending shifted more toward PCs and personal productivity. Client/server applications were also popular as a means of increasing productivity. With improving networks, the focus shifted from internal, within the organization, to external. Electronic commerce, or communicating electronically with suppliers, customers, and partners, was the emphasis. During this phase, spending and influence over information systems shifted toward the users rather than being centralized in Information Systems. Incompatible islands of automation often developed as users became frustrated with the responsiveness of the Information Systems organization and had tools available to solve their own problems.

■ The next wave of computing (1990s) focused on improving flexibility with the use of object technology and work flow management. Work flow management is a method of automating via visual diagrams. In the future, object technology will enable us to combine separate pieces of logic to form a unique solution more tailored to your business requirements.

■ Yet another phase of computing (1990–2000) is focusing on pervasive worldwide connectivity and the ability to reach people easily. The

Technology Evolution

Time

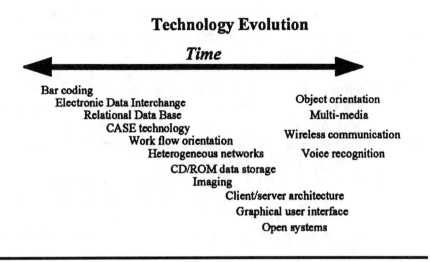

Bar coding
Electronic Data Interchange
Relational Data Base
CASE technology
Work flow orientation
Heterogeneous networks
CD/ROM data storage
Imaging

Object orientation
Multi-media
Wireless communication
Voice recognition
Client/server architecture
Graphical user interface
Open systems

Figure 4.29   Technology Evolution

Evolution of Manufacturing Concepts

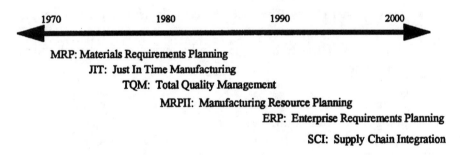

| 1970 | 1980 | 1990 | 2000 |

MRP: Materials Requirements Planning
JIT: Just In Time Manufacturing
TQM: Total Quality Management
MRPII: Manufacturing Resource Planning
ERP: Enterprise Requirements Planning
SCI: Supply Chain Integration

Figure 4.30   Evolution of Manufacturing Concepts

Internet, Intranets, and Information Highway are rapidly increasing in importance as connectivity and computing become as transparent as the telephone is today.

During this same time, there has been an evolution of technology as well as manufacturing or industry concept changes, as shown in Figure 4.29. In the manufacturing industry, manufacturing concepts have evolved and developed over the years, as depicted in Figure 4.30, and new concepts will continue to evolve. Other industries, whether finance, distribution, or others have similar developments.

It is helpful to provide management with an index or appendix of technologies and the associated definitions. You might also want to categorize technology into four tiers:

- Obsolete or trailing edge: This includes older "tried and true" technology. However, unit cost may be too high to implement due to the age and support costs of the out-dated technology. Projects may be planned to replace this obsolete technology with more up-to-date technology that is easier to support.
- Ready to implement: This includes existing technologies that are available and proven, have a defined cost saving, and in which the risk of implementation is low. These technologies may be implemented in some areas of the company, but not fully utilized or exploited.
- Emerging technologies: This includes relatively newer technologies that are being implemented commercially but are more leading edge. These technologies have a higher risk of implementation and would not be cost effective at this stage.
- Need further review: This includes technologies that are more experimental than commercial. These are typically cost effective and have a high risk. These technologies can be reviewed for possible future deployment.

Appendix 2 in the back of this book shows an example of a description of technologies. You can summarize for management what impact the industry trends have on the direction of your company. Two examples are shown in Exhibits 4.2 and 4.3.

Competitor Profiles

For management, this can be one of the most interesting sections of the plan. It is critical to find out what your *competitors* are doing with information systems. It is amazing how knowing what your competitors are doing can establish an immediate sense of urgency to improve your information systems environment!

So, how do you obtain information about your competitors? It actually sounds more difficult than it is. From the business review section (Chapter 3) of the planning process, you have a list of competitors. Following are different methods of obtaining information:

Exhibit 4.2 Technology Trend Impact — Example 1

- It will be critical in the future to have a strong internal and external network and connectivity ability. The industry and competition is demanding that organizations be faster than in the past. The network and connectivity are enabling technologies that will allow us to meet the speed expectations in the marketplace.
- We will need to focus our developments and efforts externally (for example, customers, electronic commerce, suppliers). This assumes we have our back-office systems in good shape. Technology is available to offer our customers improved service at reduced cost and time.
- Information Systems, as an organization, needs to partner and integrate with the business. As technology changes, so do business requirements and industry trends. We need to integrate the technology and business advances.
- We need to minimize the cost of our nondifferentiating functions (for example, business applications that everyone has, such as General Ledger, Accounts Payable, Payroll, etc.), so we can focus on the differentiating or unique areas. This is possible because industry advances have made application packages more available and more flexible than in the past.
- Technologies are available on the market that will allow us to reduce our costs and provide us with a competitive advantage in the marketplace. As we see competitive advantages, we need to have a flexible and open architecture in place to add the technologies to our environment.
- We need to focus our business applications environment on the new generation technology (client/server, object oriented) as well as the new generation manufacturing concepts (Enterprise Requirements Planning, Supply Chain Integration) to remain competitive with the market.

1. Ask them! You can find your competitors at information systems organizations, training classes, and conventions. Even if you are honest and explain what company you are with, it will surprise you how many Information Systems professionals are willing and even eager to tell you about their environment.
2. Talk to employees within your company who came from a competitor. This can provide a wealth of information. Typically, in the Marketing and Sales or Research and Development sections of the organization, it is common to have individuals who have come from competing companies. Interview them and find out as much as you can.
3. Review magazines, books, and journals. A literary search often reveals many different pieces about the information systems environment of a company.
4. Talk to vendors. Ask vendors to provide a list of clients utilizing their products.

Exhibit 4.3   Technology Trend Impact — Example 2

Applications Architecture Technology Impact:

- Increasing availability of integrated application packages that fulfill most of the functional requirements of the enterprise
- Use of data warehousing applications for decision support
- Availability of technology to expand applications to remote and mobile users
- Increasing availability of document and workflow management systems
- Emergence of Product Data Management applications for Product Development & Manufacturing
- Use of the Internet for electronic links to external entities
- Expanding technology for electronic collaboration

Technical Architecture Technology Impact:

- Migration to client/server as the technology foundation of commercially available application packages
- Expanding interoperability of technology components
- Availability of technology to expand applications to remote and mobile users
- Increasing availability of technology solutions that are scaleable
- Emergence of system management tools for the distributed computing environment
- Short life cycles of technology products

Service Architecture Best Practices:

- Alignment of business systems projects with strategic business priorities
- Investment in management information resources consistent with business requirements
- Partnership between business areas and management information in conducting business systems projects
- Consolidated service desk for all support activities
- Service level agreements between business systems users and management information
- Multifunctional project teams within management information

5. Look on the Internet. Review their home page and any other related information.

6. Talk to the competitor's customers. Why did they choose the competition? Did the competition offer particular functionality that was attractive? Survey information may be available through the Marketing and Sales department from lost customers showing why the companies chose your competitor.

7. Hire a consultant, provide a list of the companies, and pay to have a competitive analysis completed.

Following is some information that it is useful to learn about the competition:

1. How many employees does the company have in information systems? How many employees are there in the whole company?
2. What business application software is utilized? When did the company implement it? Is there a project in progress to replace it?
3. Do their various divisions or locations operate on a central or common Information System?
4. What is the status of their PC environment and network?
5. Can you obtain any information regarding information systems expenditures?
6. What functions does the company offer their customers? (For example, EDI, credit card, direct order entry, inventory tracking.)
7. What particular technologies does the company utilize? (For example, video teleconferencing, bar coding, point of sale, Internet, etc.)

In addition to writing any information you have in the competitive profile section (in the appendix of your plan document), it is also useful to summarize the information in the strategic plan. Do you feel your information systems environment is ahead of or behind your competition? List the reasons you are ahead or behind. What specific capabilities do you have or not have in comparison with your competitors? Some things to look for include:

- Electronic Data Interchange (EDI)
- Packaged software versus custom
- Strong or weak PC environment
- Strong or weak network, worldwide or local
- Outsourcing or staff within (for example, programming, PC HELP desk, PC acquisition)
- Integrated supply chain
- Utilization of technology (for example, bar coding, imaging, etc.)
- Use of the Internet
- Automated sales force
- Ability to take custom orders
- Speed of order delivery

Present this summary information to management.

Conclusion

You can now complete the following sections of the Information Systems Strategic Plan document from phase 3:

   V. Current Information Systems Situation — Internal
       A. Information Systems Environment
       B. Organizational Structure
       C. Expenditures
       D. Backlog
       E. Other Locations
  VI. Current Information Systems Situation — External
       A. Information Systems Industry Trends
       B. Competitor Profiles
   X. Appendix
       E. Roles and Responsibilities
       F. Information Systems Backlog
       G. Information Systems Industry Technologies
       H. Competitor Profiles

This is a critical point at which to present a summary of the information to management. It is helpful to present the information initially to the Information Systems group so they can critique and provide comments, then to the Information Systems Steering Committee, and finally to the Executive Committee.

Congratulations! Everyone is now grounded in the current situation and is ready to discuss the future!

5 Determining the High-Level Direction of Information Systems

"The great thing in this world is not so much where we stand, as in what direction we are moving."

Oliver Wendell Holmes, Sr. (1809–1894)
American physician, professor

Often, a company begins information systems strategic planning by identifying the technical requirements the Information Systems department desires in its new system. This list may include terms like open systems, client/server, relational database, graphical user interface, real time, table driven, etc. These terms mean nothing to business management, and it is not clear what requirements in the business direction are driving those technical requirements. Before determining the technical architecture and requirements, take a step back and build the high-level information systems direction based on the business direction.

The information systems project list or backlog typically includes only the projects that have been requested by certain areas. This is the "squeaky wheel" syndrome. The projects that may truly enhance the business direction are often not even on the list, or on the list with a low priority. The planning process will help uncover some of those valuable hidden business opportunities.

Through the planning process, you now have an excellent understanding of the business direction as well as the current information systems environ-

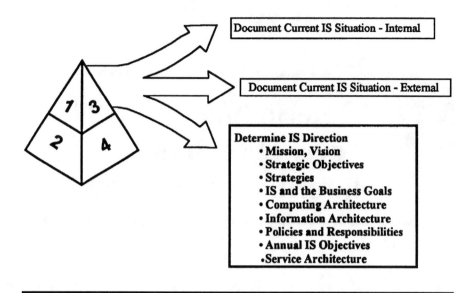

Figure 5.1   Conceptual Information Systems Plan and Vision, Determine IS Direction

ment. Now it is time to look at where information systems needs to be in the future to best meet the business requirements.

The next step of phase 3, the Conceptual Information Systems Plan and Vision, is to develop the mission, vision, strategic objectives, and strategies for information systems as shown in Figure 5.1. The higher-level information systems direction establishes the framework for the detailed plans.

I have seen several groups argue for hours about what is a mission, what is a vision, and how objectives are different from strategies. Entire books are written on the topic of developing a good mission. Rather than these statements being the end-all, it is more important to get involvement in developing these direction statements. After you have presented the business direction and current information systems environment to the Information Systems group as well as the Information Systems Steering Committee, these groups can assist in developing the statements for the direction of information systems. The Information Systems Steering Committee can update and refine a draft started by the Information Systems organization. The groups can decide what is necessary and develop the words that best fit the environment and company. Perhaps one company desires a charter, mission, vision, objectives, and strategies, while another would like to make it simpler and have only a vision and objectives. The key is to involve the group and develop statements that make sense for the company. Examples are provided here to give you ideas and initiate the thought process, but your statements must address the concerns and needs at your company.

Mission

A **mission statement** for information systems is a concise statement of what business the group is in. It is a statement of why the Information Systems group exists, what purpose and function it provides for the company. You can also look at the company mission for ideas or themes for the information systems mission.

Following (Exhibits 5.1, 5.2, 5.3, 5.4, and 5.5) are examples of information systems mission statements developed at different companies.

Exhibit 5.1   Mission Example — 1

The mission of Information Systems, in partnership with the business units, is to facilitate the availability of timely and accurate information needed to manage the day-to-day and strategic direction of the company by the deployment of systems and tools. This information will assist the company in achieving its objectives and becoming one of the top-ten in the marketplace.

Exhibit 5.2   Mission Example — 2

The mission of Information Systems in partnership with the business community is to develop, implement, and maintain worldwide business system solutions that provide secure collection, storage, and access to information. We will accomplish this by matching the business requirements with the appropriate technology.

Exhibit 5.3   Mission Example — 3

The mission of Information Systems is to develop, implement, and maintain high-quality efficient and effective business systems that provide the information needed to support the daily operation and strategic business direction of the business at a level superior to the competition with customer satisfaction as the end goal.

Exhibit 5.4   Mission Example — 4

Our mission is to facilitate improvements in operating efficiency and effectiveness by delivering worldwide integrated business systems and services. The business strategies will drive our efforts to ensure that our contributions provide the highest value to the corporation.

Exhibit 5.5   Mission Example — 5

The mission of the Information Systems organization is to provide timely, cost-effective, high-quality information systems and services that meet or exceed our customers' requirements for achieving business goals and objectives.

Vision

A **vision** is a concise statement of where you want to go, what you aspire to be. Develop this by looking at the company's vision statement and objectives and identifying how Information Systems can assist the company. Following (Exhibits 5.6, 5.7, 5.8, 5.9, and 5.10) are examples of visions developed at several companies.

Exhibit 5.6   Vision Example — 1

Vision:

- Anyone can get any information (site, geographic area, or global level) at any time, anywhere, any way, given the proper security constraints.
- The end user does not have to know the location of the data.
- Maintain data in only one master place within the organization.
- Implement systems to enhance end-user productivity.
- Systems are able to support competitive business demands with immediate response to quickly changing business needs.
- Information Systems adds a competitive edge to the company's product line.

Exhibit 5.7   Vision Example — 2

Vision:

We seek to be an integral partner in the achievement of the company's vision and mission through the appropriate application of Information Technology to business needs.

Exhibit 5.8   Vision Example — 3

We will have Business Systems that:

- Take advantage of global "sameness"
- Are purchased whenever practical
- Have integrated data that is entered only once
- Provide consistent definitions of information
- Support functional and cross-functional business processes
- Deliver the *right* information, at the *right* place, at the *right* time, in the *right* format
- Are flexible enough to support changing environments
- Can be accessed by office, home, and mobile workers
- Provide capabilities to external customers and suppliers

Exhibit 5.9   Vision Example — 4

The strategic role of Information Systems is to be:

- A provider of information technology, which means assessment and acquisition of new technology which will assure that company use of information systems and applications provide strategic advantage in our business markets.
- A provider of information services, the infrastructure, and environment that assures company-wide information sharing that meets customer requirements.
- A strategic business partner of the business units to provide timely and cost-effective information systems solutions to business needs.
- A proactive agent of change, providing management and staff with decision-making, quality information through automated and integrated information systems and processes.

Exhibit 5.10   Vision Example — 5

Vision of Information Systems:

- Have delighted customers (users).
- Proactively address business needs.
- Provide competitive advantage to the company.
- Be recognized in the industry as a world-class Information Systems organization.
- Have Information Systems employees with a passion and commitment, people that carry the fire and love their job.
- Provide enterprise-wide business solutions.
- Have a superior functioning team
- Simplify, standardize, automate, and integrate.

Strategic Objectives

Strategic objectives state how you are going to achieve the vision and mission. Following (Exhibits 5.11, 5.12, 5.13, 5.14, and 5.15) are examples of objectives from different companies.

Exhibit 5.11 Strategic Objectives Example — 1

Information Systems Objectives:

- Implement solutions in partnership with the business units. Champion each project (business-requested project, not infrastructure projects) by business management to ensure that business issues drive technical solutions.
- Align information systems projects and priorities with business priorities and direction. Likewise, the strategic direction of the company will determine the strategic direction of information systems.
- Provide responsiveness and flexibility to address changing business requirements rather than simply utilizing technology.
- Meet external customer requirements and assist in solving our customers' business issues.
- Maximize productivity and reduce costs throughout the business.
- Provide real information for business decisions (as opposed to endless amounts of data). Information must be available any time (24-hour access), anywhere in the world, in any way (flexible formats), for anyone (with security). Support worldwide information requirements and business objectives.
- Minimize information systems investments through the use of standardized hardware and packaged software, whenever possible. This will minimize support requirements and provide for maximum growth and flexibility to take advantage of future industry developments.
- Minimize risk to the company by utilization of proven, yet not out-of-date, technology.
- Educate the users and maximize their ability, through tools and training, to get information without dependence on Information Systems and utilize new capabilities and leading technology in providing a competitive advantage for the business.
- Balance Information Systems resources and expenditures with the business demands and the return on investment (ROI) to the business.

Exhibit 5.12   Strategic Objectives Example — 2

Information Systems Objectives:

- Information Systems will provide *support*, guidance, and advice to all areas of the business. This assistance will include the application and use of technology, in addition to suggestions on business process improvements. Provide continued support after project implementation to ensure you meet the business needs.
- Design systems for *ease of use* to maximize the business productivity.
- We will provide superior *communication* to ensure information sharing throughout the organization regarding technology and computing. We will understand the business and communicate in a language that is understandable. All areas of the business will know who to call for assistance.
- We will treat our technology users like *customers* and serve them with a positive attitude.
- Implement solutions in partnership with the business. *User involvement* is the key to success. Business management will own, initiate, and sell each project to ensure that business issues drive technical solutions rather than having technology looking for a problem. Do not initiate projects without the appropriate business commitment and support.
- Choose directions and tools to provide *responsiveness*, timeliness, and speed to address key business needs.
- Balance Information Systems *resources* and expenditures with the business demand and the return to the business.
- We will have a broad *knowledge* to enable us to apply various technologies and assist in all areas of the business.

Exhibit 5.13   Strategic Objectives Example — 3

Information Systems Objectives:

- Implement high-quality business solutions with a focus on customer satisfaction.
- Develop systems that support the growth and profitability goals of the company.
- Assist the company in improving its strategic position in the marketplace.
- Support the business by improving efficiency, productivity, information flow, and information access.
- Provide tools which will allow employees to make better and more timely business decisions.
- Reduce overhead costs.

Exhibit 5.14   Strategic Objectives Example — 4

Information Systems Objectives:

- Support corporate objectives and goals by providing information management technologies, systems, and services that meet business requirements.
- Communicate and execute the Information Systems organization vision and strategic plan.
- Effectively and efficiently provide and manage the company-wide information systems infrastructure.
- Team and collaborate with the business units to fulfill their information-sharing needs.

Exhibit 5.15   Strategic Objectives Example — 5

We will strive for the following long-term objectives in all systems:

- Flexibility
- Performance
- Availability
- Managed cost
- Managed risk
- Viability
- Manageability
- Support-ability
- Scale-ability
- Interoperability
- Reduced complexity
- Single system image
- Extensibility

Strategies

As you describe how you will achieve your objectives and mission, **strategies** are yet another level deeper in detail. Clearly state the strategies in the strategic plan; it can save the Information Systems group from many emotional arguments and political battles throughout the year.

One example of a strategy that, if not stated, can cause emotional arguments is the use of packaged versus custom software. In the past, companies have tended to migrate to custom solutions because both the users and the Information Systems individuals claim they have unique requirements. Due

	Grid 1:	Grid 2:
Strategic	• Spend time, money, resources	• Use Packages
Non-Strategic	Grid 3: • Outsource	Grid 4: • Use Packages or Outsource
	Unique	*Common*

Figure 5.2   Custom versus Package Solution

to the high cost of custom solutions and the increased availability of packaged solutions, many companies are migrating away from custom solutions. Yet, without a stated strategy, on a project-by-project basis it can be easy to fall into the custom "we are unique" situation or spend hours arguing about custom versus packaged solutions. Following is a suggestion on how to handle the strategy of whether the company should use custom software or packaged software.

Custom versus Packaged Business Applications

Invest the majority of resources (people and money) in areas and systems that are strategic and unique to the business. Choose the lowest-cost solution in terms of overall cost of ownership (for example, vendor package, outsourcing, etc.) on the non-strategic support systems. This will allow you to concentrate resources on areas that are most strategic to the business. Use the matrix in Figure 5.2 as a guideline to determine how to implement a system.

- Grid 1: Systems that are strategic and unique to the business must be the area where you invest time, money, and resources. Custom build systems in this area, because you will need to tailor these systems to the business. An example of a system in this area for one company was a Customer Information System which included specific information about how the customer was using their product.
- Grid 2: Purchase vendor-supplied packages for applications that are strategic but have common requirements unless you gain a strategic advantage by significantly enhancing the system in some way. An example of a system in this area for one company was a Customer Bulletin Board System.

- Grid 3: Systems that are non-strategic but unique to the business will be outsourced. This could either be a vendor-package solution with modifications or custom-built solution. However, if the needs are not strategic, you should not invest considerable resources. Determine the least costly alternative in terms of implementation and total cost of ownership. An example of a system in this area for one company was a configurator to order and build its model number.
- Grid 4: For systems that are non-strategic and common, utilize vendor packages, or outsource the function. Install and maintain systems in this area with minimum time, worry, and resources. Live with it, even if it does not fit the business exactly. Even though these systems are still very important to the daily functioning of the business, the idea is to spend little time and money on systems in this area in either implementation or maintenance. An example of systems in this area for one company were Accounts Payable, Accounts Receivable, and General Ledger.

With this basic framework and strategy, the challenge for the Steering Committee and Information Systems organization is to define what projects are strategic and non-strategic to the business. With the Information Systems Steering Committee, you can also map your application areas on the grid to determine possible solutions. Do this by examining what impact the application would have on the business goals and mission. This will focus attention on facts rather than emotions. Rather than arguments on custom versus package, the business can identify if it is strategic or non-strategic by linking it to the business goals.

Identifying and defining what is "common" and "unique" can also be a challenge. The difficulty exists in defining whether a requirement is real or a result of the way the company is currently doing business. CASE tools and information engineering concepts assist in this analysis by modeling the data and processes. Compare these basic models to the models of software packages to identify a percentage fit.

Another company provided clarity to the make-versus-buy decision with the diagram in Figure 5.3.

Following (Exhibits 5.16, 5.17, 5.18, and 5.19) are examples of other information systems strategies.

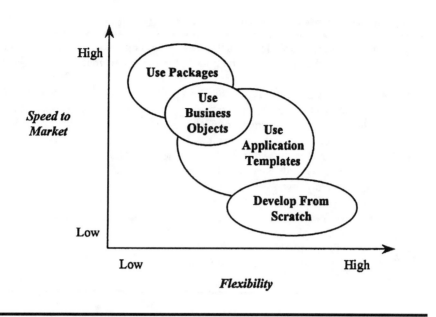

Figure 5.3   Make-versus-Buy Decision Criteria

Exhibit 5.16   Strategies Example — 1

Information Systems Strategies:

- Guide information systems directions and priorities through the Information Systems Steering Committee.
- We will treat users of our services as our customers and participate in business process improvements in business areas. Facilitate sharing of information throughout the organization regarding technology and computing by providing superior communication. We will understand the business and communicate in a language that is understandable.
- Design systems for maximum availability (e.g., 24-hour availability 7 days a week), worldwide connectivity, and optimum dependability.
- Do not constrain solutions by hardware or software platforms. Utilize the power of various hardware platforms as needed. Likewise, one software solution will not meet all business needs. Integrate solutions as business requirements dictate. Information Systems individuals will be cross-platform knowledgeable.
- Maintain information only once and have it available to everyone given proper security clearance. Information will be easily accessed, timely, and users will have the proper tools and training to be able to present the information in the desired format to support business decisions.

Exhibit 5.16 Strategies Example — 1 (continued)

- Implement new technology so that we are compatible with the industry. However, we will ensure the technology is proven to minimize the risk to the business.
- Design systems and solutions to maximize external customer satisfaction. We will also utilize technology to minimize the costs of our entire supply chain.
- Handle worldwide information exchange electronically and transport it through the communications facilities with little user effort.
- Leverage resources and solutions with other corporate entities whenever it makes sense. We will have a base of experts on staff and also manage the use of consultants where it makes sense.
- Utilize the power (for example, processing and ease of use) of the PC in our systems and projects to graphically summarize and present information so that it is meaningful to the business.
- Systems will support the ISO 9001 standards.
- Provide a process for continued evaluation of hardware and software solutions.

Exhibit 5.17 Strategies Example — 2

Information Systems Strategies:

- Implement and design systems for *ease of use*. Design systems to enhance end-user productivity. This will result in less user training and will support cross-functional users.
- Provide tools that allow for *easy access* to information. Design systems with the vision that anyone can get any information at any time, anywhere, any way, given the proper security. This means that there must be a worldwide communications network with proper security access that allows users to simply connect to the application and information required.
- We will provide *guidance* and expertise without controlling the user.
- We will provide solutions that *cross platforms* (mainframe, PC) and utilize various hardware and software tools.
- Systems and information will be available *24 hours* a day, 7 days a week.
- We will provide timely and ongoing *training* and support in applications, technical tools, and additional support as needed. This includes a value-added HELP desk for PC, printing, and Local Area Network support.
- We will implement *new technology* to keep our tools provided to the business current with the industry. However, we will ensure the technology is proven to minimize the risk to the business.
- Handle information exchange within the worldwide business electronically and transport it through the communications facilities with little user effort. Information exchanged outside the organization must also be electronic whenever possible through industry standard *Electronic Data Interchange* (EDI).

Exhibit 5.17   Strategies Example — 2 (continued)

- We will provide *worldwide* information to support the business. The Information Systems strategic direction will address the global system and information needs.
- Rather than producing endless amounts of data, we will utilize the power of the PC in our systems and projects to graphically summarize and *present information* so that it is meaningful and useful to the business. We will provide the information with minimal manual manipulation and intervention.
- We will provide tools and capabilities to automatically load data into the systems to *reduce unnecessary and redundant efforts.*
- Utilize *vendor-package solutions* whenever possible to reduce the maintenance requirements, but also tailor solutions as necessary to meet business requirements.
- We will provide updated *equipment,* including PC hardware and tools that propel the division to meeting business requirements.
- We will provide *continuous improvement* in the systems and applications for the business. Implement large projects in small pieces to reduce the overall risk to the business, and so that the projects are easier to manage, staff, and implement.

Internal Strategies:

- Personnel: We need to provide career and personal growth for Information Systems employees so that they continue to expand themselves to provide improved solutions for the business. This can be done through active career path counseling and programs, updated job descriptions which reflect the positions accurately, job rotation both inside and outside of the group to obtain exposure to the business and other areas of information systems, increased recognition, and increased training in both technical and business areas.
- Technical: Information Systems must stay current with new and emerging technologies so that we can deploy them to benefit the business at the right time. Reserve time for technical research and development to stay current with technology. Training must be a priority in this fast-changing field so that skills and methods do not become obsolete.
- Prioritization: It is critical, with limited resources and many areas in which to apply technology, that the Information Systems group carefully prioritize projects and work in partnership with the business. Follow the Information Systems Steering Committee process and priority-setting process to obtain maximum productivity.
- Communication: Communication is critical to eliminate redundant efforts and to leverage whenever possible.
- Global: Because a global focus and design are critical to our business, the Information Systems organization must become educated in what this means and in how to design systems globally.
- Standardization: Whenever possible, we must encourage common hardware and software to reduce the number of support requirements necessary.

Exhibit 5.17   Strategies Example — 2 (continued)

- Staffing: Information systems planning is critical to be proactive with the proper staff mix and knowledge base. Plan staffing in accordance with the business needs of the future.
- Documentation: Documentation is critical because it allows us to continue to support business applications. Continue to improve documentation to reduce the support requirements and learning time required for business applications.

Exhibit 5.18   Strategies Example — 3

Information System Strategies:

1. Leverage: Whenever possible and practical, we will attempt to leverage information systems solutions that exist within other divisions, as long as the solution meets the business needs of our division. This results in the lowest overall cost solution. Modularize and structure solutions to take advantage of reusable program code and allow for leveraged solutions that will result in lower cost.
2. User Partnership: User management must own, initiate, and sell each project to ensure that business issues drive technical solutions rather than vise versa. Because application systems are enablers that allow employees to do their jobs more efficiently and effectively, we will require end-user sponsors and team participants to successfully develop or implement any business application system. Do not initiate projects without the appropriate end-user commitment and support.
3. Vendor-Supplied Packages: Whenever possible, choose vendor-package solutions. Review and select vendor packages for each project unless there are significant business objectives not met through any available package. Whenever possible, implement vendor packages with no or as few modifications as possible. This minimizes the overall cost of ownership of the business application.
4. Open Systems: Develop systems with the open-systems concept for maximum cross-system portability and interoperability access. Although open systems are a vision for our future direction, true open systems are not abundant in today's vendor marketplace. As open systems become more available in the marketplace, replace existing systems with open systems. In the meantime, we must embrace vendors who are committing to open systems and use vendor products with proven portability.
5. Accessibility: Design systems with the vision that anyone can get any information at any time, anywhere, any way, given the proper security. This means that there must be a worldwide communications network with proper security access that allows users to simply connect to the application and data required. Databases must be SQL-compatible to increase the compatibility of data across the locations.

Exhibit 5.18 Strategies Example — 3

6. Systems Development Tools: Design business systems so they are able to meet the needs of rapidly changing business requirements. Utilize tools and techniques (such as Computer Aided Systems Engineering tools, Systems Development Methodology, Joint Application Design) to minimize the time and cost required to implement new or modify existing systems. Routinely utilize prototyping and well-defined specification and implementation procedures.
7. Warehousing: If the company requires worldwide information, utilize a common data warehouse rather than dictating a single worldwide solution.
8. User Interface: Design systems whenever possible and practical, to enhance end-user productivity. This will result in less user training and will support cross-functional users.
9. Data: Although we store data in several places, design systems so that we enter and maintain data in only one data storage location. Although we can duplicate the data for reporting purposes, one source must be the owner, maintainer, or master of the information. This will result in more accurate data and less overhead in maintaining the data in multiple locations and formats.
10. Information: Summarize, sort, and present information in a way that adds clarity, visibility, and meaning to the business rather than just data. Our systems and projects will strive to produce information critical to business decisions rather than endless amounts of data.
11. Information Exchange: Exchange worldwide information electronically and transport through the communications facilities with little user effort. Conversion of document formats must be available for text, spreadsheet, graphics, voice, and image. Information exchanged outside the organization must also be electronic whenever possible through industry standard Electronic Data Interchange.
12. Infrastructure: Information Systems will initiate projects requiring maintenance or enhancement to the infrastructure.

Exhibit 5.19 Strategies Example — 4

Organizational Strategies:

- All worldwide customers receive equal priority.
- All new systems must provide local flexibility while preserving strategic consistency.
- Cost, balanced against risk and benefit, should be an important factor in all architectural decisions.
- We will maintain a worldwide focus and functionality for all systems.

Business Strategies:

- Systems must accommodate a range of users — from power users to casual users.

Exhibit 5.19   Strategies Example — 4 (continued)

- Systems must strive to empower users, extending the concept of end-user computing.
- Systems must be built in a consistent, user-friendly fashion, minimizing complexity, user training, and costs.
- Systems will utilize Internet support and technologies for electronic commerce.
- The implementation of new functionality will not interrupt current business flow.
- Supporting the existing business must be the top priority.
- Systems must be available to each geographic location to support their hours of operation.
- New systems must provide acceptable levels of performance to support the business functions.
- New systems must interact with the appropriate network and systems management components.
- New systems should present a business view rather than a technical view.
- Systems should be capable of being enhanced in an efficient manner.

It is possible that in developing the objectives and strategies, you will identify new information systems projects that have not been included on the project list. Add these projects to the information systems project list.

Information Systems and Business Goals

This section of the strategic plan is probably the most interesting to business executives. There are many ways Information Systems can assist the business, such as:

- Provide unique product and service features
- Reduce product development time
- Allow the delivery of customized services
- Open new channels and market niches
- Produce higher-quality results
- Fill product positioning gaps
- Block channel access
- Increase buyer switching costs

Typically, customers have a cycle of activities in acquiring and using resources. This cycle of activities may include: establishing requirements, selecting and ordering, authorizing and paying for, testing and accepting, integrating and monitoring, upgrading, maintaining, transfering or disposing, and accounting for. You need to begin thinking of things the company could do to make this process easier for the customer. There may be opportunities anywhere within the cycle. For example, the development of the Internet is providing companies a new vehicle for providing products and services faster and making them more accessible to customers.

Start by listing each business goal directly from the business plan or from the work done in Chapter 3. Briefly list and describe any way in which Information Systems could help the company **achieve the business goal**. These are projects that business management may have mentioned but not formally requested. You may have heard an executive mention the project during your management interviews. Often, these projects have the most strategic impact on the business and typically use newer technology, yet have not been requested for a number of reasons. If the company were yours and you could use technology in any way possible, how would you achieve the business goal stated? Brainstorming sessions with the Information Systems group as well as the Information Systems Steering Committee can be helpful in uncovering some of these hidden opportunities. The purpose of this section is to get management throughout the organization thinking about how Information Systems can help the company achieve its objectives. This information can be enlightening for Executive Management as they can begin to see the true potential of information systems. This thinking may be new for Executive Management because they are more familiar with viewing Information Systems in only a back-office support role. Three examples are shown in Exhibits 5.20, 5.21, and 5.22.

Exhibit 5.20   Information Systems and the Business Goals Example — 1

Information Systems and the Business Strategies

Closely align information systems priorities and direction with the business goals and objectives. Following are some of the ways in which Information Systems can play a role in each of the business strategies outlined previously.

I. Provide superior product availability worldwide

- Information Systems must design systems that provide *real time data* that will give the business immediate information, allowing it to respond in a timely fashion to the customer and industry needs.
- Design systems solutions to be *worldwide,* which will enable us to function as a worldwide supplier. This means that we must supply what our customers want, where and when they want it. Systems must be in place so that you can take an order anywhere in the world and fill it anywhere in the world depending upon capacity and availability.

Exhibit 5.20   Information Systems and the Business Goals Example — 1 (continued)

- Design systems to be *accessible* to the customer. Research what information we could provide to the customer to make us easier to do business with as a supplier. This includes the ability for customers to enter orders after reviewing price and delivery information with the minimum amount of paperwork, providing order status and delivery information when needed.
- Utilize systems with business process re-engineering to *eliminate non-value-*added steps throughout the business.
- A closer *link between the engineering* and business systems can reduce lead times of new products and product changes.
- We can improve the *make-to-order* system (for example, Final Assembly) so that we can efficiently tailor the product to the customer's specifications with minimum cost to us.
- Implement systems to provide a more comprehensive *feedback loop* from the customers. This includes customer expectations versus delivery performance, as well as customer requests and feedback regarding the product.
- Implement systems that strengthen our *relationship* with our customers. This includes an improved forecasting and inventory management system so that we can effectively meet customer requests. Also, provide tools for improved communications such as customer access to our system, Electronic Data Interchange (EDI), e-mail, and video teleconferencing.
- Information Systems must provide vehicles that make us *easy to do business* with as a supplier. This includes tools for an improved order capture process, such as EDI, phone response order placement, customer entry, remote order entry, and bulletin board order entry systems. This also includes vehicles for ease of payment, such as credit card payment, monthly invoices, electronic payments, etc.
- We can improve the systems to handle "on sight" *inventory* management that includes replenishment and transfer.
- We can make *product selection* and configuration easier for the customer.
- We can provide the ability to make *delivery commitments* to our customers as well as create vehicles that help us meet our delivery commitments.
- We can *benchmark* other global non-competitor companies to determine how they are providing superior product availability worldwide.
- We can support the worldwide *super service center* concept by assisting with systems implementations in Germany, Singapore, and other sites as needed. We can ensure that information systems planning addresses global business needs rather than just our location.
- We can ensure that systems are in place to efficiently handle *export requirements* as well as facilitating worldwide transaction processing between subsidiaries.
- Design systems to support the quick-ship program and reduced *lead time* programs.

Exhibit 5.20   Information Systems and the Business Goals Example — 1 (continued)

II. Deliver outstanding customer service and support

- An online *bulletin board* system can provide customers and employees (for example, subsidiaries, Field Sales, etc.) with immediate access to product information, ability to place orders, messages and notifications from the factory, answers to specific questions, engineering drawings, etc.
- We could also use the voice mail system to provide *interactive voice response* for customer information and requests. We could enhance this with the video telephone to see the person with whom you are working.
- Improved Order Management systems could make the ordering process efficient so that the company is *easy to do business with as a supplier.* Back-end systems such as Electronic Data Interchange, credit card payment, monthly invoices, electronic payments, and bar coding would help the customer and reduce our order costs.
- We can provide *pursuit and selling tools* and systems to improve the sales process. This includes product sizing and selection, discounting, quoting, project pursuit, customer profiles and tracking, project forecasting, competitive assessment, installed base analysis, account and territory management, agreements, and sales presentations.
- We could provide *customer access* to order and agreement information with remote dial-in capability.
- Develop a system with the voice mail or bulletin board system to provide immediate *fax-back* of information, product literature, drawings, etc.
- A total *integrated system* would give the business the ability to add functionality quickly and allow us to respond to customer requests. It would also provide worldwide consistency for ease of management.

III. Rapidly pursue targeted growth opportunities

- Information Systems can assist by providing *worldwide reporting* through data warehouses. This will allow us to take advantage of global opportunities for new business as well as business improvements.
- Information Systems can assist by providing systems solutions that allow us to leverage the combined *family* of products and organizations.
- We can implement *worldwide communication* and systems. The worldwide network must include access from customers and vendors, as well as subsidiaries.
- Systems must have *multilingual and multicurrency* capabilities.
- We can provide tools for *Marketing tracking.* This will allow us to track project pursuit, determine areas for increased pursuit, and be aware of worldwide activities for our multinational customers. An industry database or system can provide listings of potential customers.
- We can implement a *Quotation Reporting* system that tracks quotations won and lost, competitors, reasons for loss, etc. This will allow us to improve our performance and win-ratio for quotations. Worldwide project pursuit would identify growth opportunities.

Exhibit 5.20 Information Systems and the Business Goals Example — 1 (continued)

- We can support the worldwide *super service center* concept by assisting with systems implementations in Germany, Singapore, and other sites as needed. We can ensure that information systems planning addresses the global business needs rather than just our location.

IV. Create high value, differentiated products for growth

- By integrating our environment and systems with the overall business direction, we can take advantage in the marketplace of our overall product family strength and ensure that future development is consistent to further support this strength.
- We can provide tools for online imaging for Engineering Change Orders (ECOs) and drawings that will assist in improving the process of getting *product to market* faster.
- We can have a closer tie between the business computing environment and the *engineering computing environment* since there is some common information you can share rather than duplicate. This will reduce the cost of engineering new products.
- An improved Marketing and Customer Feedback system will help ensure that we are *developing the right products* for the industry and customer requests.

V. Be the best cost producer

- By investing in information systems with business process re-engineering, we can provide tools to improve the *efficiency and productivity* of the entire division that will improve our overall cost position. Teams throughout the division continuously improve their processes. Often, these improvements require changes within the system. By continuing to change and enhance our existing systems, we can support these cost reductions as identified. Implement tools to support a paperless environment.
- The business is expanding manufacturing *globally* in various areas to reduce our cost of manufacturing. We can support this by assisting in implementing systems in other parts of the world (for example, Singapore and Germany).
- *Global financial information* can provide improved visibility to the business. Quick, easy, and timely access to information can allow for improved business decisions.
- Use tools to develop systems *quickly* to handle the changing and growing business requirements (for example, Rapid Application Development).
- We can implement systems that are *flexible* to changing business needs (for example, requiring table changes rather than programming changes).

VI. Manage the business globally

- Information Systems can provide systems that have *real time access* so that information is readily available to enable improved business decisions. This includes having systems that are available 24 hours a day and data structures that are accessible (through relational databases such as DB2).

Exhibit 5.20 Information Systems and the Business Goals Example — 1 (continued)

- Using tools, complete business processes in a *paperless environment* so that business can easily take place around the world. This will significantly reduce our costs and improve overall business efficiency.
- We can implement *portable* systems so that the company can move them to smaller or larger locations with a minimum of effort. Both software and data must be transportable to other hardware platforms and locations.
- Utilize *data warehousing* concepts and software tools to pull information from all the differing systems and worldwide locations. The company can then easily analyze the information and provide management with the information it needs to manage a worldwide business.
- Educate Information Systems personnel about worldwide culture differences and increase their exposure to worldwide systems so that we can effectively address solutions for our new *worldwide view*.
- Information Systems can assist the business in utilizing new *technology*, such as PCs, laptop PCs, and software that will improve business processing.
- We need to ensure that systems are *worldwide* in nature and that Information Systems strategic planning includes worldwide needs.
- Implement improved tools for managing the worldwide *pricing* situation.
- Modifying systems so that we function on a common *worldwide calendar* will allow us to easily interpret and analyze financial results and information.
- Ensuring that systems are in place so that the critical worldwide *information needs* required to manage the business are readily available will assist the business in worldwide management. Key measures to manage the business must be consistent and readily available on a worldwide basis.

VII. Maintain an environment where people want to work

- Support the *continuous process improvement environment* in the division by having systems that are flexible and easy to modify.
- Ensure Information Systems *job descriptions* accurately reflect the positions and responsibilities.
- *Train* and tool Information Systems personnel with up-to-date technology and skills.
- *Communicate* tools and capabilities available to the division.

Exhibit 5.21 Information Systems and the Business Goals Example — 2

Information Systems and the Business Goals

Closely align information systems priorities and direction with the business goals and objectives. Following are some ways in which Information Systems can play a role in each of the business goals outlined previously:

Exhibit 5.21   Information Systems and the Business Goals Example — 2 (continued)

1. Achieve financial targets and credibility

   - Financial Information: Information Systems can provide improved Financial Systems that, in turn, will provide management with the necessary tools to monitor the financial health of the division and enable early detection and correction of problem areas. Apply consistent financial definitions and measurements. Improved analytical tools and *ad hoc* retrieval of the information will provide improved financial visibility and "drill down" capability to isolate problem areas. Systems must also be available to improve the visibility of financial information for services, sales, and costs.
   - Financial and Product Forecasting Information: Consistent and reliable reporting of forecasts and expected financial results is critical. Improving visibility to outstanding quotations on a regular basis will provide financial and business planning for the future.
   - Project Profit & Loss Information: As the market emphasis and profitability shifts from hardware to services, we need to provide improved systems in the area of Project Management and Engineering. This will continue to increase in importance. These tools include project scheduling, change-order control, percentage complete, resource management, and financial information about projected and actual project profitability.
   - Worldwide Information: Worldwide information through a warehouse approach will provide business management with tools needed to manage the business and improve profitability on a worldwide basis.
   - Increase Productivity: One of the main goals of Information Systems is to eliminate waste and increase productivity throughout the division. This will reduce our overhead costs and allow us to meet or exceed our financial targets. Information Systems can play a very important role in facilitating and coordinating the elimination of non-value-added tasks through business process redesign initiatives.

2. Merge to a common architecture

   - Common Computing Tools: Information Systems can provide a common set of tools that will assist Technology in communication and migration of the platforms. This includes a seamless electronic mail system as well as common tools for business communication such as technical documentation, word processing, presentation graphics, and spreadsheets.
   - Engineering: For our customers, our product and services integrate the control system to their business application systems. Although we do this for our customers, we could do a better job of integration internally by coupling the engineering and manufacturing of our product closer to our business application systems. This results in a more timely solution to market. For example, engineering tools could provide worldwide access to designs and interface directly to the manufacturing system.

Exhibit 5.21   Information Systems and the Business Goals Example — 2 (continued)

3. Transition selling and servicing organizations to achieve competitive advantage

- **Customer Information:** It is imperative that we know exactly who our worldwide customer base is. Our customer base is an important asset for our future, and we need to treat it as such. We need an accurate, worldwide, easily accessible database with information about customers and what equipment they have. Understanding this information will allow us to improve customer service as well as increase potential sales. Examples of the kinds of information to include are:
  - Who the customer is
  - What hardware and software they have and how long they have had it
  - What industry and application it is used for
  - What devices it interfaces with
  - When and how it was serviced
  - All conversations and issues that have taken place
  - Customer contact individuals for various functions
  - Company contacts for various functions
  - Sales volume
  - Any agreements or special terms
  - Special notes about the customer
- **Order Entry and Quoting:** It is critical that we structure our business and computer systems so that it is easy for customers to do business with us. Every point at which a customer comes into contact with us (configuration, quotation, contract negotiations, order, invoice, order status) must be easy, quick, and accurate.
- **Enhancement and Bug Information:** We need to be responsive to customers who request an enhancement or discover a deficiency in the product. Information Systems can provide a tool to track and report these enhancements and bugs. This will allow us to track it through the process and effectively manage completion of the effort, track and improve our quality, and communicate with the customers. The customers could have direct access to status and enter problems.
- **Technical Information:** Today we are wasting expensive engineering and technical resources by "reinventing the wheel." A customer asks a question that has been asked and researched before within the organization. Utilize a tool to store all technical information with extensive "key-word" search capabilities to allow us to respond to our customers in a more timely, consistent, and cost-effective manner.
- **Service Tools:** Information Systems can become an integral part of servicing the customer. Use tools to monitor customer call tracking, but also aid in diagnostic expertise, questioning, and trouble-shooting. A computerized system with artificial intelligence could have electronic documentation, automatic logging and reporting capability, problem detection information, a direct interface to service management, and could also provide failure and servicing information for quality analysis.

Exhibit 5.21   Information Systems and the Business Goals Example — 2 (continued)

- Skills Inventory and Resource Availability: Provide a worldwide warehouse of resources and skills available so that the individuals can be used as needed.
- Customer Tools: Information Systems can assist in many areas to make it easy for the customer to communicate with us and improve customer service. One example of this would be an online bulletin board system with product announcements and alerts, ordering information, and new product releases. Link customers into an online communication system to send messages directly to employees. Other examples include direct access to our systems, Electronic Data Interchange (EDI), voice mail, video teleconferencing, graphical order entry and configuration, and "one-stop shopping" concepts. All of these methods can provide a partnership approach to ensure continued business.
- Pricing Information: We need accurate and thorough information on profit margins.

4. Develop strong third-party relationships

- Information Systems can assist by using common third parties for additional services such as PC outsourcing support, application vendor packages, computer equipment purchases, etc.

5. Develop a strong corporate identity

- Information Systems can provide a clear direction for migration to common business application systems. Operating on common systems will improve the leveraging and communication, and allow us to function better as a single entity.

Exhibit 5.22   Information Systems and the Business Goals Example — 3

Following are five business goals and possible ways in which Information Systems could help the company achieve them.

1. Customer Delight

- Design systems so that customers can access information easily and directly. Customers should be able to design and enter orders, obtain cost, delivery date, and shipping information directly via technology (e.g., Internet, phone response, direct entry).
- Systems should utilize electronic exchange, such as EDI, electronic payment and invoicing, quotes, and acknowledgments.
- Product selection and configuration of custom orders should be easy and feed directly into manufacturing.
- Systems and processes should be designed to ensure maximum quality delivered to the customer. This includes catching design errors through the use of a configurator.

Exhibit 5.22   Information Systems and the Business Goals Example — 3 (continued)

- Provide services and information to ease customer responsibilities (e.g., bar coding on furniture for asset management, space management software).
- All output of systems that touch the customer should support the corporate image.
- Systems can provide business simulation capability to answer "what if" questions.
- Systems should provide complete error checking to catch errors immediately.
- Systems should be able to adjust quickly to changing customer needs. These changes should be possible, for the most part, without IS involvement.
- Systems should be easy to use to support the internal customer, or the next person in the process.

2. Superior Sales Growth
   - Provide pursuit and selling tools and systems to improve the sales process. This includes product configuration, time and territory management, sales pursuit systems, target market development, automated marketing lead information, and target market potential.
   - Systems should be flexible for changing sales territories, and should actually proactively suggest optimum territory alignment.
   - Provide online bulletin board, fax-back, or Internet system to provide immediate access to product information, ability to place orders, answers to questions, and product literature.
   - Have tools and systems that can integrate new products.
   - Provide distribution planning systems.
   - Provide systems and tools that are easy and add value to the dealers and representatives.
   - Provide tools that can analyze the impact of future price increases to maximize value and minimize customer costs.
   - Provide systems and tools to support the design and introduction phase of product development.
   - Provide systems with simulation capability.
   - Provide forecast information to drive manufacturing planning so that we can build the volume we sell.
   - Provide configuration editing so that we can manufacture what we sell (ensure manufacture-ability).
   - Interface to industry databases and information to proactively build pursuit information.

3. Financial Excellence
   - Utilize business process re-engineering to eliminate non-value-added steps throughout the business.
   - Implement tools and processes to support a paperless environment.
   - Standardize tools and equipment to reduce support costs. Utilize standard software packages whenever possible.

Exhibit 5.22   Information Systems and the Business Goals Example — 3 (continued)

- Provide tools that provide immediate financial feedback and information in a format that is understandable so that corrective actions can be taken.
- Provide improved tools for inventory management and inventory-turns accuracy.
- Have flexible systems that can integrate future acquisitions.
- Provide improved visibility to maintain and monitor standard and variance cost information.
- Provide cost of quality measurement information, such as margin analysis, estimating tools, and quotes.

4. Employee Excellence

- Provide systems that are easy to use and make it easy to obtain information.
- Train employees in the tools and processes to minimize frustration and to improve their ability to do their jobs.
- Provide up-to-date tools and technology.
- Provide systems to track employee training and capabilities.
- Provide employee performance tracking.

5. Business Process Improvement

- Provide systems that are flexible in handling changes in business processes.
- Provide training and tools to facilitate business process re-engineering.
- Provide a structure and process for business process improvement.
- Provide a tool to track and prioritize business process improvements.
- Provide quality measurements, such as value-added ratios.
- Provide documentation and procedures for processes.

The process of looking at business goals has probably identified additional information systems projects that were not previously on the backlog list. Add these projects to the list. Do not panic if the backlog seems to be growing; you will soon identify priorities that will ensure that the correct projects are in progress.

Computing Architecture

For a complex environment with many different components to work together, it is necessary to have agreed upon a common **computing architecture**. As you expand the information systems environment in the future, the additions must conform to the computing architecture to ensure that all components will continue to function together. Update this architecture on an ongoing basis with technology advances and changes. Start with the business operating vision in building the computing architecture rather than just focusing on technology itself. You must have a business requirement or problem to solve before deploying technology.

Looking at the information systems mission and objectives developed above, you can determine what technical requirements are necessary to meet the business objectives. An example of this is depicted in Figure 5.4.

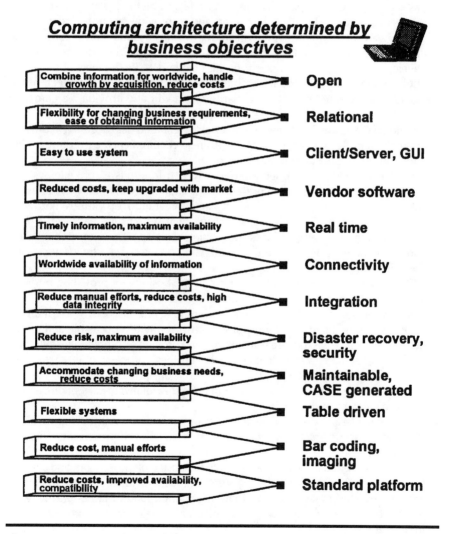

Figure 5.4   Computing Architecture

You can also provide a detailed description of the computing architecture components in terms that the business can understand. An example of this is included in Exhibit 5.23.

Exhibit 5.23   Computing Architecture Description

- **Open** (or Open DataBase Compliant — ODBC): Implementation of systems based on open technology will be the most effective method to meet the business requirements of worldwide information and to provide solutions independent of hardware platforms. ODBC will allow technically different systems to be interfaced to share any information the business requires. Purchased or internally developed software must conform to this standard as the benefits obtained by implementing an open systems architecture can be eroded if one piece of the architecture does not meet the standards. Open will also provide the company with a leveraged position for negotiating with vendors.
- **Relational Database Structure:** A relational (SQL) based data access will provide the maximum flexibility for changing business requirements, ease of obtaining information, and maximum data integrity.
- **Client/Server, Graphical User Interfaces (GUI):** In efforts to provide systems that are easy to use and which present information in meaningful ways to users, we will utilize the power of the PC and integration of various hardware platforms. Standard GUI designs will ensure that systems are easy to use with minimal training. It also reduces application development time. Both the PC and network environments are critical components of a client/server GUI environment.
- **Vendor-Supported Software:** We are not in the business of providing business application software. Other companies are, and can do it better and less expensively than custom-writing our software to fit our business. We will utilize packaged, unmodified, vendor-supplied software whenever possible and utilize our resources in areas that are truly unique and provide a competitive advantage in the marketplace. We will change the business process to fit a standard package rather than changing the system to fit our process. Although we will not utilize beta software, our strategy will be to stay relatively current on vendor-supplied releases and rewrites.
- **Real Time:** Design and implement systems in such a way that updating of information occurs immediately rather than through batch processing. This will support the objective of 24-hour availability as well as the timely information requirements. Build backup measures into the design of the network and systems to ensure continuous availability. Systems must be reliable with minimum downtime. Design systems so that information is available online with distributed printing capability to minimize handling costs and provide timely information.

Exhibit 5.23   Computing Architecture Description (continued)

- **Connectivity:** Design the computing environment for optimum connectivity rather than stand-alone islands. The objective is to be able to electronically share and pass information from anywhere in the world to anywhere in the world. We can obtain significant value for the business by sharing information, eliminating redundancy of efforts, and increasing the speed of communication through a solid networked environment. We will leverage this network with the entire organization for efficiency and cost reasons. This connectivity requires compliance with certain technical standards and guidelines.
- **Integration:** Design systems such that you enter information only once. This will reduce effort, eliminate redundancy of data, and improve data integrity.
- **Data Integrity:** The accuracy and dependability of our information are foremost. Therefore, we will implement application solutions that ensure the data are correct at all times. This implies sufficient edits to ensure the user enters the data properly as well as taking sufficient data collision precautions through application design standards.
- **Software Design:** The core of tightly integrated applications (Financial, Manufacturing, Distribution) will be provided by one software supplier to minimize the amount of bridges and interfaces necessary.
- **Electronic Exchange:** Information exchanged within or outside the organization must be electronic whenever possible and through industry standard Electronic Data Interchange (EDI).
- **Disaster Recovery:** Design recovery in the event of disasters or problems with each application. Design recovery up to the last business day, with disaster recovery within one business day.
- **Security:** Implement applications and software with the utmost security to ensure that we protect our critical business information. Protect and secure the worldwide network as much as possible. Take sufficient measures for overall security, including virus checking and password protection, and design other software security measures.
- **Documentation:** Appropriate online and printed system HELP will be available for users of the systems. This will provide immediate aids to system navigation as well as minimizing training time for new and existing users.
- **Maintainability:** For areas of the business whose requirements you cannot meet with standard vendor-supplied software applications packages, design systems that are easy to modify and quickly tailored to changing business needs or business process improvements.
- **CASE Generated:** Computer Aided Systems Engineering improves the quality and consistency of the systems while also increasing productivity and communication during the systems development process. Over the life of the systems, the company will be able to reduce costs because systems are easier to maintain.
- **Table Driven:** Systems developed with tables rather than hard-coded values are more flexible for changing business needs. Maintenance costs of systems are considerably less because users are able to make changes to meet business needs.

Exhibit 5.23   Computing Architecture Description (continued)

- **Bar Coding:** Utilize bar coding whenever possible to reduce the amount of manual labor required to maintain information.
- **Imaging:** Whenever possible, store and retrieve documents online for efficiency.
- **X.400 or X.500 E-Mail Standard:** Use this standard electronic mail protocol to allow for compatible communications.
- **ISO Certified Suppliers:** If possible, we will select suppliers that are ISO certified for our software providers.
- **Other Technologies:** Deploy other technologies, such as video conferencing, pen-based computing, CD-ROM, Executive IS, as the business requirements dictate.

Exhibits 5.24 and 5.25 show how other companies described their computing architecture and technical strategies.

Exhibit 5.24   Technical Computing Architecture

The technical computing architecture will:
- Provide system performance, availability, and reliability consistent with business needs
- Support client/server architecture
- Enable office, home, and mobile computing
- Use scaleable components
- Minimize variety within each architecture component
- Include tools for managing utilization of components
- Rely on a minimum number of vendors that:
  - Have a global support infrastructure
  - Support multiple prior versions of their products
  - Provide products that are compatible with multiple brands of other components

Exhibit 5.25   Technical Strategies

- The computing architecture will be adhered to for all future systems.
- Systems will be developed with a client/server model. A three-tiered application architecture (presentation, logic, data) will be employed on a three-tiered technical architecture (workstation, application server, enterprise server).
- Data and function should be distributed as necessary to meet business and performance needs.
- Systems will employ graphical user interface design when appropriate.

Exhibit 5.25   Technical Strategies (continued)

- Object technology will be used where appropriate to develop flexible, timely systems.
- A global network will be in place to service users worldwide.
- Data integrity, concurrency, and throughput should be managed by a transaction monitor.
- Elimination of a single point of failure should be balanced against cost.
- Systems should provide national language support where reasonable.
- Products selected should adhere to industry-accepted standards (open).
- There should be a high degree of interoperability between the application development tools and the systems management tools.
- Systems will be deployed using relational database technology.
- Systems will be displayed graphically.
- Multimedia will be deployed as necessary and will be balanced against cost.

You may find it useful to separate the detailed technical architecture plan into a stand-alone document. This will provide the details necessary for the technical group, and this level of detail may not be necessary for business management. Following are the components of a separate technical architecture plan which was developed at one company:

- Executive Summary: Provides summary information on the technical architecture plan. This section should also be included in the Information Systems Strategic Plan for all business management.
- Architecture Overview: Describes specific architectural principles, as well as identifying main system anchor points. Anchor points are technology or tools in which the company has a significant amount of money invested, and will not change in the near future.
- Client Architecture: Presents an examination of the hardware and software components that comprise the client architecture (PC, workstation). Details any assumptions made in the client architecture design, along with an analysis of implicit risks and concerns associated with its deployment and use.
- Work-Group Server Architecture: Presents an examination of the hardware and software components that comprise the work-group server architecture. Details any assumptions made in the work-group server architecture design, along with an analysis of implicit risks and concerns associated with its deployment and use.
- Enterprise Server Architecture: Presents an examination of the hardware and software components that comprise the enterprise server

architecture. Details any assumptions made in the enterprise server architecture design, along with an analysis of implicit risks and concerns associated with its deployment and use.

- LAN Architecture: Presents an examination of the hardware and software components that comprise the LAN architecture. Details any assumptions made in the LAN architecture design, along with an analysis of implicit risks and concerns.
- WAN Architecture: Presents an examination of the hardware and software components that comprise the WAN architecture. Details any assumptions made in the WAN architecture design, along with an analysis of implicit risks and concerns.
- Other Enabling Technologies: Provides a detailed look at the architecture associated with other add-on technologies.
- Performance: Describes the physical placement of data and applications within the system, along with an analysis of its impact on performance. Outlines performance criteria and service level expectations.
- System Management Integration: Outlines the hardware and software necessary to manage the entire environment.

Information Architecture

In large, global companies with various divisions and locations, the question is often raised as to what **information** resides at each site, what information is necessary at a corporate level, and what information must be shared across sites. It is important to resolve this issue in the strategic planning process. Information systems expenditures at a local or site level may not be necessary, or would not be approved if the direction is different at a corporate level. Although there are common corporate information needs, there are often different information needs at the site level, or information that must be shared by the remote sites. Agree upon the information architecture in advance, even though it is possible to bring together the corporate information in a data warehouse. The locations and corporate must decide who is responsible for what information. The following diagram (Figure 5.5) depicts the different information needs that exist.

As information needs migrate toward the center (for example, global or company group level), the cost and complexity of providing the information systems solution are higher and the degree of flexibility is reduced. This is

Information Needs

Figure 5.5   Information Needs

because consistent systems and processes must be in place to transfer and collect the worldwide or group information in addition to the site information. Therefore, unless there is a business need to migrate the information to the center of the circle, it is best that it remain close to the site level. Even though an information need would be at the global or group level, the actual transaction-based system needs to exist at the site or geographic area. The global or group solution would typically be a data warehouse for reporting purposes.

It can be helpful to develop a grid with the information needs that were developed earlier (in Chapter 3) and identify what Information Systems group is responsible for that information. This means that the information is needed at the particular level or site, to report the data or to update it. There may or may not be a separate Information Systems organization or separate information systems business applications at each of the sites. In the event there are multiple systems and organizations, typically the lowest level that is responsible for updating the information is the owner of the information and systems to maintain the information. See the following example in Table 5.1. "Y" denotes that that business group has a requirement for the information.

Information Systems and the business can further clarify the table with the use of the CRUD criteria. The CRUD criteria identify which entity is responsible for creating, replacing, updating, and deleting the information. You can also note if the organization only requires the information for reporting purposes. This table can then become the basis for future system development. There are tremendous business ramifications and questions

Table 5.1   Information Architecture

Information Need	Sales Site	System Eng. Site	Mfg. Site	Geo. Area	Global	Process Group
Marketing:						
Customer Information	Y	Y		Y	Y	Y
Pricing and discounts	Y	Y		Y	Y	
Quote	Y	Y		Y	Y	
Forecasting	Y	Y	Y	Y	Y	
Technical Reference	Y	Y		Y	Y	Y
Agreements, Contracts, TC	Y	Y		Y	Y	Y
Sales Goals, Credits	Y			Y		
Pursuit Information	Y			Y	Y	Y
Competitor	Y			Y	Y	Y
Training Course	Y	Y		Y		
Sales Tools (Bulletin Board)	Y	Y		Y	Y	Y
Order:						
Order Information	Y	Y	Y	Y	Y	Y
Project Information	Y	Y	Y	Y	Y	Y
Bookings	Y			Y	Y	
Backlog			Y	Y	Y	
Item and Model Level	Y	Y	Y	Y	Y	
CAD Design Information		Y	Y	Y	Y	
Configurator	Y	Y		Y	Y	
Sales	Y			Y	Y	Y
Distributions Req Plan	Y		Y		Y	
Shipping	Y		Y			
Invoicing				Y	Y	Y
Order Status	Y	Y	Y			
Project History	Y	Y		Y	Y	
Service Level	Y	Y	Y	Y	Y	
Table of Denial	Y					
Project Engineering:						
Project P&L	Y	Y	Y	Y	Y	
Resource Availability		Y		Y	Y	
Project Scheduling		Y		Y		
Resource Skills		Y		Y	Y	

Table 5.1   Information Architecture (continued)

Information Need	Sales Site	System Eng. Site	Mfg. Site	Geo. Area	Global	Process Group
Quality:						
Internal Failure			Y			
Shipment and Warranty	Y		Y	Y	Y	
Quality Procedures	Y	Y	Y	Y	Y	
Hold Information	Y	Y	Y			
Field Failure Information			Y	Y	Y	
Field Service:						
Call Tracking	Y			Y	Y	Y
Installed Base Information	Y	Y	Y	Y	Y	Y
Diagnostic	Y	Y		Y	Y	Y
R&D and Technology:						
Bug and Enhancement		Y		Y	Y	
Manufacturing:						
Bill-of-Material			Y			
Engineering Change			Y			
CAD			Y			
Inventory and cycle count			Y			
Manufacturing Item			Y			
Master Scheduling			Y			
Material Req Planning			Y			
Manufacturing Order			Y			
Purchasing			Y	Y	Y	Y
Vendor Information			Y	Y	Y	Y
Capacity Planning			Y			
Mfg Routing and Hours			Y			
Financial:						
Product Cost			Y	Y		
Budgeting		Y	Y	Y		Y
Functional P&L	Y	Y	Y	Y	Y	Y
Balance Statement				Y	Y	Y
General Ledger		Y	Y	Y	Y	
Accounts Payable		Y	Y	Y		

Table 5.1   Information Architecture (continued)

Information Need	Sales Site	System Eng. Site	Mfg. Site	Geo. Area	Global	Process Group
Fixed Assets		Y	Y	Y		
Accounts Receivable				Y	Y	Y
Credit	Y			Y	Y	Y
Sales Tax				Y		
Foreign Currency				Y	Y	
Human Resources:						
Employee, Position				Y		Y
Payroll			Y	Y	Y	
Employee Hours	Y		Y	Y		
Benefit Information				Y	Y	
Salary Planning				Y		Y
Applicant Tracking				Y		
Employee Training, Skills				Y	Y	Y

within each of the information needs. Closely review and discuss this list with management.

It is possible that the discussion of information needs also initiates some information systems projects that were not previously identified on the backlog list. Add these new projects to the list. You may discover that key information needs are kept by manual methods or Excel spreadsheets with a significant amount of labor associated to obtain the information. It is common that, after years of using a constant system with changing business processes and needs, that the users are actually printing off data, rekeying it into separate manual spreadsheets or systems to get the real information needed.

Policies and Responsibilities

As information systems technology is moving into the business, the Information Systems organization finds it has less and less control of the environment. Yet, it is even more critical now for all the pieces to function together. Therefore, it is useful to establish certain guidelines, or **policies and responsibilities,** within which the business can operate while not jeopardizing the larger picture by conflicting with other objectives or tools in the environment.

Some of these items may already be established in a corporate policies and procedures manual, in which case you can just reference the documents. Having policies and procedures well documented can save hours of frustration for both users and Information Systems personnel. Be sure to update this information frequently and provide all users with convenient access to it. Following are some examples of items that you should include in this section:

1. What is the standard PC hardware that users can acquire that Information Systems supports? What is the process for hardware acquisition? What hardware requires the approval of Information Systems?

2. What is the standard PC software that the users can acquire that is supported by Information Systems? What software is available on the network? What is the process for software acquisition? What requires the approval of Information Systems?

3. Who is responsible for budgeting acquisition and depreciation of PCs? To whom does the PC belong? For example, can Information Systems redeploy PCs to match the business need?

4. Who is responsible for ensuring optimum pricing on PC hardware and software? For example, is it Purchasing's or Information Systems' responsibility?

5. Who is responsible for budgeting PC software, standard desktop software as well as the necessary special software? How do you ensure software license compliance?

6. How does the company manage PC retirement, and who is responsible? What methods do you utilize for PC disposal?

7. What standards does the company follow for user-developed PC applications? When does a PC business application become the support responsibility of Information Systems? What methods of back-up and documentation are necessary? What is the policy and responsibilities for other user department tools that may be used, such as Intranet, Internet, customer bulletin boards, EDI, and Lotus Notes applications.

8. What is the company policy regarding PC games and Internet access?

9. Who is responsible for organizing and funding PC training?

10. Who is responsible for ensuring a virus-free environment?

11. What is the responsibility of any remote sites? What is the responsibility of the remote site and what is the responsibility of the central Information Systems department?

12. What are the responsibilities of the users and Information Systems for new business applications or projects?

Annual Objectives

Clearly state what Information Systems will do and will not do in the coming year so that everyone has common expectations. This is done through agreed-upon and prioritized **annual objectives**. The annual objectives may change once the planning process is complete and a new direction is formulated. However, in the meantime, projects need to be worked on and should be formally prioritized. The priorities can then be modified once a direction is agreed upon.

Information Systems projects must be aligned with business objectives through the prioritization process. The Information Systems Steering Committee completes the prioritization process. Often, the prioritization can become an emotional and political event. With a solid process agreed to by the group (which is outlined below) before beginning, you can complete the prioritization process quickly and easily.

After completing the prioritization process in one company, an Information Systems Steering Committee representative was asked what he thought of the process: "Of course I'm disappointed that my projects didn't come out on top, but I understand the process, and agree that other projects have higher priority for the company." In another company, through the prioritization process, it was discovered that Information Systems was working on projects in the wrong area of the company: manufacturing projects were being completed because of the involvement and pressure of the Vice President of Manufacturing. After going through a structured prioritization process, it was discovered that Marketing projects were more important to the strategic direction of the company.

Complete the prioritization only for projects above a certain level of effort or cost. This level should be set by the Information Systems Steering Committee. The level should be high enough so the group is not evaluating every minor change, but low enough so the Steering Committee can direct the majority of time. Information Systems can prioritize day-to-day individual requests and small projects with copies of the requests and priorities going to the Information Systems Steering Committee for their information. However, projects must all be sponsored and represented by a member of the Information Systems Steering Committee. Information Systems presents only infrastructure projects.

Before beginning the prioritization process, the Information Systems Steering Committee must understand the business purpose of each project. Ask each member of the Information Systems Steering Committee to talk briefly about each project that has been requested from his or her area. The

Steering Committee member can explain the purpose of the project and why it is important to the business.

Following are three different processes to prioritize projects. You can utilize whatever process best fits your environment and the recommendation from your Information Systems Steering Committee. The processes are:

1. Prioritizing by Business Objective
2. Prioritizing by Forced Ranking
3. Prioritizing by Business Criteria

1. Prioritizing by Business Objective
   a) List the business objectives. The business objectives were identified in Chapter 3.
   b) Rank the importance of each business objective on a scale of 5 to 15, with 15 being the most important. If the company only has a few objectives, use 6 to 10 for mathematical purposes. The Executive Committee or the Information Systems Steering Committee can help in this process.
   c) List all the Information Systems projects. If the list is too long, have the Steering Committee identify any low priority projects that will not be prioritized and just list the projects to be prioritized.
   d) Identify the impact (1 to 10) each will have on business objectives. With the Information Systems Steering Committee, go through each project and discuss the impact the project will have on each business objective. Typically, the sponsor of the project is the best able to score the project, but other members can challenge the rating. It is important to do this in a group setting rather than as an assignment because the entire group can gain appreciation for the importance of projects outside their areas. Open debate and discussion should be encouraged, not avoided.
   e) Multiply the impact times the business goal ranking and total the score for each project.
   f) List projects in descending total score for a prioritized list of projects.
   g) This mathematical model can only provide a starting point or recommended list. The Information Systems Steering Committee can then review the list in total and make adjustments as needed. There may be other factors, not identified in the business objectives, that impact the projects, such as dates required or project dependencies.

2. **Prioritizing by Forced Ranking**

   a) List all the Information Systems projects. If the list is too long to prioritize, have the Steering Committee identify any low-priority projects that will not be prioritized and just list those projects to be prioritized.

   b) Go through a force ranking process by comparing the first project with the second, the first project with the third, fourth, and so on through the entire list. Then compare the second project with the third, fourth, fifth, and so on. With each pair of projects, ask the Information Systems Steering Committee for a vote. If they could have only one of the two projects, which would they choose? The project with the most votes gets a mark. Do not spend time arguing, but rather ask for a vote, note the majority, and move on to the next project. Remind the Steering Committee that it is their job to objectively determine projects with the most impact, rather than just voting for their own efforts.

   c) Add up all the marks for each project. List the projects in descending order based on the marks for a prioritized list. Again, review the list in totality because this mathematical model only provides a starting point or recommended list.

3. **Prioritizing by Business Performance Impact Criteria**

   This process is similar to the prioritization process identified earlier for business processes.

   a) Identify basic opportunities to impact performance, such as:

      1. Impact on external customers or entities (for example, customers, subsidiaries, buying groups, government agencies, ISO).
      2. Impact on quality of service or product.
      3. Reduction of business costs.
      4. Impact on internal customers.
      5. Impact on the speed of the process.

   b) Rank the importance of the performance impact on the company using a scale of 7 to 10. This number will become the project multiplier.

   c) List all the Information Systems projects.

   d) With the Information Systems Steering Committee, agree on the impact the project will have on each of the performance impacts. Rate that impact on a scale of 0 to 10, with 10 having the highest impact.

   e) Multiply the project multiplier times the rating for a score. Add up the total points for a project score.

f) List the projects in descending score order for a prioritized list of projects. Again, review the list in total as this mathematical model is only a starting guide.

After the prioritization process is complete, you can then balance against available project resources to determine how far down the list you can get during the next year. List the projects in priority order with the estimated hours. From your work in identifying resources and backlog, you have the number of project hours which you can accommodate with current resources. Draw a line at the point at which resources are depleted for the year. You may also need to consider skill type and availability required for the projects. The Information Systems Steering Committee can then review the projects below the line. If the projects must be completed this year, the Steering Committee has the choice of adding resources, either full-time or contract, to accommodate the need.

You can then assign resources and develop a detailed timeline and estimated completion date of the prioritized projects. Be sure to account for day-to-day support. For example, a 120-hour project may take significantly longer than 3 weeks due to vacation, other activities, etc.

Information Systems Service Architecture

Service architecture is the blueprint that specifies which information systems processes and what kinds of people are required to support the business systems and computing architecture. The people side of the equation and direction cannot be overlooked, because without the properly skilled people you will not reach even the best-planned direction.

The service architecture includes:

- Processes: major functions of the management information systems organization
- People: hiring, development, and compensation practices
- Organization: internal structure of the management information systems organization
- Culture: values held within the management information systems organization
- Technology: characteristics of implemented technology
- Metrics: methods of providing and ensuring quality

Exhibit 5.26   Service Architecture

People

Business Area Experts

- Specialization by business processes
- Specialized knowledge of business systems that support those business processes
- General knowledge of technology

Application Experts

- Specialization by type of business system
- Specialized knowledge of business systems capabilities, operations, and supporting tools
- General knowledge of technology and business processes

Technology Experts

- Specialization by technology component
- Specialized knowledge of technology component capabilities, operations, and supporting tools
- General knowledge of business systems and business processes

Processes

Projects

- Deployment of new systems
- Substantial additions to existing system capabilities
- Substantial revisions to existing system capabilities

Enhancements

- Minor revisions to existing system capabilities
- Minor additions to existing system capabilities

Support

- Operations
- Maintenance
- Troubleshooting
- Consulting

One company summarized the service architecture direction as shown in Exhibit 5.26.

Some of the questions you should consider include:

- Are you providing all the information systems functions that are necessary? Are user areas providing support that the Information Systems organization should?

- Are the information systems processes efficient? Have they been mapped and reviewed for efficiency? Are user inquiries handled quickly and efficiently? Are users satisfied with the support? Why or why not?
- Are you hiring people with the skill set you require in the future? Are you providing the proper development for employees? Can employees cross into other areas of Information Systems and obtain cross-training?
- What has been the turnover within Information Systems? What have been some of the reasons for leaving?
- Are compensation policies aligned with market demands? Have you had significant turnover due to salaries?
- Is the organization structured efficiently? Do you have the functions you will need in the future? Do job descriptions and titles accurately depict the functions that are needed today as well as in the future?
- Are the values reflected through daily decisions?
- Does the organization understand the direction?
- How do you measure Information Systems efficiency and effectiveness?

Through this process, one company found it was necessary to totally change job descriptions, titles, salary grades, and organizational structure. Although it may be necessary, major changes such as these should be thoroughly considered before implementing, because they can cause severe havoc in an Information Systems organization, even if implemented carefully.

The company looked at the client/server technology of the future and determined it had a significant impact on the resources. In the past, resources were very focused in narrow areas of network, PC, and business application. As client/server applications were implemented, they were falling through the cracks of the Information Systems organization because no area of Information Systems claimed responsibility. To successfully assist the users, they needed knowledge and skills in all three areas: PC, network, and business applications. It was also desired to provide more growth opportunities and reward for breadth of knowledge. Some companies have implemented a "pay for skill" program for this very reason. Job descriptions were also not indicative of the new technology and roles. Flexible and broad job descriptions were necessary so they would not require updating as the technology changed. Rather than having different titles for each function of Information Systems (PC, network, business application), the company chose generic titles and job descriptions to be used across all the functions. The jobs also encompassed several salary grades to accommodate the growth that was necessary. This also provided a technical career path that extended as high as the management ranks. An example of generic titles includes:

- Information Systems Associate
- Information Systems Specialist
- Information Systems Analyst
- Senior Information Systems Analyst
- Information Systems Architect
- Information Systems Manager

The company also reviewed each open information systems job and identified the specific skill that was desired, from both a personality side and a technical side. The desired skills were prioritized (H: high, M: medium, and L: low). A high priority meant that an individual (no matter how good), would not be hired unless he or she had this skill. This became a checklist and rating sheet for each individual interviewed. The list can also be used to provide candidates with a checklist of what you are looking for. Ask them to rate their skills in each area. The list should be developed by the people interviewing individuals for the position. It can be amazing to discover that each interviewer is looking for slightly different skill sets and individuals. You can also formulate interview questions to directly correlate to your desired criteria. An example is provided in Exhibit 5.27. You can also further define each adjective in a glossary.

Exhibit 5.27   Skill Set Criteria

- Senior Information Systems Support Analyst (Application)
  - H-Team player   H-Analyst skills
  - H-Independent   M-AS/400 skills
  - H-Flexible   M-Financial systems
  - M-Decision maker   M-Multi-platform skills
  - M-Leadership   M-Years experience
  - M-Dedication   M-Specific vendor experience
  - M-Career focus   M-Desktop experience
  - L-Company fit   L-Education
  - L-Visionary

- Senior Information Systems Support Analyst (Network)
  - H-Communication   H-Network architecture/design
  - H-Team player   H-Network monitoring

Exhibit 5.27   Skill Set Criteria (continued)

• H-Independent	H-Server monitoring
• H-Flexible	H-Capacity planning
• H-Decision maker	H-Security design
• H-Visionary	H-Network performance tuning
• M-Dedication	H-WAN experience
• M-Career focus	M-Desktop experience
• L-Company fit	M-UNIX experience
	M-C++ experience
	L-Object orientation
	L-Education
	L-Experience

■ Information Systems Support Architect (DBA)

• H-Team player	H-Oracle experience
• H-Independent	H-Database security experience
• H-Flexible	H-Backup/disaster recovery experience
• H-Decision maker	M-Worldwide replication
• H-Visionary	M-Data warehouse, query tools
• H-Communication	M-UNIX experience
• M-Leadership	M-NT experience
• M-Dedication	M-Database performance tuning
• L-Career focus	M-C++ experience
• L-Company fit	L-Database design
	L-Education
	L-Experience

■ Senior Information Systems Support Analyst (Scientific)

• H-Team player	H-DEC VAX VMS skills
• H-Independent	H-Years experience
• H-Flexible	H-PC programming
• H-Dedication	M-Analyst skills
• M-Decision maker	M-Statistical analysis
• M-Leadership	M-Multi-platform experience
• M-Career focus	M-UNIX experience
• L-Company fit	M-Desktop experience
• L-Visionary	M-Sybase/Oracle experience
	L-Education

■ Information Systems Manager

• H-Communication	H-Management experience
• H-Leadership	H-Cross-platform experience
• H-Worker, set example	H-Network management
• H-Quick learner	H-Data communication experience
• H-Decision maker	H-Desktop management
• H-Visionary	H-Experience
• M-Career focus	M-AS/400 management
• M-Company fit	M-Technical background, programming
• M-Dedication	M-Education

Exhibit 5.27   Skill Set Criteria (continued)

■ Senior Information Systems Support Analyst (PC)
  - H-People person   H-Microsoft Office knowledge
  - H-Open minded   H-PC hardware knowledge
  - H-Creative   H-PC programming, application development
  - H-Conviction   H-Cross-platform connectivity
  - H-Team player   H-Middle-ware experience
  - M-Company fit   M-Network experience
                             M-Database experience
                             M-Microsoft certification
                             M-Multi-platform experience
                             M-Experience
                             L-Education
                             L-UNIX experience
                             L-Oracle experience
                             L-Notes experience

Also review the skills of the existing resources and identify any training that will be necessary for each individual.

If you are changing the organization significantly or shuffling responsibilities, it can help to add clarity by providing a matrix with a column for each individual. For each individual, identify a list of his or her primary objectives as well as secondary objectives. Each area of support should be identified under someone's name. It would be advisable to have items listed under more than one name to provide backup and depth of coverage.

Conclusion

Congratulations! You are now well on your way to having a solid information systems direction. You are now able to complete the following sections of the information systems strategic plan document from phase 3:

VII. Information Systems Direction
  A. Mission
  B. Vision
  C. Strategic Objectives
  D. Strategies
  E. Information Systems and the Business Goals
  F. Computing Architecture

G. Information Architecture
H. Policies and Responsibilities
I. Information Systems Annual Objectives
J. Service Architecture

Present this information to all your planning groups, including first the Information Systems Steering Committee, Information Systems Organization, and finally, the Executive Committee.

6 | Determining the Gap Between Your Current Situation and Where You Want to Be in the Future

"Change is the law of life. And those who look only to the past or the present are sure to miss the future."

John F. Kennedy (1917–1963)
35th President of the United States

Phase 4 of the Process: Planning Option Analysis and Action Plan

Now that you understand where you are today and where you need to be in the future, the next step is to determine how to get to where you want to be. The gap may be large or small, but you need to bridge it in all areas of information systems, whether it is the business application, network, or desktop computing environment. This is the beginning of phase 4 of the planning process, the Option Analysis and Action Plan as shown in Figure 6.1.

Business Operating Vision Assessment

First, go back to the **Business Operating Vision** that was developed in Chapter 3. With the Information Systems Steering Committee, grade your

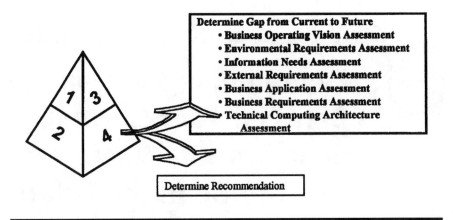

Figure 6.1   Phase 4, Option Analysis and Action Plan

current systems against how well your systems meet the requirements in the Business Operating Vision. The grades can be the same as those assigned in school (or any other rating that the group agrees upon):

A: Excellent
B: Good
C: Average
D: Below Average
F: Fail, doesn't meet requirement at all

It may take a short discussion of each requirement to come to an agreement. Typically, this can be very beneficial in identifying strong and weak areas. Exhibit 6.1 shows an example of one company's grades on its Business Operating Vision.

By reviewing the grades, the group may be able to come to some initial observations. Perhaps all the systems are in bad shape, or perhaps several areas are in excellent shape while only a few areas are poor. This will determine where your focus will begin.

Environmental Requirements Assessment

Turn back to the **environmental requirements** identified in Chapter 3. With the help of the Information Systems Steering Committee, again grade your current systems against how well the systems meet the environmental requirements. Additional observations can indicate some weak areas, or perhaps the business has grown into some new areas and the systems have not kept pace with the changes.

Exhibit 6.1   Business Operating Vision Gap

- ■ Manufacturing
  - • Process manufacturing — D
  - • Discrete manufacturing — D
  - • Make-to-stock manufacturing — D
  - • Make-to-order manufacturing — F
- ■ Operate the business on a worldwide basis
  - • Partial design or manufacturing anywhere — F
  - • Consistent manufacturing processes/products — F
  - • Take an order anywhere, fill anywhere — F
  - • Coordinate worldwide project teams — F
  - • Worldwide procurement and sourcing — F
  - • Common customer support and service — F
  - • Multi-currency, multilingual — F
- ■ Utilize technology to operate efficiently and effectively
  - • Worldwide electronic mail — D
  - • Paperless environment — D
  - • Minimize manual efforts — F
  - • Easy to use, flexible — F
  - • Electronic commerce — F
  - • Easy interfacing of systems — D
- ■ Easy to do business with from a customer standpoint
  - • Electronic commerce — F
  - • Capability to bundle sales — F
  - • Handle complex and multiple site customers — D
  - • Utilize Internet for customer information — F
  - • Utilize external electronic services — F
  - • Interface to customer system — F
- ■ Have worldwide information needed to manage the business
  - • Provide timely visibility to key metrics — D
  - • Track and report contract compliance — C
  - • Timely roll-up of subsidiaries, financial numbers — D
  - • Timely financial close process — D
  - • Track the success of marketing techniques — F
  - • Sales force information — F
  - • Worldwide forecasting, budgeting, planning — D
  - • Worldwide inventory information — F
  - • Worldwide customer complaint/call information — F

Information Needs Assessment

Next, go back to the **information needs** identified in Chapter 3. Again, with the help of the Information Systems Steering Committee, assign grades to how well your current systems are able to handle your information needs. Key information needs should be readily available in the desired format to provide the business with the information necessary to make business decisions. It should not require manual manipulation or rekeying to get the information. In your environment, if it requires a tremendous amount of manual labor, spreadsheets, or manipulation to obtain the information, the grade would be lower. If the information exists and is readily accessible to anyone needing it, the grade would be relatively high.

External Requirements Assessment

Using the **external requirements** developed in Chapter 3, assign grades with the assistance of the Information Systems Steering Committee. Perhaps your systems rate well with the internal requirements, but have not had an external focus.

Business Application Assessment

By **business application** area (Manufacturing, Distribution, Finance), list the strengths and weaknesses of each application. Ask each Information Systems Steering Committee member to meet with his or her group and send you a list of strengths and weaknesses. Typically, those that utilize the business applications on a regular basis are able to quickly formulate this list for you. Getting involvement from the rest of the business in the analysis will be very beneficial. Another way to obtain assessment information is to conduct a user survey. Exhibit 6.2 shows an example of an assessment done at one company.

After submitting the detailed strengths and weaknesses, in a meeting with the Information Systems Steering Committee, brainstorm and list the strengths and weaknesses for the business applications as a whole. The interaction during this process can help some areas of the business understand the situation in other areas. Exhibit 6.3 shows an example of the overall strengths and weaknesses assembled by one company.

Exhibit 6.2   Business Application Detailed Assessment

Order Management and Marketing:

Strengths:

- Order entry is accurate
- Sales system provides a lot of good sales information (although difficult to use)

Weaknesses:

- System has no online verification of inventory, availability, restriction codes, storage temperatures, and order versus forecast.
- Inability to accept an order anywhere in the world, have visibility to it worldwide, and manufacture or fill the order anywhere in the world, depending on capacity, availability, and inventory.
- Inability to handle order entry for shipments from all current distribution centers.
- Inability to handle international orders.
- Inability to support multi-currency and multi-languages.
- System does not currently support electronic commerce with customers, including invoicing, money transfer, payments, or ordering. Systems are not able to do EDI, direct entry, or direct interface from a customer purchasing system.
- Inability to bundle sales and share information with other entities to support joint sales, common customer and membership information, or joint contracts. Inability to produce a combined sales report for customers with corporate information.
- Cumbersome program for handling credits and debits.
- Usage control program is inadequate for the international business needs of today.
- Inability to support a combined warehouse with other divisions.
- Cannot easily handle make-to-order.
- Inability to easily handle international shipping and receiving.
- Inability to handle complex and multiple-site customers and track membership of group purchasing organizations and hospital chains. Inability to interface with customer third-party intermediaries or distributors.
- No Internet home page for customers to have access to training availability, communications, product information, etc.
- No usage of external services and sources of customer information.
- Contract compliance information not meeting all the needs.
- Inability to track the success of various marketing techniques.
- Sales force has very limited information available, and it is not timely. Marketing has limited visibility to the consolidated sales information, it takes much manual effort to obtain it, it is not timely, and is of questionable accuracy. This includes won/lost information, placement information, customer information, and general visibility to what is happening in the field.

Exhibit 6.2   Business Application Detailed Assessment (continued)

- Inability to interface information from the customer system for automatic re-ordering or test result information.
- No visibility to worldwide customer complaint and call information.

Manufacturing:
  Strengths:
- Provides the basic inventory management and MRP tools
- Systems built around capabilities of IS
- Personnel is trained and experienced on it
- Above average lot control and tracking system
- Above average expiration and ship date logic

  Weaknesses:
- Does not handle worldwide sourcing and procurement
- Limited cost information
- Not user friendly
- Limited visibility to hours required to build a system
- No tie of shop floor hours to Payroll
- Poor CRP capabilities
- Poor inventory, supplier, distribution management tools
- Inaccurate allocation screens
- No "what-if" capabilities
- Limited visibility to change
- No visibility of run rate versus standard
- Must do quality check on all reports before using for inaccurate and incomplete information
- Many manual work-arounds to bridge the needs with system capabilities
- Overall limited reporting capabilities on manufacturing activities
- Below average Distribution capabilities (for example, back orders have to be tracked manually)
- No system expert (however, we do have module experts)
- Does not support consistent manufacturing processes and products. No common bill-of-material or part numbering.
- Limited cost information

Finance:
  Strengths:
- Data are accurate in cost to six decimal places to the right.
- Ability to transfer information from Sales system and General Ledger to Excel.

  Weaknesses:
- Financial close process very cumbersome, time consuming, and not timely. It takes 3 weeks to close the books for a month and disseminate financial information. By the time management has the information, it is too late to be useful or make timely business decisions.
- Different worldwide calendar makes financial comparisons difficult.

Exhibit 6.2   Business Application Detailed Assessment (continued)

- Roll-up of subsidiaries' financial information not timely.
- Limited capabilities for forecasting and budgeting.
- Financial reports are time consuming and cumbersome to generate. Limited worldwide information available.
- No visibility to worldwide inventory.
- Chart of accounts maintenance is complicated and labor intensive.
- It is very difficult to budget spending at a project level. You cannot easily accumulate expenses for projects which continue over a year end.
- Inability to track customer profitability.
- Foreign currency is not handled properly.
- Limited reporting capabilities in Accounts Receivable. Reports not available other than month-end.
- No online visibility to spending or budget. Find out after it's too late.
- Unable to point sales from one division to different General Ledger account numbers.
- Requires many manual journal entries in General Ledger.
- Unable to keep financial data on the system for more than 3 years.

Exhibit 6.3   Business Application Summary Assessment

Strengths:
- It works! The system is getting the job done and allowing the business to function today.
- It is reliable and is generally available during the stated daytime hours.
- Overall, the systems are tailored to our business rather than fitting the business to the system. This allows us to continually make process improvements in the business and change the system to meet those requirements. Therefore, we have flexibility in how we do our business, rather than being constrained by the system (provided we have the resources to accommodate the changes in a timely fashion).

Weaknesses:
- Although our systems collect a lot of data, all areas lack ease of ability to analyze the data and turn it into valuable information. Simple analysis questions or "what if" questions require significant manual manipulation and independent searching. As a result, there is considerable demand on the programming group and a large backlog of projects.
- Due to the high degree of custom systems, the systems require a high level of maintenance and support to keep them functioning.
- Many of the key measures to manage the business are not available from the systems, or are derived through extensive work on PCs and manual processes.

Exhibit 6.3   Business Application Summary Assessment (continued)

- The systems are not user friendly. A lot of training is required to become proficient in them and therefore a limited number of individuals have access to information.
- Reporting is cumbersome. Users need to submit a programming request to see a different view of the data.
- System does not currently support a paperless environment. All processes utilize considerable manual effort.
- Requires much manual maintenance, duplicate entry, and external manipulation of data. Many workarounds and external "islands of information" have developed over the years to accommodate deficiencies in the system.
- Quality of data is questionable.
- Information is stored in several different places, and labor is required to keep information updated in several places. Information is inconsistent.
- The system is slow, and has capacity and space issues.
- Nightly processing requires too large a time window, reducing system availability.
- Limited capabilities currently for worldwide communication, interaction, and sharing of files.
- Current systems (other than the new software) do not meet the desired computing architecture requirements outlined in subsequent sections. The systems are not open, which means they are difficult to integrate for worldwide information and ease of obtaining information. The systems are not client/server or Graphic User Interface-based which means utilizing the power of the PC so that they are easy to use. The systems are not a packaged supplier solution because the systems have been significantly modified and without supplier maintenance. The systems are not real-time which means that they are not available 24 hours.

Business Requirements Assessment

As mentioned in Chapter 3, if you use an external company to assemble your detailed **business requirements**, you will have a very extensive database of your detailed requirements. The same company also has a database of the ratings of the various business application systems available on the market and how well the vendor packages meet the requirements. The company will typically give you a database with the detailed ratings as well as a list of the top 10 with a total score. You can typically assemble these requirements in a day and a half with the right people in the organization involved. These individuals are typically those who work with the systems daily.

It can also be extremely beneficial to take the same people, in another session (it typically goes faster than the first session when you must understand each requirement), to grade how well your current system meets the requirements. For one company, the following ratings were used:

9: The current system has the full functionality now.
8: We will have the full functionality within 3 months.
7: We have the functionality with automated workarounds.
6: We can get the information with query changes.
5: Minor program modification to get this.
0: The functionality does not exist in our system.

This will give you an overall score, as well as a score by business application area, in addition to the detailed requirement ratings. You will be able to compare this rating with what is available in vendor-supplied packages on the market. One word of caution — typically vendors rate their own systems. Although vendors say their package has a particular requirement, the vendor software may not do the requirement exactly as you require. Unfortunately, this analysis does not take the place of detailed demonstrations, but it can save a significant amount of time limiting the field of potential software packages.

Using software typically supplied by these companies, you can also get a report of key requirements, or of the areas of gap between your current system that you rated and the highest-ranked application system. If you are doing this manually, you can also get this information from a spreadsheet.

This analysis at one company showed their current systems met 57% of their requirements, as opposed to 98 to 99% with typical packages. This can be an excellent data point when making the case for entirely new business application systems, or even a portion of systems.

In addition to this mathematical evaluation, you can also look at the systems to identify any gaps that this analysis missed. For example, are your systems currently capable of handling the year 2000?

Technical Computing Architecture Assessment

Next, go back to the **technical computing architecture** outlined in Chapter 5. Again, grade the current environment against your desired computing architecture. Typically, you will be able to do this best with the involvement of the Information Systems organization. Exhibit 6.4 shows an example of the grading at one company.

Exhibit 6.4   Computing Architecture Assessment

■ Open	D	■ Software design	F
■ Relational	D	■ Electronic exchange	F
■ Client/Server, GUI	F	■ Disaster recovery	F
■ Real time	D	■ Security	B
■ Connectivity	D	■ Maintainability	F
■ Integration	D	■ CASE generated	F
■ Data integrity	C	■ Table driven	D
■ Bar coding	F	■ EDI, Imaging	F

Table 6.1   Technology Architecture Gap

Technology	Going From	Going To	Business Drivers
Platform			
Operating Systems			
Data Management Systems			
Networking			
Network Management			
Electronic Communication			
Systems Development			
Development Languages			
Applications			

Another company effectively summarized the technical gap with Table 6.1.

Service Architecture Assessment

If you introduce a new direction into the Information Systems organization, there is a good chance that individuals will become very nervous unless you adequately address the people side of the equation. Fear is a common reaction of individuals who might not have the skill set required in the new direction. As with other areas, assess the gap and determine the appropriate action plan with the people and internal information systems processes.

The **service architecture gap** can be assessed by conducting a self-assessment through interviews or surveys of the Information Systems organization. For each category defined earlier (for example, processes, people, organization, culture, technology, metrics), determine the relative strength or weakness and the level of importance. For example, one company identified opportunities for improvement in the following areas:

- Processes
  - Project justification/prioritization
  - Use of service level agreements
  - Use of efficiency/effectiveness metrics
  - Strategic planning
- People
  - Project management skills
  - Project-oriented structure
  - Team approach

Another company identified the need to develop client/server skills, have resources with broader knowledge base, provide improved career paths, and provide salary structures more competitive with the market.

One company identified the new information systems skill set that would be required for the future. It balances technical, leadership, and business knowledge skills that lead to greater resource optimization and more well-rounded information systems workers. In addition to investing in skills enhancement and staff retention, the company found it necessary to create new roles and responsibilities for both technical and business liaisons. The skill sets needed were summarized as in Figure 6.2.

Summary of the Gap

It should now be apparent how large the gap is and if it exists in all areas or only in a few isolated areas of information systems. Next, **summarize the gap.** Go back to the building blocks identified in the current environment (business application, PC, network) and summarize your findings. Exhibit 6.5 shows an example from one company.

One large multidivisional company summarized the gap in the business application systems by placing them on a grid identifying efficiency, effectiveness, and number of systems as shown in Figure 6.3.

Another company summarized the gap in business applications by taking all the groups of information needs that were necessary to meet the business objectives and ranking them on a grid of economic value and strategic value. This grid identified those areas that were definite "home runs" for the company and those with high economic and high strategic value, as opposed to those that were applications they should not bother with because they had low economic and strategic value. The grid is shown in Figure 6.4.

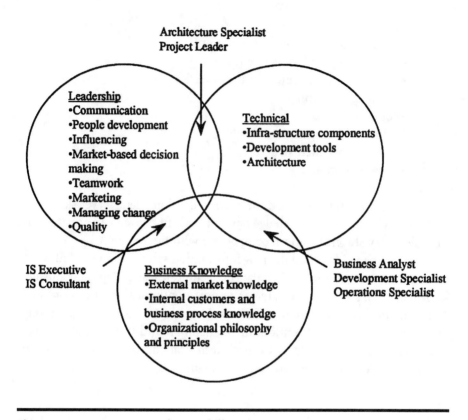

Figure 6.2   Future IS Employee Skill Set

Exhibit 6.5   Gap Summary

- **Business Applications:** The business applications that run on the AS/400 have the largest gap from where we need to be. The majority of the items listed above in the business operating vision are a result of deficiencies in our business application systems. The strengths and weaknesses also provide more specific information on the gaps. The area of the business application is of most concern, and will take the most time and resources to improve. Rather than building upon what we have, this area requires total overhaul and replacement.
- **PC and LAN:** This area of our environment is positioned for the future. There are, however, improvements necessary in the areas of support, communication, consistency, and tools to better utilize this environment. Standards and controls, although not perfect, are moving in the right direction. During the past few years, the company has invested fairly well in this area. Although our PC environment continually needs upgrading, it is not significantly lacking.

Exhibit 6.5　Gap Summary (continued)

To meet our future computing architecture of client/server, and the business requirements of easy access to information in a meaningful format, the PC is a critical piece of our environment. We must aggressively continue investments and upgrades in this area. In the past environment, a dumb terminal or low-end PC could get information as you would the majority of the processing on the server or AS/400. With new technology and business systems, you complete processing at the client, or PC end, in addition to the server end. We have recently experienced this requirement with the new software requiring high-end PCs.

- **Product-Related Computing:** We can make improvements in this area, but in general, the systems here seem to be meeting the requirements. The systems are old, patched, added-on over the years, written in a variety of languages, and have redundant and inefficient data structures. Redesign and changing the technical architecture of these systems would help significantly but is not as urgent as the improved business application systems. These systems are very company specific, and we would probably not find packages that would address our requirements. Once we obtain a new technical environment for the business application systems, we must evaluate these systems to be re-written in the new environment and possibly eliminate a separate environment.

- **Network:** The basic infrastructure of the local network is such that we can build upon it for the future. There are weak areas and links that we must strengthen, and we must increase the capacity to handle our new client/server computing architecture. The network will become the most critical piece of our environment in the future. We must focus on strengthening our external network to other locations, customers, suppliers, and other external entities. Our networking capabilities will become our advantage or disadvantage in the marketplace in the future.

In summary, our business application systems currently on the AS/400 are the area of largest concern and are in need of improvement at this time. We need to continue to build upon and strengthen the PC and network areas. We can migrate the product-related computing on the DEC to the new architecture over time.

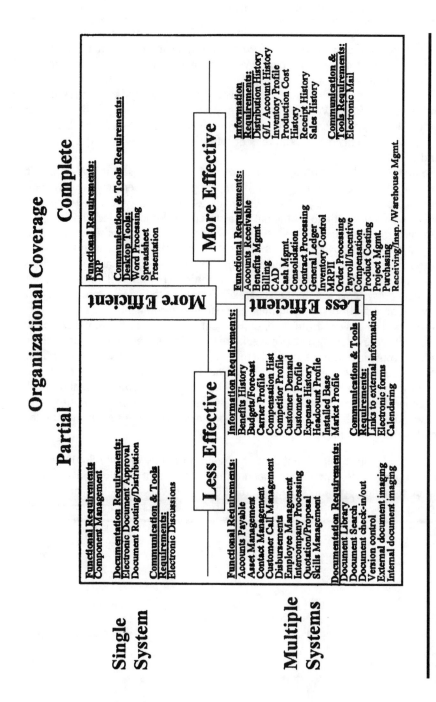

Figure 6.3   Application Summary

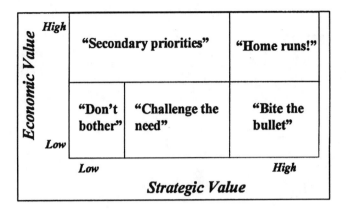

Figure 6.4   Strategic Grid

Conclusion

You can now complete the following section in your plan document from phase 4:

VIII.   Gap Analysis

Present the gap analysis to the Information Systems Steering Committee, the Executive Committee, and the Information Systems Organization. By now you have the attention of the organization, and you need to rapidly start formulating action plans, because management's first question will be: What are we going to do about it?

7 Determining How to Get to Where You Want to Be

"People are afraid of the future, of the unknown. If a man faces up to it, and takes the dare of the future, he can have some control over his destiny. That's an exciting idea to me. Better than waiting with everybody else to see what's going to happen."

John H. Glenn, Jr. (B. 1921)
American astronaut, U.S. Senator

Now that you have assessed the gap between where you are to where you want to be, you are ready to begin the next part of phase 4 — determining the recommendation. This is shown in Figure 7.1.

So, how do you get from where you are today to where you need to be in the future? There is often more than one solution or one event that must happen for the transformation to occur. It can be helpful to summarize the characteristics of your current (or prior) state, as well as your future state in addition to transforming events that must occur. For example, one company summarized its situation as shown in Figure 7.2.

Identify the issues in the current state from your interviews with management (Chapter 3) and the Information Systems group (Chapter 1) which you held at the beginning of the strategic planning process. Once you clearly identify the current issues, you can determine the future state, and what must happen to get to it.

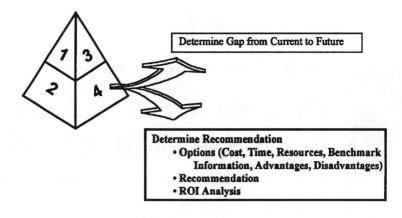

Determine Gap from Current to Future

Determine Recommendation
• Options (Cost, Time, Resources, Benchmark
    Information, Advantages, Disadvantages)
• Recommendation
• ROI Analysis

Figure 7.1   Determine Recommendation

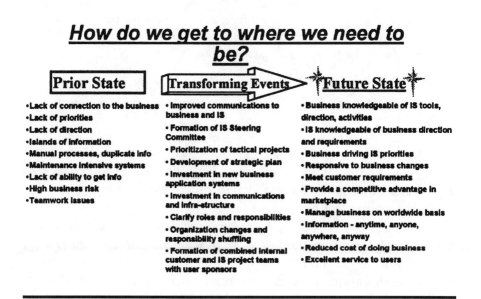

How do we get to where we need to be?

Prior State	Transforming Events	Future State
•Lack of connection to the business •Lack of priorities •Lack of direction •Islands of information •Manual processes, duplicate info •Maintenance intensive systems •Lack of ability to get info •High business risk •Teamwork issues	• Improved communications to business and IS • Formation of IS Steering Committee • Prioritization of tactical projects • Development of strategic plan • Investment in new business application systems • Investment in communications and infra-structure • Clarify roles and responsibilities • Organization changes and responsibility shuffling • Formation of combined internal customer and IS project teams with user sponsors	• Business knowledgeable of IS tools, direction, activities • IS knowledgeable of business direction and requirements • Business driving IS priorities • Responsive to business changes • Meet customer requirements • Provide a competitive advantage in marketplace • Manage business on worldwide basis • Information - anytime, anyone, anywhere, anyway • Reduced cost of doing business • Excellent service to users

Figure 7.2   Transforming Events

Option Identification

The next step in the process is to identify all available **options**. It is important to do a thorough job investigating the options because many times when the cost estimates start accumulating for the project, management will want to go back to review the options again. You will save time if you do a thorough job of option evaluation at the beginning. At this level, your options are high level and generic. For example, rather than identifying a particular software application package, one option would be to implement new packaged software, whether it be package x, y, or z. You can also consider the option of continuing on the current path, or doing nothing. Identify options for each area of major change or investment. Exhibit 7.1 is an example of how one company identified its options for business application systems.

Exhibit 7.1   Options

A. Options — Business Applications

We have the following options for our business application systems:

1. Continue on current path. This would mean that we would complete the project to address the year 2000 and continue to make incremental improvements in our current custom systems to address the changing business needs.
2. Implement upgrade to our current system. With this option, we would purchase and install the new release of our vendor-supplied software. Although the vendor has addressed the year 2000 in its new release, there would be very little additional improvement or enhancement in the release. We would need to transfer over 70% of our current modifications to the new release of software. Although we would address the year 2000, we would find ourselves in a situation similar to today's, in that the modifications would force us to go off maintenance and we would essentially have custom software.
3. Implement new packaged software. There are virtually hundreds of options for us to choose from for our business applications systems. As mentioned in the business requirements section, to quickly determine our requirements and narrow our options, we utilized a company to assist in analyzing our requirements against a database of information from over 500 suppliers of business application systems.

Following are the top suppliers and the percentage fit the vendor-supplied packages had to our total requirements (including our company-unique requirements).

In summary, there were numerous application packages that meet over 95% of our requirements. As outlined in the "Gap Analysis" of this document, this compares with our current custom application systems meeting 57% of our requirements. A Request for Quotation was sent to the above suppliers to obtain additional information. Considering the information returned in the quotations, the following vendors were selected by the Vendor Review Team for additional review.

Information Gathering — Request for Quote

You need to obtain additional information to formulate the option analysis. If one of your options is a new business application system, you will need costs as well as other information about the vendor and software package. This involves sending several vendors a **Request for Quotation (RFQ)**. This can also be referred to as Request for Proposal (RFP), or Request for Information (RFI). No matter how thorough a Request for Quotation is, use it only as initial scanning and qualification. Nothing will take the place of in-person vendor demonstrations to determine the true viability of a package in your environment. However, if you structure a quotation request well, you can narrow the field. Send the Request for Quotation to the top 10 (or fewer) vendors that met your requirements if you use a company for the requirements definition as recommended in Chapter 3.

What does a Request for Quotation include? Your Request for Quotation must be as concise as possible. Vendors do not want to wade through inches of paper before qualifying you as a potential customer. Fortunately, you have already done much of the work with various sections of the strategic plan. If you utilized a vendor for the requirements definition, you will also have detailed responses by requirement for each of the business requirements. Following is a general outline for a typical Request for Quotation that you can modify for your particular situation:

A. **RFQ Guidelines**. This includes the following information:
   1. Where and to whom should RFQ responses be mailed?
   2. When are responses due?
   3. To whom should the vendors direct any questions or inquiries?
   4. What should be the format of the response?
   5. What documents should the vendors include with their response? This list includes:
      - Signed confidentiality agreement (included in RFQ).
      - Responses to questions regarding company and software (RFQ section C-2).
      - Responses to company-specific requirements (RFQ section C-3).
      - Any changes, updates, or notes to the vendor requirements (RFQ section C-4).
      - A copy of their contract along with any required license agreements so you can begin legal review.
      - A summary of the pricing with any tier, volume, or platform pricing indicated.

- A copy of the training schedule.
- A company brochure, annual report.
- List of customers with names, addresses, phone numbers for contact, implementation date, and software version. You may need to sign a vendor confidentiality agreement for this information.
- Include any online demonstration disks available.
6. What is the next step for the vendor if the vendor makes the cut to the short list?
7. Statement of confidentiality of RFQ information.

B. **General Information**
1. Company: This is a brief (one-page) description of your company. Include the following:
   - What business is the company in?
   - How old is the company? Include a short historical perspective.
   - How large is the company in terms of sales and employees? Is it public or privately owned?
   - Is this quotation for one division, one location, or the entire company? Provide information on parent, subsidiaries, and divisions.
2. Current Environment: This is a short (one-page) description of your current information systems environment. Include the following:
   - What hardware environments are you utilizing? Are your plans to change hardware environments?
   - What software is the company currently utilizing?
   - How many utilize the system you are replacing?
   - What network is in place? What locations are connected?
   - How many PCs do you have? What is the typical PC configuration?
3. Business Requirements
   - Scope: This can be the scope section of the strategic plan.
   - Environmental Requirements: This can be the Environmental Requirements section of the strategic plan.
   - Business Direction: This is a summary of the business mission, objectives, and goals. Obtain approval from internal management before sending this information to an external company.
   - Information Requirements: This can be the Information Needs section of the strategic plan.
   - External Requirements: This can be the External Requirements section of the strategic plan.

■ Information Systems Requirements: This is a summary of the computing architecture requirements of the strategic plan.

■ Project: This is a summary of the project in progress, including when it started, how you got to this point, and where you plan to go.

■ Reason for Change: What are the key motivating factors for the business to implement this project? What is the case for action?

■ Key Issues: This can be a list of the key issues as identified with a vendor in the requirements definition step as outlined in Chapter 3. This is not an entire list of all the requirements, but rather the key requirements for your environment. Include the responses for that particular vendor which were in the database of the automated tool, if you used one. The vendor can correct, change, or modify the responses previously supplied.

C. **Vendor Response**
   1. Confidentiality Agreement: This is an agreement ensuring that the responses to the RFQ are accurate, as well as keeping any information supplied confidential.
   2. General Company and Package Information: This includes general questions of interest to you about the vendor. An example prepared for one company is included in Exhibit 7.2.

Exhibit 7.2   RFQ Questionnaire

Please respond to the following questions:
Company:
   Company name: _____
   Software name: _____
   Date company formed: _____   Public/Private: _____
   Annual sales: _____
   Targeted markets or customers: _____
Employees:
   Number of employees worldwide: _____
   Number of employees in development: _____
   Number of employees in support: _____
   Number of employees in area: _____
   Number of employees in area with > 2 years experience: _____
Customers:
   Number of customers that have one module or more implemented in production: _____
   Number of customers that have full suite implemented in production: _____
   % of customers on annual maintenance: _____
   % of customers on current release: _____

Exhibit 7.2   RFQ Questionnaire (continued)

Average length of time for customers to implement modules: _____
Average length of time for customers to implement new release: __
Is there an active user group in area? _____
List any customers in our business:

_____

Software:

Handle process manufacturing: _____Discrete: _____
Repetitive: _____Job shop: _____
Make-to-stock: _____Make-to-order: _____
Language code written in: _____
Year majority (>75%) of code written in: _____
Databases supported: _____
Relational database: _____
Windows compliant: _____
Hardware necessary: _____
Operating system necessary: _____
Date of last release: _____Date of next release: _____
Major re-write planned: _____ When: _____ Why: _____
Approximate cost (range) of various modules included in
Manufacturing, Distribution, and Finance for 600 total users, 200
active, including database and development tools needed:
_____
Developed with CASE tool: _____
Developed with methodology: _____
Object oriented: _____
Major areas of planned enhancements: _____

_____
_____

Training:

Is public training offered in area: _____
Cities public training offered: _____
Average cost of training class: _____
Number of days training needed for   Order Entry person: _____
                                       Master Scheduler: _____
                                       Information Systems: _____

Support:

Approximate cost of annual maintenance: _____
24-hour support available: _____
Cost for support: _____
Product guarantee: _____
Implementation support available for turnkey: _____
Any automated conversion support or tools available from our
current software:

_____

3. Company-Specific Requirements: This is a list of the requirements specific to your company identified in the requirements definition phase (Chapter 3). These would be only the requirements not included in the generic requirements in the database of all vendor information. Since these requirements were not in the database, you will need to send the company-specific requirements to the vendor for response.
4. General Requirements: Include a disk of the requirements identified with the responses for that particular vendor included from the outside company in Chapter 3. Ask them to review the responses provided to ensure accuracy and only provide updates if any discrepancies exist.

D. **Appendix**
1. Company Brochures, Annual Report: Include any company literature that will help the vendor understand your business.

RFQ Response Review

After **reviewing the RFQ responses,** select the best three or four vendors for additional review. This can be done with a subset group from the Information Systems Steering Committee. It may be easiest to assemble a key criteria sheet to evaluate the vendors. An example is provided in Exhibit 7.3.

Exhibit 7.3   Vendor Evaluation Summary Sheet

	Vendor 1	Vendor 2	Vendor 3
Company:			
Name of company			
Name of software			
Date company formed			
Public/Private			
Annual sales			
Targeted markets			
Employees:			
Number of worldwide			
Number in development			
Number in support			
Number in our town			
Number in our town > 2 yrs experience			

Exhibit 7.3   Vendor Evaluation Summary Sheet (continued)

	Vendor 1	Vendor 2	Vendor 3
Customers:			
Number in production			
Number with full suite			
% on annual maintenance			
% on current release			
Implementation time			
Time to implement new release			
Active user group in area			
Customers in our industry			
Software:			
Make/Engineer to order			
Discrete/Make to stock			
Repetitive/Job shop			
Integrated configurator			
Language of code			
Year code written			
Databases supported			
Relational database			
Windows interface			
Current release			
Date released			
Year 2000 compliant			
Hardware needed			
Operating system			
Date of last release			
Date of next release			
Major re-write planned			
Reason for re-write			
CASE developed			
Methodology used			
Object oriented			
Planned enhancements			
Cost:			
Software			
Database, tools			
Hardware			

Exhibit 7.3   Vendor Evaluation Summary Sheet (continued)

	Vendor 1	*Vendor 2*	*Vendor 3*
Training			
Consulting			
Bolt-on's			
Training:			
Public training in our area			
Cities training offered			
Average cost of class			
Number of days Order Entry			
Number of days Master Scheduler			
Number of days Information Systems			
Support:			
Cost of annual maintenance			
Is 24-hour support available			
Cost for support			
Does product have guarantee			
Implementation support			
Local partner consultant			
Conversion support			
Requirement Ratings:			
Industry Rating			
Industry Comments			
Other:			
Date received			
Quality of response			
Notes			
Contact name			
Contact number			
Comments			
Comments			
Group thoughts			

The RFQ response provided some cost information, but you will want to validate that information with the vendor. You are obtaining very generic cost information for approval from management before proceeding with in-depth reviews and analysis. Work with three or four vendors to obtain high-level cost estimates. Initially, vendors are very reluctant to do this at this point in the process. You can get them to cooperate by explaining that you are trying to save their time by determining how serious business management is before proceeding with in-depth reviews. Keep in mind that vendors will be tempted at this point to low-ball estimates, and you will need to temper them with your own experience and that of industry experts.

It may be helpful to utilize a structured decision-making process to select three or four vendors from the larger group. This can be done with the Information Systems Steering Committee through the following steps:

1. Identify the criteria key to making the decision. If it were your money and your company, how would you evaluate and select an option? This list should be high level and have no more than 15 criteria.
2. Force rank the key criteria. Ask the group if they had to choose between the first criteria and the second, which would they choose? First and third? First and fourth? Follow this for each combination. Count the votes for each criteria. The one with the most has the highest priority to the group.
3. Weight the criteria. Assign a weight using 8 to 10. The higher-priority items would be a weight of 10, while the lower items would be an 8. This will become the multiplier.
4. Rate the criteria against each option. If you have 10 vendors, rate all 10. Use a scale of 1 through 5. A 5 would indicate the vendor does an excellent job at meeting the criteria, 3 average, and 1 poor.
5. Multiply the rating by the weight. Total the scores for each vendor. The highest scorers are the preferred vendors.

This method should be used as one indicator and should be reviewed in total. An example is provided in Exhibit 7.4. In the example, option 2 would be the preferred option.

Exhibit 7.4 Key Criteria Decision Table

Priority	Requirement	Weight	Option 1 Rate	Option 1 Weight* Rate	Option 2 Rate	Option 2 Weight* Rate	Option 3 Rate	Option 3 Weight* Rate
1	Stable vendor for future	10	5	50	3	30	3	30
2	Meets business requirements	10	3	30	5	50	5	50
3	Technical architecture	10	3	30	3	30	5	50
4	User friendly	9	3	27	5	45	5	45
5	Flexible	9	3	27	5	45	5	45
6	Support re-engineering processes	9	3	27	5	45	5	45
7	Vendor support	9	3	27	3	27	3	27
8	Cost	8	5	40	3	24	1	8
9	Resources	8	5	40	3	24	1	8
10	Time	8	3	24	3	24	3	24
	Total			**322**		**344**		**332**

Option Analysis

The next step is to **analyze the various high-level options**. This includes assembling the following information for each option:

- **Costs:** Be extremely careful to not underestimate costs at this point. You need to include all your costs, not just the vendor software costs. Once you provide management with these high-level numbers, it can be amazing how good their memory is if you come back with higher costs than your original estimates. It is always easier to start high and find ways to reduce costs rather than starting too low. Whatever numbers you provide at this stage, be sure management understands they are preliminary and you need to do a significant amount of work to formulate actual budgetary numbers. Include all costs, such as:
  - **Hardware and servers:** You may require more than one server. Will your query or data warehouse application reside on a machine separate from your transaction processing? Will you require a test or development server in addition to the production machine? Will you have additional disk or backup (for example, mirroring) requirements? Will you have to design an architecture for high availability? Will you need additional hardware peripherals for things like bar coding? Will new printers be necessary?
  - **Software:** In addition to the core software application package, will you require additional software for specific requirements? Will you need to buy additional licenses for existing software to port to a new hardware environment?
  - **Consulting or contracting:** You typically require consulting for conversion programming, consulting in the new business application package, network or technical consulting, business process re-engineering consulting, project management, etc. Also include travel and expenses incurred by consultants.
  - **Training:** Include training of the users and the Information Systems group in the new software. Does the Information Systems group require additional technical training due to new platforms?
  - **Travel:** Will travel be necessary to obtain input from worldwide users or locations? Will you have to train other users in various locations that will be utilizing the software?
  - **Supporting software packages:** Are additional software packages necessary for utilities and other support areas?

- **Network costs:** Are any network enhancements necessary to support the new application software?
- **PC costs:** Are any PC hardware or software upgrades necessary to support the new application software?

As a general check, one consultant uses a rule-of-thumb to estimate total project costs at $20K to $30K per concurrent user. If you require a lot of work on the infrastructure or planned for consulting use, use the $30K number. If the infrastructure is currently in place, and you have enough internal labor, use the $20K number. If you have named users rather than concurrent users, use the $20K number. Therefore, for 100 concurrent users, this consultant would plan to spend approximately $3M for the total project, including software, hardware, consulting, and network.

- ■ **Time:** What is the total amount of time you need for the project and when is the latest you must begin the project? Time is also like the cost area — do not underestimate the time to do the project. It often takes longer than you think, and management has an excellent memory for the first number you provided. Try to provide a fixed time upon project approval. For example, the project will be completed 18 months after project approval.
- ■ **Resources:** How many user resources and how many Information Systems resources are necessary? Will the resources be part-time or full-time? One word of caution on part-time resources — to do a large project effectively, you need some commitment of full-time resources. With part-time resources, production and day-to-day issues always take precedence, and you often get fewer resources then you anticipated.
- ■ **Benchmark Information:** Why should management believe your time and cost estimates? Can you give them examples from other companies, or report what consultants or research organizations are saying similar projects cost?
- ■ **Advantages:** List the high-level advantages this option would have for the company.
- ■ **Disadvantages:** List the high-level disadvantages this option would have for the company.

The example in Exhibit 7.5 is how one company summarized its options.

Exhibit 7.5   Option Analysis

A review indicated three available options. These options were studied in-depth, including estimates on costs, time, resources, benchmark information, advantages, and disadvantages.

1. **Continue on Current Path.**
   a. **Costs:**

Hardware:	$ X K
Software:	$ X K
Consulting:	$ X K
Total:	$ X M

   Since we are at capacity on our current hardware, we would need to purchase a larger machine, and would keep our existing machine for testing of the year 2000 changes. Upon completion of the project, we could sell the current hardware. We would need to purchase upgraded licenses for all our programming tools and other software for the increased CPU size, as well as additional licenses to copy the software during the project.

   The software costs are to purchase licenses from our current vendor. Our current agreement is CPU based. Moving to a larger CPU requires us to purchase licenses, as well as making a duplicate copy of the software during the year 2000 project.

   Consulting is based on utilizing X programming contractors for XX months ($XX-$XX per hour as we would likely get one vendor resource and two local resources).
   b. **Time:**
   This project is estimated to take XX months minimum, and would need to begin early 1999.
   c. **Resources:**
   IS: XX full-time equivalents. There would be no enhancements or maintenance to the existing systems during this time.
   Users: XX part-time (25 to 75%) key users at various times during the XX month time frame.
   d. **Benchmark Information:**
   The vendor spent 12,000 person hours converting the same software we have to the year 2000. These resources were very experienced with the software. We have additional modules and software that also require changes.

   In 1995, we completed a small portion of the year 2000 project because it was necessary for expirations that were going out to the year 2000. About 5% of the large project was completed, for a total of X,XXX IS person hours investment.

   An article in *Information Week* on 2/5/96 emphasized the year 2000 issue. "Companies must deal with a bomb that's ready to explode. Never before in the history of computers has there been such a threat as the one posed by the year 2000. Now less than four years away, the turn of the

Exhibit 7.5   Option Analysis (continued)

century promises to wreak havoc on the world's legacy systems unless the systems are fixed or replaced." The estimated cost for a single large company to fix its 2000 problem is $40M. The article goes on to say, "The cost and hassle of fixing the date change may be sufficient reason to purchase and install client-server software that's 2000 capable ... this can be a catalyst for change if you're considering migrating."

Gartner Group estimates that worldwide, the cost of fixing the year 2000 problem will reach $400B to $600B. So, at least we are not the only company in the situation.

e. **Advantages:**
   - This would address the year 2000 issue.
   - Minimal user training would be necessary.
   - Short-term, least expensive option.
   - No IS re-education would be necessary.

f. **Disadvantages:**
   - Long-term, most expensive option.
   - There would be no enhancements or changes during the XX month time frame of the calendar project. This would be difficult for the business, as many requested changes are necessary to accommodate changes in the business or urgent priorities.
   - With over 70% of our current modifications needing to carry forth to the new software, we would find ourselves in a situation similar to today's — going off maintenance with custom software.
   - We would still have the inefficient processes in the user areas that we have today.
   - This would be a short-term solution, and we would still need to address the strategic direction. This option would not move us closer to our strategic direction as it would not meet our business requirements any better, or our operating vision, or computing architecture.

2. **Upgrade Current System.**
   a. **Costs:**

Hardware:	$ X K
Software:	$ X K
Consulting/training:	$ X K
Total:	$ X M

   As we are currently at capacity and the new software requires additional CPU, we would need to upgrade our hardware.

   Software costs are to re-purchase the vendor software. In addition, we would incur an ongoing 15% annual maintenance fee.

   The consulting and training costs are for 2 consultants from the vendor and training costs for the various classes necessary.

   b. **Time:**
   We anticipate this project to take XX to XX months, and we would need to begin the effort in early 1999.

Exhibit 7.5   Option Analysis (continued)

c. **Resources:**

IS: X full-time equivalent resources. There would be no enhancements, modifications, and minimal user support during the project.

Users: X key users (50+% of their time for 18 months). This would include a user project leader, and key individuals from Planning, Order Management, Finance, Shop Floor, and Distribution.

An additional XX part-time users would be needed (25 to 50%) at various times during the XX months. This includes key users from areas listed below.

d. **Benchmark Information:**

When we last upgraded in 1991 to the release of software we are currently utilizing, it took XX months, with XX Information Systems full-time equivalents and XX contractors.

Several customers of the vendor were contacted who have completed the upgrade to assess the level of effort. Much depends on how many modifications the companies have made and how the modifications are done. One company in San Francisco is currently deciding between implementing another software package or upgrading their software. The company estimates the two efforts to be very similar in cost and time. Another manufacturing company has stayed on maintenance and upgraded each release. The company estimates X months, X people for each single upgrade. After hearing how our modifications have been done and the extent as well as our operating system, the company indicated ours would be a significantly larger effort.

e. **Advantages:**

- Addresses the year 2000.
- Brings us to the current vendor release.
- We would be able to add on modules for future enhancements, such as EDI and bar coding.
- Minimal IS re-education would be necessary.

f. **Disadvantages:**

- The vendor has done very minimal enhancements other than the year 2000.
- Over 70% of our modifications would need to carry over to the new software release. This would result in the same situation we have today; going off maintenance with a custom system.
- No business process re-engineering. Would have the same processes as today.
- This would also be a short-term fix because there would be no movement toward our strategic direction. This includes not meeting our business requirements, our business operating vision, or our computing architecture.

In a Gartner Group research paper, Gartner ranked this vendor-supplied software as very low in functionality and technology quotients, the worst of all worlds. Gartner Group advises "users that have invested in these vendors' products to review the products to determine the potential for long-term viability and the rationale for continued investments."

Exhibit 7.5   Option Analysis (continued)

3. **Implement New System.**
   a. **Costs:**

Hardware:	$ X M
Software:	$ X M
Consulting/training:	$ X M
Total:	$ X M

   These costs are estimates until we select the specific package. The hardware costs would be for a new computer or a totally different hardware platform, depending on the requirements of the software selected. The software includes not only the basic manufacturing, finance, and order management, but the other modules that we have added to our current environment, such as the functionality provided today for sales reporting, database manager, programmer tools, etc. In addition to the costs, we would pay a 15% maintenance fee. Significant training and consulting would be necessary for users and Information Systems in the new software.

   b. **Time:**
   This option is estimated at XX to XX months elapsed time. This effort would need to begin in early 1999.

   c. **Resources:**
   Information Systems: X full-time Information Systems equivalents. Again, there would be no enhancements, modifications, and minimal support of the existing systems during the project.

   Users: X key users (100% of time for 18 months). This includes a full-time user project leader, and individuals from Planning, Order Management, Finance, Shop Floor, and Distribution.

   X additional part time (25 to 70%) users would also be necessary at various times during the XX months. This includes individuals from Canada, Sales, QC, Purchasing, PPD, QA, Product Support, Document Control, and Cost Accounting.

   d. **Benchmark Information:**
   Our parent organization is in the process of implementing a new software package. The company has an approved project budget for $XXM, which excludes manufacturing. The project began in 10/97 and is scheduled for completion 1/99.

   Various consultants have provided a variety of examples of companies of similar size and industry that have made comparable investments on such an effort.

   e. **Advantages:**
   - This option would address our long-term strategic direction.
   - This option would give us the opportunity to re-engineer our business processes, change the way we are doing things, and eliminate wasteful processes.
   - We would implement a vanilla vendor package, which would allow us to stay current with the vendor enhancements in the future.

Exhibit 7.5   Option Analysis (continued)

- A new vendor package would be more flexible for changing with the business requirements. Many options are table driven rather than requiring programming changes.
- A new system would allow us to obtain information easily, meet the business operating vision, meet the business requirements and information needs, as well as the computing architecture.
- A new system would position us so that we could handle additional business growth in the future.

f. **Disadvantages:**
- Additional costs.
- Requires significant user commitment. To be successful, it must become a key business issue. This is a major issue as we would need the same resources that are being sought for other projects. We cannot begin the project without key full-time user commitment!

Recommendation

Now it is time for another Information Systems Steering Committee meeting. Present the information you have received to date. Outline the various options and associated information. Typically, with all the quantification completed so far, the **recommended solution** is obvious and obtained with complete consensus. If it is not, you will need to formulate a smaller representative group from the Information Systems Steering Committee to work through the details and recommend a solution to the group. A sponsor or vocal member of the Information Systems Steering Committee may begin to emerge. It is extremely useful to involve that person because he or she will be a key resource in the selling process. In one company, this person was extremely well respected by upper management and was actually the individual who presented the recommendation to upper management rather than Information Systems! It can be extremely powerful if it appears to upper management that it is the recommendation of the entire business rather than just Information Systems.

In addition to the recommendation in the area of business applications, remember the other components of information systems. Include recommendations on the network environment, PC or desktop environment, engineering environment, service architecture, or any other information systems areas that you have in your environment. Use a similar approach in each area, that of identifying options, estimates, presenting to the Information Systems Steering Committee, and developing recommendations.

ROI Analysis

Before presenting the final recommendations to Executive Management for approval, you often need a **Return On Investment Analysis**. This could also be a net present value or internal rate of return depending upon the requirements at your company. Executive Management typically needs to know how much it will cost and how much benefit it will have to the business before making an investment decision. Depending upon your company culture, this step may or may not be significant. Again, it is extremely helpful if the business groups complete this economic analysis because they need to sign up for and deliver the anticipated savings. Exhibit 7.6 shows one example of an ROI analysis for a company.

Exhibit 7.6   ROI Analysis

The business recognizes that improving our information systems is a critical action and key enabler for our future business direction. We recognize that improving information systems is the number-two overall divisional business priority during the next year. Although we will outline benefits of implementing a new system in more detail in the Appropriations Request, this section will outline an overview of the key benefits.

The ROI for the implementation of the new system is XX%. This ROI is based on a capital request of $XK and implementation costs of $XK. The expected benefits for this program have been segregated into four categories: sales impact, direct material savings, manufacturing resource improvements, and asset management. The detailed ROI forms and schedules are included in the Appendix.

■ **Sales Impact:**
   A conservative estimate of the sales impact from implementing a new information system is X% of market share (for example, with the system, we expect worldwide market share to be XX% in FY 1999; without the system, we expect worldwide market share to drop to XX%). The dollar impact of this improvement is $XXK in operating profit five years after implementation.

   One of the reasons for this market share improvement is better customer interfaces. Customers are currently demanding greater access to our system, which we will be able to provide with the new system. Additionally, the new system will allow us to more accurately process orders, update orders for changes, and provide more timely information on order status. We will provide improved responsiveness to customer needs with immediate information, which we do not have today. Ship complete logic, available to promise, customer credit card processing, and customer bar coding are just a few examples of customer requests that we are unable to meet today. These benefits are critical to ensure that we protect the market share we currently have.

Exhibit 7.6   ROI Analysis (continued)

The new system will also allow us to improve lead times, improve service levels, and reduce the time to market on new products and line extensions. Time to market will decrease through concurrent engineering, preferred vendor and parts lists, commonality of product design across multiple products, and a seamless integration between our engineering systems and business systems. These are key attributes that a system will need to provide for the division to grow its market share.

- **Direct Material Savings:**
Direct material savings will come from two areas: yield improvements and reduced purchase costs. The model assumption is that yields, with the new system, will improve from 94.9% in FY 1994 to 96.7% in FY 1999. However, without the system, yields will improve only slightly, from 94.9% to 95.1%. These yield improvements are possible by improved feedback within the shop control system that will allow for more timely response to process problems.

   We will improve purchase costs since the system will provide our suppliers with better access to our forecasts and specs, as well as improved supplier management, common parts, and common designs. With worldwide purchasing information available, we will be able to leverage global procurement and planning strategies. We will also realize cost savings through a streamlined interface to our suppliers with electronic document transfer. The ROI model assumes that with the system we will be able to reach our net inflation goal of .9%. However, without the system we assume that net inflation will be 1.2%.

   Together, these material cost reductions will generate material cost savings of $XXXXK in FY 1999 (X% of sales).

- **Manufacturing Resource Improvements:**
The new system will not only allow us to do what we currently do more efficiently, but it will also allow us to grow the business without adding resources as soon as we would have to without the system. Depending on the function, the new system will provide an opportunity for efficiency gains of X% to XX% over our current head count, as outlined in the efficiency comparison. Additionally, the new system will allow the division to continue to leverage head count additions, estimated to be XX% of sales (same as the past 5 years), whereas, without the new system, the next 5 years' high expected sales growth will cause that leverage factor to drop (head count growth expected to be XX% of sales in FY 1999).

   These labor savings will come mostly from the areas of Contracts, Purchasing, Planning, Marketing, and Accounting. This labor will be reduced through re-engineering efforts of the business processes, including decreased rework of product and processes, and eliminating non-value-added tasks.

   We expect the value of these savings to be $XXXXK in FY 1999.

Exhibit 7.6   ROI Analysis (continued)

- **Asset Management:**
  Improvements made in the front end of the booking process will yield corresponding improvements in Days Sales Outstanding (DSO). Additionally, the EDI and credit card capabilities of the new system will also yield improvements in DSO. The model assumes that domestic DSO will improve by 2 days.

  We will also improve inventory turns. Through reduced internal lead times, yield improvements, improved forecasting, and reduced safety stock, the model assumes that domestic turns will improve by XX%.

  Finally, the model assumes that there will be a small improvement in capital utilization; better utilization of capital assets will reduce the amount of new assets that we need to purchase. The model includes a 1% improvement in asset utilization. These three operating capital improvements; improved DSO, higher inventory turns and better capital utilization, provide a $XXXK improvement in incremental operating cash flows in FY 1999.

This system will affect practically all areas of the business. As a result, the impact of these expected benefits are spread evenly among the above factors. A sensitivity analysis of these benefits is outlined below:

ROI

• As presented	53%
• Assume no market share improvement	38%
• Assume no purchase costs reduction	44%
• Assume no material yield improvement	49%
• Assume no labor efficiency gains	44%
• Assume no labor efficiency gains nor any additional leverage	40%
• Assume no DSO improvements	49%
• Assume no ITO improvements	50%
• Assume no capital utilization	51%

Additional benefits not included in the ROI calculation are:

- **Supports quality initiatives**
  - ISO 9000. ISO certification requirements will be easier and less expensive to implement.
  - Reduce process variability. Our product will be consistent on a worldwide basis.
  - Regulation compliance. This includes compliance to U.S. and worldwide government regulations such as hazardous material and licensing.
- **Information Systems Opportunity Costs.** There are many information systems projects that have been requested which we would not need to complete as a result of implementing this system. These projects with approximate information systems effort are as follows. Detailed project descriptions are listed in the Appendix.

Exhibit 7.6   ROI Analysis (continued)

• Customer credit card	6 months, 2 people
• Shipment bar coding	6 months, 2 people
• Purchasing credit card	6 months, 2 people
• Purchasing EDI	6 months, 2 people
• Order Link and Sales Link Interface	3 months, 2 people
• Order Link file transfer	6 months, 1 person
• General Ledger release	4 months, 2 people
• Accounts Receivable release	5 months, 2 people
• Focus solution and replacement	3 months, 1 person
• Available to promise	6 months, 2 people
• HR Payroll	6 months, 3 people
• Configurator	9 months, 3 people
• Expand online system availability	9 months, 4 people
• Print improvement	2 months, 2 people
• Shop floor control	6 months, 2 people
• Link engineering, business systems	2 months, 2 people
• Worldwide forecasting system	6 months, 2 people
• Field failure returns	6 months, 2 people
• Bar coding in manufacturing	6 months, 2 people
• Project management	6 months, 2 people
• Invoicing and adjustments	8 months, 3 people
• Purchasing system	8 months, 3 people
• MRO Purchasing	4 months, 1 person
• Final assembly system	8 months, 4 people
• Worldwide key measures	4 months, 2 people
• Year 2000 conversion	6 months, 8 people

Conclusion

Congratulations! You are ready to present the high-level recommendation to Executive Management. This will be discussed further in the next chapter. You have now completed the four phases of the planning process and are ready to obtain approval. You are also able to complete the following sections in the strategic plan document from phase 4:

IX. Recommendation
    A. Options
    B. Recommendations
    C. Return On Investment Analysis

8 | Selling the Recommendation

"All things are possible until they are proved impossible — and even the impossible may only be so, as of now."

Pearl S. Buck (1892–1973)
American novelist, humanitarian

The best plan in the world is worthless if you can't sell it to Executive Management and the entire organization. Often, changes in information systems result in millions of dollars of investment for an organization. Management must see a solid and thorough process for determining the direction. Management must also understand the level of effort, investment required, and the risks to the organization.

If you have followed the process outlined in this book, by now you have increased communication and support of information systems activities throughout the organization. Now it is time to obtain Executive Management approval before spending additional time investigating the options in detail.

Management Overview

First, you need to build the case for action. Do this by writing the **Management Overview**, Section I in the Information Systems Strategic Plan document. This is a succinct summary (1 to 3 pages) of what must change (the vision), why (the need — survival, growth, security, etc.), how much it will cost, and how long it will take. The summary conveys what you must become, and how you will impact the external customer and the business. It generates passion and persuades people that the obvious best alternative is what is recommended. A description of the business environment summarizes what is happening or what has changed to cause concern. A diagnosis also explains why the current process and systems are unable to meet the demands. Finally, emphasize the cost of inaction or the consequence of staying as you are.

Exhibit 8.1 shows an example of the case written at one company.

Exhibit 8.1   Management Overview

I. Management Overview

Through the strategic information systems planning efforts, our company was able to:

- Understand our current environment, organizational structure, level of investment and expenditures, project backlog, and environment outside of this location
- Review our competitors' use of information systems
- Understand current and emerging technology in the marketplace
- Understand our business objectives and how the company wants to function in the future
- Understand what our customers are requesting from an information systems perspective
- Objectively evaluate the strengths and weaknesses of our current systems
- Formulate improved interim strategies for managing resources and project requests

Although there are several aspects of our current information systems environment which can be built upon to take us into the future (such as in the areas of PC, Network, and Product Computing environments), it became evident that the existing business application systems are not adequate and will not propel us into the next century without major overhaul or replacement. These systems do not meet the business requirements outlined in our business operating vision, nor do they meet our external customer requirements. Our old, custom, patched systems simply cannot keep pace with changing business needs. Additionally, the base architecture of our current systems is not sufficient to build on for the future as indicated by the significant gap between our current system and our desired computing architecture resulting from the business requirements. Finally, like many companies, our current systems will not handle the year 2000. The project to change our current systems to handle the year 2000 is a significant cost and time effort, and we need to decide if we want to continue to invest money in our old custom application systems.

Exhibit 8.1   Management Overview (continued)

Following is a summary of reasons, as identified by business management, which lead us to conclude that a new business system solution is necessary:

- **Access to information:** It is very cumbersome to obtain information from our current systems. As a result, information needed to help manage the business is not readily available. Requests for special reports and information are difficult to respond to in a timely fashion. With the proper architecture in place, tools are now available on the market that will allow users to readily obtain the information themselves.
- **Business process re-engineering:** Processes throughout the business are laden with inefficiencies, manual workarounds, and duplicate efforts due to the inefficiencies in our systems. The current systems restrict our ability to effectively eliminate manual workarounds and inefficiencies.
- **Inability of custom systems to keep pace:** Not only do we not have the capability to meet our future business goals, our systems do not meet our current business goals and requirements. It is very expensive and time consuming to modify and maintain the systems to meet the changing business requirements, as shown by our nine-year backlog of projects. We are too small to maintain custom systems, and much larger organizations are finding custom software inflexible and too expensive to maintain. One example of this is the inability of our current systems to handle the year 2000. Just this project alone is a major effort that we would need to begin shortly, with no increased value to the business.
- **Changing business requirements:** When the current systems were selected and implemented in 1986, the company was in the process manufacturing business. Our business has grown considerably and we now manufacture and market large discrete products. Future business changes are also inevitable, and the current systems do not provide sufficient flexibility to handle these changing requirements.
- **External customer requirements:** Our customers are requesting electronic capabilities such as Electronic Data Interchange, bar coding, credit card processing, subscription services, and information regarding contract compliance and cost per reportable test. Additionally, customers would like to see electronic communication, including drawings, literature, access to technical information, and product information. Today we are unable to provide these capabilities and as a result, the company is finding itself at a competitive disadvantage in the marketplace. Providing secure customer access is essential to our expanded customer focus; our current systems close the window to important information necessary for business decisions.
- **Competition:** Our competitors provide capabilities to our customers that we are unable to provide today and are gaining a competitive advantage by making their systems more responsive to the management of the worldwide business.

Exhibit 8.1   Management Overview (continued)

- **Ability to manage the business on a worldwide basis:** Our current systems are not "open" technology, which means it is difficult to interface with other systems to obtain worldwide information needed to help manage the business. Our current systems meet only some of our domestic manufacturing requirements and do not have the capabilities to integrate worldwide information, process international orders, deal with international regulatory issues, and handle foreign currencies and foreign languages.

Following are the various options we have for our current business application systems:

1. **Continue on our current path.** This involves continuously making incremental improvements to the current custom systems to address the business needs as has been done in the past. We would need to complete a major project to address the year 2000 in our current systems. The total cost of this option is $XM, with an XX month completion. This option would be a short-term solution to address the year 2000, as it would provide us with no progress toward meeting our strategic direction, business requirements, operating vision, or desired computing architecture.

2. **Upgrade our current system.** This involves implementing the new release of our current software. The total cost of this option is $XXM, with an XX month completion. We would need to carry over the majority (70%) of our current modifications to the new release, so that we would essentially be in the same "custom" situation we are in today. Again, this option would be a short-term solution to address the year 2000, with no progress toward meeting our strategic direction, business requirements, operating vision, or desired computing architecture.

3. **Implement new system.** This option involves reviewing, selecting, and implementing an entirely new software (and potentially hardware) environment for our business application systems. It is estimated at $XXM over an XX month time frame. This option would address our strategic direction, allow us to re-engineer our business processes to eliminate waste throughout the business, provide improved abilities to access information, allow us to meet our business operating vision, our business requirements, and establish our desired computing architecture.

The recommendation of the Information Systems Steering Committee is to implement new business application systems. Developments within the past few years within the information systems industry coupled with our need to address the year 2000 have made *NOW* an opportune time to pursue new business application systems. Changes in technology toward open and client/server systems make improvements in the above areas possible. Additional enhancements and investments are also necessary in the Network area to build on what we currently have because our infrastructure has not kept pace with the growth of the company.

Exhibit 8.1   Management Overview (continued)

To be successful, this project must be a priority for the company, because it will require a significant effort and commitment from all areas of the business as well as upper management. Not only is it an expensive project for the company, but it will also utilize critical resources in the company and these critical resources will then be unable to address other business issues. However, we feel the benefits to the company are also significant and worth the effort, considering the other options available.

The purpose of this document is to communicate the results of the planning process and the logic used to reach our conclusions and recommendations.

Plan Document

You are now able to update the information systems strategic **plan document** in its entirety. Distribute the plan document in draft form to the Information Systems group and the Information Systems Steering Committee and ask for input and changes. Have another meeting with the Information Systems Steering Committee to confirm that the committee agrees with the recommendation. Also ask for their support by asking each of them to talk to their corresponding member of Executive Management and voice their support for the recommendation. It can also be helpful to ask the group for suggestions on how to present or obtain the support of the Executive Management group. You can ask for volunteers to help you make the business case because it is significantly stronger if the business makes the recommendation rather than Information Systems alone.

Executive Committee Presentation

Now you are ready to tackle the **Executive Committee**. Begin by distributing a copy of the document. Since it is a fairly long document by this time, attach a cover memo indicating why it is important for them to read the document and identify a few key sections that are particularly important in case they are unable to read the total document. Also mention that the recommendation is a joint decision from the Information Systems Steering Committee, and Executive Management can contact their representative if they have any specific questions. This way you are enlisting the Information Systems Steering Committee to be your salespeople. In the memo, indicate a date and time

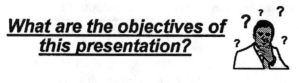

What are the objectives of this presentation?

- Provide an overview of the Information Systems Strategic Planning process, summarize information and findings

- Review our basis for recommendation to implement a new business application system

- Provide an understanding of scope of effort

- Discuss priority and timing of effort relative to other business issues

Figure 8.1   Objectives of Presentation

for an overview presentation once they have had an opportunity to review the information.

The presentation to Executive Management should be no longer than two hours. You should have at least one member from the business who is on the Information Systems Steering Committee with you for support, if not presenting a portion of the presentation. You need to begin the presentation by letting them know the purpose of the presentation and why the group should listen. Figures 8.1 and 8.2 show examples of the initial slides used at one company to introduce the presentation.

Next, explain the agenda of the presentation. Figure 8.3 shows an example of an agenda used at one company.

You can see from the timing of the agenda, the presentation needs to move rapidly to keep the interest of Executive Management.

It is often helpful to summarize your recommendations at the beginning of the presentation so that management understands where you are heading. One company summarized the recommendation as shown in Table 8.1 and also included a summary of the costs.

Early in the presentation, recognize the Information Systems Steering Committee, stressing that the recommendation you are presenting is from the whole group of business representatives that Executive Management appointed, rather than coming from the Information Systems organization. Figure 8.4 identifies the members and reconfirms the purpose of the group.

Review the process the group used to arrive at a recommendation (example shown in Figure 8.5), emphasizing that the process is not complete, that

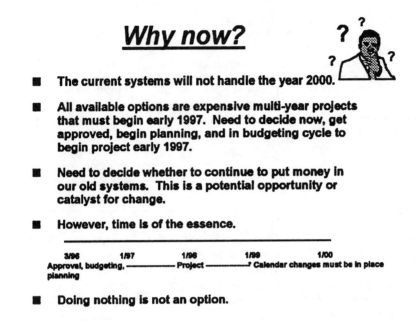

Figure 8.2   Why Now?

Figure 8.3   Agenda

you are in the stage of a high-level recommendation, and want their approval before completing a detailed analysis. The next one to two slides can summarize the scope as outlined in Chapter 2. Summarize the current situation as outlined in Chapter 4, including environment, expenditures, and organization. After outlining the internal environment, summarize the external environment as outlined in Figure 8.6. One slide per item can convey the message.

Table 8.1   Management Summary

Assessment Where we are today	Direction Where we want to be	Plan How we will get there
Different systems that address the same requirements Current systems that do not completely fulfill existing business requirements	A portfolio of common integrated systems that satisfy business requirements for all geographies	Transition to common systems, primarily relying on commercially available application packages, supplemented by new development and/or existing systems
Different technical environments that support similar systems A technical environment that does not have the necessary attributes nor capacity to support future mission-critical systems	A technical environment that is compatible with commercially available application packages, supportable throughout the world, and based on scaleable and interoperable components	Identify technology components that are compatible with commercially available application packages Acquire and/or upgrade components as necessary to support the implementation of those packages
Business systems solutions and services that are based on functional instead of enterprise needs and priorities	A partnership with business process owners in using accepted methods to deliver business systems solutions and services in accordance with enterprise needs and priorities	Develop and implement processes that apply enterprise needs and priorities to the evaluation and prioritization of request for business systems solutions and services

Now you are ready to talk about the future direction as outlined in Chapter 5. Explain that the business components determined the information systems direction, as shown in Figure 8.7. Again one slide for each of these components can convey the message.

Next you are ready to discuss the gap between your current situation and where you need to be in the future, with the work you completed in Chapter 6. Use a diagram such as Figure 8.8 to introduce the components of the gap, with no more than one or two slides for each component.

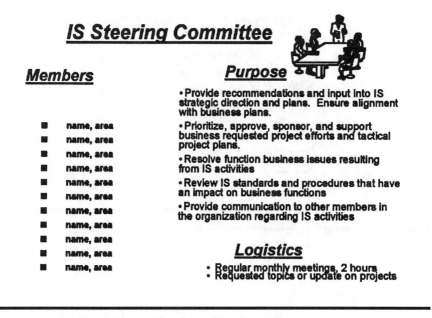

Figure 8.4   Information Systems Steering Committee

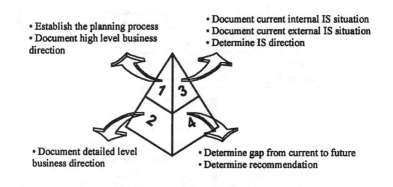

Figure 8.5   Process Utilized

You are now ready to outline the various options available to the organization. Introduce the components as shown in Figure 8.9. You need no more than three to four slides to thoroughly discuss each option. At the end of the options, you can have one slide which summarizes all the costs (direct and internal resources) for each option. You can also have a summary slide of

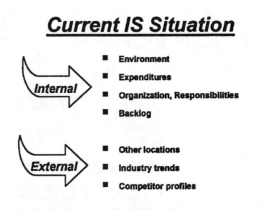

Figure 8.6   Current IS Situation Summary

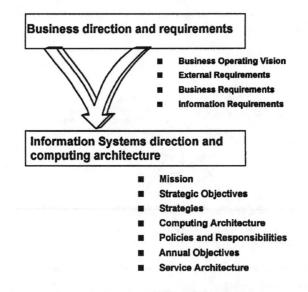

Figure 8.7   Business Direction Determines IS Direction

how each option matches with the objectives, as shown in Figure 8.10. This slide can be very effective if color-coded with red for undesirable impact, green for desirable impact, and yellow for medium impact.

What is the gap?

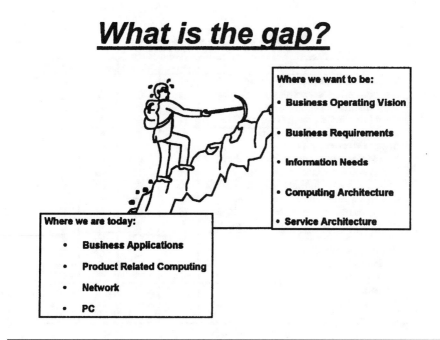

Where we want to be:

• **Business Operating Vision**

• **Business Requirements**

• **Information Needs**

• **Computing Architecture**

• **Service Architecture**

Where we are today:

• **Business Applications**

• **Product Related Computing**

• **Network**

• **PC**

Figure 8.8 Gap Analysis

Costs? Advantages?

Time? Disadvantages?

Resources? What are other companies doing?

Figure 8.9 Option Analysis

In closing, you can outline the next steps, with an associated timeline. It is often helpful to break the recommendation down into phases. Phases are more manageable and can spread the costs over a number of years. One company summarized their recommended phases in Figure 8.11.

The company based the sequence of projects on the following criteria:

Option Summary

	Current	Option 1	Option 2	Option 3
Meet business operating vision	●	●	●	○
Meet technical computing architecture	●	●	●	○
Meet business requirements	●	●	●	○
Meet information needs	●	●	●	○
Meet customer requirements	●	●	●	○
Align with competition	●	●	●	○
Provide easy access to information	●	●	●	○
Business process re-engineering	●	●	●	○
Keep pace with industry developments	●	●	◉	○
Change with business requirements	●	●	●	○
Ability to manage worldwide business	●	●	●	◉
Provide foundation for enhancements	●	●	●	○
Minimal user impact		○	◉	●
Minimal IS impact		○	◉	●
Total project cost		$xxxM	$xxxM	$xxxM
Capital cost		$xxxM	$xxxM	$xxxM
Discounted ROI		n/a	n/a	1-20%
Payback period		none	none	5-7 yrs
NPV of cash flows		$(2.4-2.9)M	$(2.8-3.4)M	$0-6.9M

Figure 8.10   Option Summary

- User dissatisfaction with the existing system as reported through surveys and interviews
- Potential business benefits and alignment with the business goals
- Number of areas that will receive benefits
- Number of existing systems that are replaced

You can again summarize the need for implementing your recommendation, as shown in Figure 8.12.

After the presentation, lead a short discussion to identify if the group should continue on the recommendation and outline the exact costs and benefits in more detail and choose a specific vendor package. The next step is to prepare the actual request for money where you would obtain signatures to formally begin the effort.

At this point, management has confidence in your process and recommendation. Still, they might be struggling with the size of the investment necessary. Stand firm to your recommendation and refer to the detail and

MIS STRATEGIC PLAN OVERVIEW

Processes	Functional Requirements	Information Requirements

Customer Interaction	Contact Management
	Quotation/Proposal
	Customer Call Management
	Order Processing
	Billing
	DRP
	Warehouse Management
	Inventory Control
	Accounts Receivable
	Diagnostic Tools
		Profiles:
		  Market, Competitor, Customer
		  Product Inventory, Carrier
		Histories:
		  Sales, Distribution, Service,
		  Expense
		Sales Forecast
		Customer Demand
		Installed Base

Product Development and Manufacturing	CAD
	Component Management
	Project Management
	Product Data Management
	Purchasing
	Receiving/Inspection
	Accounts Payable
	MRP II
	Product Costing
		Profiles:
		  Market, Competitor, Supplier,
		  Product
		Histories:
		  Project, Purchasing, Receipt,
		  Payment, Production Cost,
		  Expense
		Product Quality
		Product Test Results

Finance & Administrative Support	General Ledger Asset Management Consolidation Cash Management Disbursements Intercompany Processing Employee Management Payroll/Incentive Compensation Benefits Management Skills Management	Product Development Information Product Manufacturing Information Customer Interaction Information Budgets & Forecasts G/L Account History Expense History Headcount Profile Benefits History Compensation History Training History

Functional Automation & Decision Support Systems Projects

- ☐ Customer Interaction Systems
- ☐ Finance Systems
- ☐ Manufacturing Systems
- ☐ Human Resources Systems
- ☐ Product Development Systems

Figure 8.11 Phase Summary

Why do we need a new business application system?

Access to information

Manage worldwide

Business Process Reengineering

Cost reduction

Competition

Customer requirements

Custom systems can't keep pace

Changing business requirements

Figure 8.12   Summary

solid foundation you have carefully laid. Call upon other experts in management to support the business case on why the recommendation is important for the company. You may need to alter the speed of the spending, determine creative ways of funding the investment, or have self-funding phases, but you can stand firm in that the direction you have chosen is the direction the company must head.

Don't forget ... you are never finished with the strategic planning process and selling the recommendation. You need to constantly communicate, communicate, communicate. Communicate both what has been done and where you are going. Everyone in the organization must be aware of the information systems direction and plan. Continue building relationships with all levels of management and the Information Systems organization. Provide the leadership that is necessary in times of change.

9 What to Do Next

"Even if you're on the right track, you'll get run over if you just sit there."

Will Rogers (1875–1935)
American actor, humorist

So, now you know where you want to be, how to get there, and you have obtained initial management approval. Your work is done, right? Wrong!! Unfortunately, this was the easy part. Now the real work begins!

Next is the selection of a specific package or solutions to meet the needs of areas determined to be deficient. You may have found that your whole computing environment requires replacement.

Vendor Review and Implementation Team

Now it is time to form a critical team of individuals, the **Vendor Review and Implementation Team**, who will actually select the business application package as well as lead the implementation effort. Try to have the same group select the package as well as implement it because they will have the ownership in the decision to make the package work. The individuals must have a strong understanding of the business requirements as well as an open mind to make improvements and change the way the business is functioning today.

Selecting the project leader is critical. The leader must be from the business area because the project is a business project, not an Information Systems project. If desired, the project can have a co-leader from Information Systems, but the primary leadership must come from the business. In addition to being a strong leader, the person must have excellent communication and planning skills, a good overall knowledge of the business, decision-making skills, and the respect of the organization. During the vendor selection phase of the project, the participants can be part-time. However, during the implementation, it is strongly recommended to have several full-time business representatives in addition to a full-time business leader. Typically, organizations have a very difficult time giving the key resources to work on the project full-time. However, to be successful, it is necessary. With part-time involvement, the project will always struggle to get the necessary involvement. The people who should lead and be involved in a software package selection and implementation are those you can least afford to commit.

Project Plan

Begin the project by developing a project name, logo, and **project plan**. To publicize the project and get involvement from the organization, one company had a "Name that Project" contest, with the winner receiving a team sweatshirt with the project logo. Continuous communication is essential to get and sustain interest throughout the organization. It is also a good time to publish articles about the project in the company newsletter. Figure 9.1 shows an example of a logo for one project.

Figure 9.1   Project Logo

Exhibit 9.1 Project Mission

To strengthen the company's ability to meet worldwide customer expectations and company profitability goals by:

- Re-engineering global business processes to improve efficiency and lower costs;
- Providing common business operating systems with advanced computing architectures which will improve cooperation and communication between functional and geographical areas within the company; and
- Providing high-quality, consistent, and timely information both locally and worldwide which will improve management decision-making capabilities.

You are now ready to develop a project plan. What is included in the project plan? Following are some of the components that you can include:

- **Project Mission:** What is the purpose of the project? What is the project trying to achieve? Exhibit 9.1 shows an example of a project mission for one company.
- **Scope:** State very specifically what you will include in the scope of the project as well as any areas you will specifically exclude (for example, business applications, business processes, hardware environments, geographic locations or divisions that you will include or exclude). If you know of phases of the project, identify those as well.
- **Project Goals:** Identify specific expectations of the project. How will you know if the project is a success or not? What does management want the project team to accomplish? Project goals should be SMART: Specific, Measurable, Attainable, Realistic, and Trackable.
- **Project Team Organization:** List the names of all the business and Information Systems participants. Identify the specific time commitment if it is a part-time role. Form a project steering committee for overall project responsibility and authority.
- **Roles and Responsibilities:** Identify the roles and responsibilities for each member or group of members who participate in the project. Exhibit 9.2 shows an example of roles and responsibilities for one project.

Exhibit 9.2 Roles and Responsibilities

Following are the specific roles and responsibilities for the various team members.

Project Steering Committee: 5% of time

- Provide communication to upper management of project status and issues
- Ensure you meet project schedule and costs targets. Resolve resource constraints.
- Provide communication to project team of upper management requirements
- Responsible for the decision and selection of package based on findings and recommendation of project team
- Resolve interdepartmental or geographic conflicts that cannot be resolved by the business project leader
- Meet on a monthly basis (via video conferencing), or more frequently if necessary
- Involved with vendor negotiations as necessary

Business Project Leader: 100% of time

- Main, key leader and voice of project
- Decision maker for any conflicts which arise in functional or geographic areas
- Communicate recommendation of team to Project Steering Committee and worldwide management
- Responsible for communication and coordination with other parts of the world
- Prepares the formal request for funds
- Responsible for project communication infrastructure and process
- Responsible for determining and adhering to project schedule
- Responsible for determining and adhering to project budget
- Responsible for negotiating with vendors
- Organize and lead regular team meetings
- Management and selection of implementation consultants
- Prepares management project status report

Information Systems Project Leader: 80% of time, with other 20% going to regular IS activities

- Assist the business project leader in determining actions, schedules
- Communicate recommendation of team to Information Systems Steering Committee and worldwide management
- Assist with communication and coordination with other parts of the world
- Assist with preparation of the formal request for funds
- Assist with establishment of project communication infrastructure and process
- Communicate any technical impacts
- Communicate hardware requirements
- Communicate programming requirements
- Lead the programming effort required
- Determine and adhere to IS schedules

Exhibit 9.2 Roles and Responsibilities (continued)

- Assist with negotiations with vendors
- Assist in organizing and leading regular team meetings
- Lead or facilitate the Project Steering Committee meetings
- Management and selection of implementation consultants
- Prepare management project status report

Primary User Representatives: 50 or 100% of time

- Responsible for communicating requirements, developing demo scripts
- Responsible for gathering input and communicating back to the organizations which they represent
- Responsible for reviewing packages and making recommendations
- Responsible for business process re-engineering
- Responsible for worldwide harmonization of terms, fields, measurements
- Responsible for establishing parameters in system to fit the business
- Responsible for establishing new processes, set-up
- Responsible for testing system
- Responsible for training users
- Responsible for user documentation, procedures
- Responsible for ensuring accuracy of information (for example, conversions)
- Responsible for providing input and adhering to project schedule and budget
- Responsible for providing written monthly status reports to the Project Leaders by the last day of each calendar month
- Responsible for leading sub-projects as necessary

Primary Information Systems Representatives: 80% of time, with other 20% to IS activities

- Assist users with business process re-engineering and the tasks outlined above under Primary User Representatives
- Responsible for developing technical requirements
- Responsible for determining hardware requirements
- Responsible for installing hardware
- Responsible for installing software
- Responsible for programming, testing of conversions
- Responsible for programming, testing of interfaces
- Responsible for providing input and adhering to project schedule and budget
- Responsible for technical documentation
- Responsible for providing written monthly status reports to the Project Leaders by the last day of each calendar month

Supplemental User Resources: 10 to 50% of time

- Assist the full-time representatives with duties as outlined above

Supplemental Information Systems Resources: 10 to 50% of time

- Assist the full-time representatives with duties as outlined above

It is also helpful to include a matrix of each project participant, what business application they are responsible for, and which departments within the company they represent. This can ensure that no area will "fall through the cracks" during the project. Also identify the role of consultants on the project.

■ **Project Communication**: Lack of communication is the number-one reason projects fail. You can never communicate enough. Identify in the project plan how communication will take place and who is responsible. How will you update the average employee on the project? How will you update project members? How will you involve managers in the decisions? How often will the project steering committee meet, and who will run the meetings? What is the format of monthly project status reports? How will you run, record project meetings? How will you document decisions? Do not forget all the various people that you will need to communicate with, as shown in Figure 9.2.

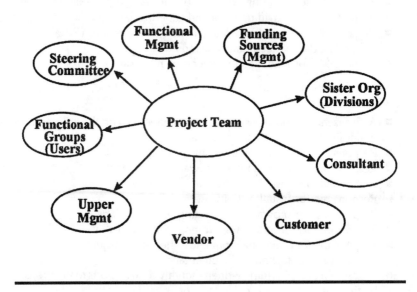

Figure 9.2   Communication

■ **Quality Assurance Compliance Guidelines**: What specific internal or external guidelines or procedures must you adhere to during the project life cycle? Do you have any ISO requirements?

- **Project Schedule:** Identify the high-level phases as well as the detailed tasks in the project. Identify the person responsible, estimated hours, and estimated time frame for completion.
- **Project Budget:** Identify how you will capture expenses for the project. How will team members record time spent on the project? Who is responsible for budgeting and assuming costs related to the project that occurs within the business departments? What are the capital and expense budgets for the project?
- **Training Plan:** What training classes are necessary for the participants to be productive? You will have additional training requirements once the specific hardware and software are selected, but are there any initial training classes needed for the selection team (for example, business process re-engineering).

Project Kick-Off Meeting

Since a journey begins on common ground, it is important to establish that common ground when beginning a new project through a **project kick-off meeting**. Participants can be unclear about the specific objectives of the project, or exactly what their role will be. Ground everyone with the same information and establish a clear vision of the group direction so each member of the group feels comfortable in his or her new role. Since obstacles are what we see when we take our eyes off the goal, the project goals and objectives must be absolutely clear in everyone's mind. The information you share can include an understanding of the project mission, scope, goals, responsibilities, schedule, and initial tasks. It is helpful to have an all-day meeting with the entire team to initiate the project.

Since everyone knows the project will be a lot of hard work, you need to initiate the project with enthusiasm, fun, and a teamwork orientation. It is helpful to organize a day with teamwork challenges, project sweatshirts, brain-teasers, competition, or anything you can think of to add some spirit to the project initiation. Begin the presentation by explaining why management selected them to participate in the project.

It may be a new role for many of the team participants to function in a project role with members from other parts of the organization. Let the team know there will be some frustrating and unclear times, but as project team participants, it is their role to help the team get back on track. It is helpful to explain the four stages of team development as outlined in Appendix 3.

Vendor Review

After obtaining the responses from your RFQ, you can review all the information and assemble the answers to **compare the vendors.** Try to narrow down the vendors to no more than three for a detailed review. If after reviewing the information, you have not narrowed the selection to three or four, you might want to bring in several vendors for a two-hour presentation. Tell each vendor that he has two hours to explain why he should be on your short list. After choosing three or so vendors to review in detail, you need to prepare for the demonstrations.

It can be very difficult to ascertain in a demonstration how the software will work in your environment. Software demonstrators are typically very good at showing you the best features without allowing you to see the deficiencies until it is in your own environment. To get the most out of the vendor demonstrations, you need to direct and guide the demonstration for your particular requirements. Following are items that you can prepare before your vendor review:

1. Script
2. Data package
3. Key requirements
4. Rating methodology
5. Demonstration guidelines for the vendor
6. Demonstration guidelines for the team participants
7. Vendor introduction to company

Each of these is discussed in more detail below.

Script

First, you need to assemble a detailed **script** of what you want to see and how you want to see it. Since demonstrations can be very time consuming, focus on the areas critical to your business rather than those that any software package can do. Develop the script by the various areas of the business that are evaluating the package. A script can be very generic or very detailed, and you can complete it at a level the particular team is comfortable with. Appendix 4 in the back of this book shows one example of a detailed script. The demo is your opportunity to "test drive" the software for your particular business requirements.

Data Package

The next item you can assemble is a **data package**. This is a package of your own company data that you would like to see used in the demonstration. Typically, this consists of the major information requirements of the system, such as:

- Customer
- Item, Bill of Material
- Order header and line items

Key Requirements

If your script is extremely long, assemble a short list of the **key requirements** the company needs from the vendor or in the new software package. These are differentiating items that are critical for your business and upon which you would rate the vendors. See an example of key requirements for one company in Appendix 5.

Rating Methodology

Decide upon a ranking or **rating methodology** before viewing any vendors. Decide if you will rank each requirement on the script, or only the key requirements. Average all participants' ranking, or give a weighted average with the most weight going to the expert in that functional area.

Demonstration Guidelines for the Vendor

Prepare **demonstration guidelines for the vendor.** An example is provided in Exhibit 9.3.

In addition, develop a high-level agenda of how you want the demo to flow. An example is shown in Exhibit 9.4.

Demonstration Guidelines for Team Participants

In addition to guidelines for the vendor, also establish **guidelines for your project team.** Several of them may not have experienced demos before and should be prepared on what to expect. An example of team guidelines is shown in Exhibit 9.5.

Exhibit 9.3   Vendor Guidelines

Demo Guidelines

- If you have both UNIX and AS/400 software, demo the UNIX version.
- If you have "green-screen" and GUI software, demo the GUI software.
- Demo your current release that would be generally available if we signed the purchase agreement today. Do not show or discuss vaporware (unless talking about future directions). If you answer a question with future availability ... make sure you clearly state that. If you answer a question, make sure you answer it for the version software we are looking at (i.e., UNIX, GUI).
- Use the actual software ... not canned screens or demonstration.
- Follow our script as much as possible. !f you need flexibility, let us know.
- You can create the agenda after reviewing our proposed script and agenda and adjust accordingly considering how long the areas typically take to review in your software and your availability of resources.
- If your software cannot do what we ask, please just say so.
- Please make sure you have knowledgeable resources to answer our questions. If they don't know the answer, don't guess ... take notes and get back to us. We'd rather hear "I don't know" than the wrong answer.
- If we don't ask about an area that you feel is a key differentiator, please tell us.
- Feel free to go through the manufacturing flowchart and then go back to answer detail questions so as not to interrupt the flow of the main example.
- You can use standard demo data that you have set up rather than our data, but make sure the examples are of sufficient complexity to demo what we are requesting. Let us know if you would prefer us to supply data.

Exhibit 9.4   Demo Agenda

Proposed Demo Agenda

- Day 1:
  - a.m.: General (company overview, general software questions, system navigation, reporting, interfaces)
  - p.m.: Manufacturing
- Day 2:
  - a.m.: Manufacturing
  - p.m.: Financial break-out
  - p.m.: Technical break-out
- Day 3:
  - Distribution

Exhibit 9.5   Vendor Guidelines for the Project Team

Demo Guidelines — Project Team

- Keep an open mind until you have seen all three suppliers. Don't "lock-on" or "lock-out." The groups may prefer different packages, and we will need to work through the differences.
- If a key requirement is not met, do not shut the vendor out. Again, keep an open mind. If all other areas are great, perhaps we can meet the missing requirement with a "bolt-on" package or re-thinking the business requirement. Do not shut-out the vendor as you will need to discuss the complete reasons that you liked or did not like the package.
- Don't "tip your hand" to the vendor and look totally discouraged or encouraged. You can show enthusiasm for the software.
- If a requirement is not met, take note and move on. Do not rag on them; the software is not going to be perfect, so don't expect it.
- Give the demo your complete attention, we need everyone to have a thorough understanding of each package to reach a decision.
- Do not leave the demo for phone calls or other business. Come on-time and stay until the end. Stay attentive. It will be boring after a while, but you need to stay focused and pay attention.
- Take good notes of ratings, advantages, disadvantages, and other information. It will get confusing on the features and functions that are included in each package. Stay organized from the beginning.
- Manage time and questions. Each application area will have an allocated amount of time. Watch your questions and level of detail to make sure you make it through all your key points. Do not de-rail on a detailed topic. Take notes for follow-on questions that can be handled in another session if needed.
- Attend all three suppliers. You will not be able to compare if you only see one or two packages. Each sub-group can coordinate if additional participants are needed or if the group does not need everyone seeing the entire demo.
- Be flexible on following the script. Their package may require significant set-up to show exactly what we want.
- Feel free to ask questions (as time allows). This is your time to see the package and obtain answers. We need to make a decision based on what we see. If you need more information, ask for it.

Vendor Introduction to Company

Once you prepare for the demonstrations, have each vendor visit your site to learn more about your business and processes. This typically takes a full day. An example of an agenda of items to cover in this day is shown in Exhibit 9.6.

Exhibit 9.6   Vendor Visit Agenda

Vendor Visit

- Background
- Project
  - Mission
  - Scope
  - Team
  - Schedule
- Demo
  - Guidelines
  - Agenda
  - Script
- Business Overview
- Business Tours

Congratulations! You are now ready to conduct thorough and useful demonstrations of the software packages.

Vendor Selection

After viewing each vendor, assemble a list of strengths and weaknesses in addition to the vendor rankings. Obtain input from all project participants. This is good to discuss in a group setting, as different areas can have different opinions that are helpful to discuss as a group. As a group, you can easily reach a consensus as to the **recommended software** with the process you have utilized.

Recommendation

The next step is to obtain detailed cost estimates so that you can complete the **recommendation**. Be sure to include all the components:

- Base business application software
- Any bolt-on software packages or additional software needed for the full business functionality necessary
- Database software
- System tools and operating system software

- Consulting, including technical consulting, network, application, business process re-engineering, and business consulting
- Consulting travel
- Team travel to obtain worldwide buy-in from other locations if necessary
- Hardware, including the various servers that are necessary, including the transaction processor, any data warehouse, and any test environments that are necessary
- Network costs
- PC software and hardware upgrades that are necessary
- Training classes, including both application as well as technical
- Training travel costs

Upon assembling the detailed costs, you can now update the Information Systems Strategic Plan and present the final recommendation to the Information Systems Steering Committee and the Executive Committee.

Risk Management

The recommendation should also address how you plan to **manage the risk**. Any large effort, particularly those that involve major change, have chances for failure. Identify reasons the project could fail and what you plan to do to avoid disaster.

Following are some reasons that projects fail that you should consider:

- Communication. How do you plan to keep the entire organization abreast of the project?
- Inadequate project planning and control. How will you ensure all phases of the project are planned? What will be the method of ensuring control of the project? Who is responsible for planning? Who is responsible for controlling the project?
- Unrealistic timetable. Have you received several opinions on the timetable for implementation? If the time frames are unrealistic at the beginning, they are bound to get worse!
- Not prepared for extra work. Are both your user community and Information Systems organization prepared for the level of resource commitment necessary?

- Attempt to modify package. If you have identified benefits to be gained by implementing a standard vendor-supportable package, how will you ensure that modifications will be kept to an absolute minimum?
- Too much reliance on vendor. What will be the role of internal resources and consultants? Who has ultimate responsibility for the project?
- Unrealistic expectations. Can the project attain the objectives established?
- Inadequate training. Is a training plan and costs included for both the Information Systems organization as well as the user community?
- Poorly defined requirements. Are the objectives of the project clear and understood by everyone?
- Lack of management involvement. Do you have all the right players involved in the project?
- Inadequate hardware configuration. Have you received benchmark information on the hardware sizing? Do you have contractual arrangements relative to the hardware sizing?
- New technology. Is the technology proven? If not, how will you address the risk?
- Package fit. Will there be a conference room pilot to confirm the software choice?
- Skills. Will you train? Will you utilize consultants? What will be the role of the consultants?
- Inadequate testing. What will be the testing phases? How will you assess readiness to implement?

With the process utilized and information gathered and communicated throughout the planning effort, the recommendation now has the support of the entire organization. You have completed all the groundwork for a successful project implementation! You are now on to the fun task of implementing your new strategic direction!

In subsequent years, you will want to go back and update or revise your information systems strategic plan. Particularly if there are major business changes, you may want to redo portions of the plan. Long-range planning in today's fast-changing information technology industry is at most a three-year window. Strategies for the Information Systems organization to help business units meet or exceed their information management and sharing requirements need to be reviewed and redirected on a regular basis. Updates to the documented and communicated plan should be done annually. This allows opportunity to make timely changes to technology and business process

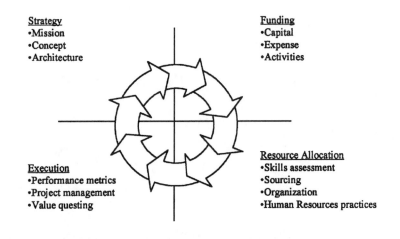

Figure 9.3   Iterative Strategic Planning Framework

strategies and direction. An iterative strategic planning framework allows for flexibility and practicality in strategy formation, funding planning, resource allocation and execution. Figure 9.3 shows the concept of continuous review and planning of strategies, funding, resource allocations, and execution.

Although you do need to modify the plan with technology or business changes, you must also be careful not to change the direction too frequently. Once you state a strategy and provide a plan or direction, it is important to stick to the plan and not revise it constantly or unnecessarily. A strategy or plan is a long-term direction and must tolerate occasional losses in addition to the wins. You need to stay the course to get good at your direction and prove its success. The purpose of a strategy or plan is to determine how to do things over a period of time in the face of high change. With the process you have completed, you should have a solid plan which is supported by the entire organization. It will be able to stand the test of time and prove to be a success!

"Men never plan to be failures; they simply fail to plan to be successful."

William A. Ward (1812–1882)
English theologian, writer, editor

"Make no little plans; they have no magic to stir men's blood ... make big plans, aim high in hope and work."

Daniel H. Burnham (1846–1912)
American architect

Appendix

Contents

1. Business Application Description
2. Technology Description
3. Stages of Team Development
4. Detailed Script
5. Key Requirements

1.
BUSINESS APPLICATION DESCRIPTION

Business Application Descriptions

Manufacturing:

- **Inventory Control:** This module allows the company to minimize the investment in inventory, while meeting customer orders and maintaining desired service levels. It maintains up-to-date inventory balances, including on-hand, allocated, and on-order quantities. It handles receipts, adjustments, warehouse transfers, and miscellaneous issues.

  Inventory has the following functions:
  - Maintains accurate and up-to-date inventory data. This includes current inventory levels by stocking locations, historic data, prediction of future levels; provides inventory management and valuation statistics.
  - Captures a detailed audit trail of all inventory level changes
  - Captures inventory movements from raw material to finished goods, as well as open order, and in-transit. Handles availability status for use in promising inventory to customer orders, purchasing and shop floor.
  - Reporting includes ABC analysis, stock status, and inventory valuation
  - Handles lot tracking, multiple warehouses, random stores
  - Supports physical inventory audits and cycle count functions

Inventory interfaces with the other systems as follows:
- Purchasing and Receiving: Obtains the quantity on order and quantity received
- Order Entry: Obtains the order allocations and returns
- Product Standard Costing: Obtains the inventory information
- WRO: Updates the allocations, in-transit inventory
- Shop Floor Control: Updates the on-hand inventory allocations, issue of material to work orders, and receipts from work orders
- Distribution Requirements Planning, Master Production Scheduling, Material Requirements Planning: Sends these systems the on-hand inventory information
- General Ledger: Sends the information from the inventory transactions that occurred so it is reflected in the inventory valuation

- **Product Structure:** This module is a foundation that provides the product structure, or bill-of-material, utilized in many applications. It represents how the product is constructed with sub-assemblies defined level by level with parent and child relationships. The product structures are the basis for all planning and costing done in the system.

The Product Structure application has the following features:
- Provides audit trail of activities with bill
- Provides engineering change control with effective dates
- Provides different types and classifications
- Supports features and options, planning bills, and substitute components
- Provides reporting for single and multiple level where used or indented bills
- Provides a planning bill-of-material that is used for forecasting

The Product Structure application interfaces with the other systems as follows:
- Order Entry: Provides the features and options entry
- Inventory Control: Multiple issues
- Material Requirements Planning: Uses the lead time offset and required manufacturing quantity per
- Master Production Scheduling: Uses the planner and bill explosion

- Shop Floor Control: Used for allocation to work orders, "features and options" processing, back flushing
- Product Standard Costing: Used for cost roll-up of assembly's component costs

■ **Master Production Scheduling (MPS):** This application is the interface between the strategic Marketing and Production Plans, and the formal build plan defining material requirements. This build plan, called the Master Production Schedule, helps to resolve conflicts between manufacturing priorities and marketplace demands allowing management to effectively plan, monitor, and control inventories. MPS drives the production of product by balancing the demand against inventory and planning factors to get the master build plan by product, quantity, and date. It translates the sales plan by family group into specific end items recognizing capacity constraints via rough-cut planning. The MPS process takes demand from forecasts and customer orders and nets against on-hand inventory and existing MPS build orders to suggest new or changed MPS orders based on lot size and planning parameters. An accepted or firm MPS schedule is the prime input into Material Requirements Planning.

MPS has the following features:
- Bucket-less system (the Master Schedule can be defined with variable time periods)
- Can generate forecast for MPS items based on planning bill
- Can utilize two time fences for demand rules, and utilizes various lead time offsets
- Provides a production plan report and MPS valuation report

MPS interfaces with the following modules:
- Inventory Control: Obtains on-hand balances
- Product Structure: Obtains the planner and bill-of-material
- Forecasting: Obtains the forecast
- Order Entry: Obtains the open customer orders
- Purchasing: Obtains the open purchase orders for MPS items
- Shop Floor: Obtains the open work orders
- MRP: Provides MRP with the Master Production Schedule

- **Material Requirements Planning (MRP):** The purpose of MRP is to provide a time-phased priority planning system that explodes the master production schedule via the bill-of-material into demand for lower-level components. Demand is netted against inventory and open orders to recommend action for release of planned orders, suggested work orders, and suggested purchase orders. Action messages are generated to keep inventory as close to the desired stocking level as possible.

  MRP has the following functions:
  - Updates planned order releases for future release, including suggested work orders, suggested purchase orders, and provides input into Capacity Requirements Planning
  - Exception messages are produced to reschedule orders, change quantity, dates, excess inventory, past due orders, etc.
  - Can peg requirements to trace the source of demand
  - Daily buckets of data are maintained; reporting buckets are variable
  - Processing is completed level by level. It assumes suggested action is taken at the upper levels in calculating the lower-level demand.
  - Handles phantom assemblies
  - There are filters to control the exception messages generated by MRP and the nervousness of the system

  MRP interfaces with the following modules:
  - Master Production Schedule: Obtains the master schedule, MPS orders
  - Product Structure: Obtains the bill-of-material
  - Inventory: Obtains on-hand inventory amount
  - Purchasing: Obtains the open purchase orders, updates suggested purchase orders
  - Work Orders: Obtains the work orders outstanding and updates the suggested work orders
  - Order Entry: Obtains the customer order information
  - Capacity Requirements Planning: Provides input of suggested work order information

- **Manufacturing Control:** This module creates and maintains the manufacturing database that controls production activities, such as product routing, production labor data collection, shop floor input and output monitoring. Work center and routing information are maintained. Work center information defines how the work is completed in each step of the manufacturing process, including the number of shifts, shift length, employees, utilization, efficiency, standards, queue time. Routing information defines the tasks required to manufacture a product, including primary and alternate operations, lead times, standards, operation codes, set up information.

- **Capacity Requirements Planning (CRP):** This application determines the workload for each work center based on planned orders and open work orders. CRP calculates and forecasts load information for equipment and resource centers. It pinpoints bottlenecks before orders are released, and helps reschedule work center activity. The tool shows the feasibility of the MPS and MRP plans.

  Rough-cut capacity planning is a moderate- to long-range planning and simulation tool providing an approximate measure of load that MPS, forecasts, and work orders will place on critical resources. This will promote early identification of resource constraints, and allows adjustments to be made to the master schedule before generating MRP.

CRP has the following features:
- Generation can be run for all products, a product range, or a product group
- Allows online inquiry and reporting on last rough-cut generation
- Reports all bills that utilize a specified resource, and lists the critical resources by product
- Provides daily or bucketed reporting
- Ability to vary capacity by date and planned variances
- Ability to define both machine and labor standards, efficiencies, and utilization percentages
- Provides online inquiry of work center and line load analysis

CRP interfaces with the following modules:
- Master Production Schedule: The Rough Cut Capacity Planning (RCCP) interfaces with MPS
- Material Requirements Planning: The Capacity Requirements Plan (CRP) interfaces with MRP for the planned orders
- Product Structure: Obtains the bill-of-material needed
- Manufacturing Control: Obtains the planned capacity for work centers, and updates the work center variance

■ **Discrete and Repetitive Manufacturing Execution:** Manages work orders through completion, creates daily dispatch lists, provides visibility to work-in-process inventory status and value, provides production performance reporting.

Manufacturing execution features:
- Handles work order splitting, automatic allocation of lots to work orders, material issues from multiple lots and locations, back flushing of materials, outside operation processing
- Provides reporting on pay point, material shortage, production performance, line
- Handles reporting and capturing of scrap
- Handles repetitive line rate scheduling, automatic issues of material and absorption of labor at standard through multi-back flushing and pay points, CRP load by line
- Generates consolidated pick lists

Manufacturing execution interfaces with:
- Order Entry: Obtains the customer orders
- MPS: Obtains the work orders
- MRP: Obtains the work orders and planned orders
- Product Structure: Obtains the bill-of-material and product information
- Manufacturing Control: Obtains the work center and routing information
- Purchasing and Receiving: Updates outside operations
- Inventory: Updates allocations, issues, and receipts
- CRP: Updates work orders
- Payroll: Updates with hour's information
- Standard Costing: Updates with actual cost information

■ **Purchasing and Receiving:** The Purchasing and Receiving application provides the capability to execute, monitor, and control the purchasing aspects of the material plan. The module covers the generation of requisitions and then receipt of the goods into stock. Purchase orders can be created using requisitions, planned orders, or manual input.

Purchasing has the following features:
- Handles dock-to-stock, and expediting for work order shortages
- The system supports requisitions, approval and quotation control, and lot tracking
- Receives purchase materials into stock and updates inventory
- Provides lot tracking, receiver document
- Blanket and MRO purchase orders are supported
- Vendor and buyer performance analysis are provided
- Provides reporting on early, late, and on-time shipments, return to vendor, and rework

Purchasing interfaces with:
- Accounts Payable: Provides invoice matching
- MPS: Provides scheduled receipts
- Inventory: Provides order information, receipts, lots
- General Ledger: Provides inventory, accrued payable, purchase price variances
- Shop Floor: Provides information on outside operations
- Costing: Provides actual material costs
- Material Requirements Planning: Updates suggested orders and scheduled receipts

■ **Forecasting:** The Forecasting workbench aims to develop accurate forecasts through the use of statistical analysis and modeling techniques. Simulation capabilities provide the ability to see effects of changing forecasting techniques and inventory parameters without affecting live data. It also monitors the accuracy of forecasts and monitors sudden demand changes.

Forecasting functions include:
- Provides simulation capabilities for what-if analysis
- Assists in inventory management by calculating safety stock levels, suggested order quantity, economic order quantity
- Supports various forecasting techniques, such as simple moving average, exponential smoothing including seasons, trends, focus forecasting

Forecasting interfaces to:
- MPS: Can transfer the forecast information to the MPS
- DRP: Can transfer the forecast information to the DRP

Distribution

- **Customer Order Entry:** Provides the ability to enter customer orders, allocate inventory at time of order placement, track orders, and provide information of customer service levels.

  Order Entry functions include:
  - Ability to copy orders, handles multiple levels of pricing, credit checking, multiple order types, multiple ship-to addresses
  - Produces customer acknowledgments, bookings register, pick slips, bills of lading, quotes

  Order Entry interfaces to the following applications:
  - General Ledger: Updates with order information
  - Accounts Receivable: Updates with order information
  - Billing: Updates with invoice information

- **Billing:** Billing produces the customer invoices so we can get paid

  Billing functions include:
  - Handles multiple warehouses, multiple plans, credit and debit memos, multi-currency
  - Invoices can be printed and reprinted if necessary

  Billing interfaces to the following applications:
  - General Ledger: Updates with invoice information
  - Accounts Receivable: Updates with billing information
  - Order Entry: Receives order information

- **Shipping:** Shipping interfaces with the order entry system to create the shipment information and documentation. Provides the ability to ship customer orders, allocate inventory, and print appropriate documentation accompanying the shipment.

  Shipping functions include:
  - Printing pick slips so the product can be retrieved from the appropriate stocking location
  - Generating export documents that accompany the shipments through customs
  - Entering quantities being shipped

Shipping interfaces to the following applications:
* Order Entry
* Inventory Control: Relieves inventory
* General Ledger: Updates with shipping information

Finance

- **Fixed Assets:** Fixed Assets tracks and reports the financial value of all of the company's assets.
- **General Ledger:** The purpose of the General Ledger system is to accurately reflect the financial condition of the company.

General Ledger interfaces with the following applications:
* Accounts Receivable: Obtains receivable information
* WRO: Obtains the inventory transfers
* Inventory: Obtains receipt, issue, and adjustment information
* Purchasing: Obtains receipt information
* Accounts Payable: Obtains payable information
* Shop Floor: Obtains labor and material transactions
* Payroll: Obtains wages information

- **Costing:** The purpose of the standard costing module is to develop, monitor, and revise product cost information. Standard costs are used for developing manufacturing plans, controlling manufacturing costs, budgeting, inventory valuation, and pricing. The system uses bills of material, routings, and outside operations to develop material, labor, set-up, burden, and outside operation costs.

The cost module has the following functions:
* Captures labor, material, overhead, outside operation, and set-up costs
* Handles standard as well as next year's going to standard
* Either full absorption or direct costing of overhead can be used
* Provides variance analysis to pinpoint the accountability and focus on out of control costs. Variance reporting is available when comparing frozen standard, current standard, and actual costs.
* Up to five overhead costs can be assigned as fixed or variable
* Planned shrink or scrap costs can be included in the cost
* Ability to roll-up all costs or selected costs

The cost module interfaces with the following applications:
- Product Structure: Obtains component costs, bill-of-material, and where used for the cost roll-up
- Production Control: Using routing, labor cost, overhead cost, set-up cost, outside operations, scrap
- General Ledger: Updates inventory transaction variance information
- Inventory: Updates the valuation of inventory
- Order Entry and Billing: Updates the cost of goods sold
- Shop Floor Control: Updates the valuation of WIP; this is the basis for variances

■ **Accounts Payable:** The Accounts Payable system provides control and management over the cash outflow. It provides control by matching invoices with purchasing receipts, and tracks open invoices and activity by supplier. Provides reporting mechanisms for cash planning and vendor performance.

Features of Accounts Payable include:
- Online matching of invoices with receiving function
- Reporting including General Ledger interface, trial balance, discount analysis, vendor analysis, aged open payables
- Can process two open periods simultaneously, multi-currency, check reconciliation, multiple bank processing

Accounts Payable interfaces to:
- General Ledger: Updates General Ledger with cash information
- Purchasing: Obtains receipt and purchasing information for matching

■ **Accounts Receivable:** Accounts Receivable aids in the collection of money, reduces bad debts, and monitors cash flow. Provides information on customer accounts and activity.

Accounts Receivable functions include:
- Posts cash received
- Handles adjustments, invoice, non-AR cash receipt's entries, multi-currency, transfers, check reversal
- Provides online customer account inquiry, including credit limits, exposure amounts, open and closed item detail
- Prepares customer statements and finance charges, aged trial balance

Accounts Receivable interfaces with:
* Order Entry and Invoicing: Obtains the order and invoice information
* General Ledger: Updates General Ledger with receivable information.

■ **Budgeting:** The budgeting system assists in the development of the annual budget. This internally created system creates a secondary database of select files for the manufacturing portion of the budget. Blank sales files are distributed out to the field, forecasts are returned to us by diskette and we combine the data through an upload using Showcase middle-ware.

2.

TECHNOLOGY DESCRIPTION

1. Ready To Implement Technologies:

a. **Bar coding:** The capability to automatically scan coding rather than keying the information. It reduces manual labor and improves accuracy.

b. **EDI:** Electronic Data Interchange is a computer-to-computer interchange of information conforming with specified standards over a communications network. If entered directly to the computer, it can significantly reduce manual labor, accelerate processing time, and improve accuracy.

c. **Local Area Networks:** A LAN is a limited distance network connecting computers, printers, and other peripherals. The network exists within a building or several buildings close together. It allows sharing of resources, provides better data backup and security capabilities, provides access to all computer systems and information on the network.

d. **Open Systems:** Systems having been developed to conform to a set of internationally agreed-upon standards. This is more of a strategy than a technology. It allows you to move software to multiple hardware platforms without modifying the systems. Open systems allow for hardware scaleability to fit the size of business, easier multivendor integration, and gives a leveraged position for negotiating with vendors.

e. **Video Teleconferencing:** Video teleconferencing provides visual and audio communications with two or more parties via a common carrier network. It can function within a PC or as a stand-alone unit. This reduces travel time and expenses and provides for improved communication resulting in better business decisions.

f. **X.400 E-mail Standard:** Standard based protocols and services supporting a comprehensive electronic messaging service. It allows differing mail systems to communicate and reduces the expense.

g. **Rapid Prototyping:** Rapid prototyping improves the system development process by letting users see proposed systems quickly before actual development begins.

h. **CASE Tools:** Computer Aided Software Engineering and a standard systems development process (Systems Development Methodology) improve the systems development process to ensure consistency, increases system quality, enhances communication, and increases productivity.

i. **CD-ROM:** A CD-ROM stores large volumes of information on a disk similar to CD audio disks.

j. **Client/Server:** Separates processes on differing hardware platforms interacting with each other over a network. The PC is the "client" front end and allows for easy-to-use systems, while the processing is done in the back-end on a server. This takes advantage of each hardware platform's capability and provides an increased flexibility to meet the needs of users and customers.

k. **Imaging Processing:** A tool to replace paper documents with an electronic facsimile and then store, retrieve, display, print, fax, and distribute the image. It can dramatically improve the entire work flow of an organization.

l. **Relational Databases:** Relational databases allows data to be stored in tables with accessibility from other platforms.

m. **Wide Area Networks:** A Wide Area Network (WAN) connects computers across distances, countries, or the entire globe.

n. **Work Group Software:** Work group software is used on a LAN to provide users with an easy method of sharing information. Office productivity can be improved by better access to information, teamwork, decision making, and improved quality.

o. **Internet and Other Vendor-Supplied General System Access:** The Internet is a generally available network that is used for many different purposes. For example, we could use the Internet for communication of test results and product information to customers. Suppliers of other industry information also exist, such as FedEx and other shipping companies.

p. **Network Faxing:** This is the capability to fax documents and files directly from a network.

q. **Executive IS:** Executive Information Systems allows management to access and analyze key information without technical computer knowledge.

2. Emerging Technologies:

a. Object-Oriented Programming: Independent software modules containing programming and data behaving like independent objects and can be re-used. This reduces programming time for development and maintenance as code is reused.

b. Pen-Based Computers: Pen-based computers use electronic pens to input data instead of a keyboard. Hand printing is translated into typed text.

c. Wireless Communications: Computers can be connected by using cellular modems on a cellular phone network. On a LAN, it uses spread-spectrum radio technology. Cellular modem technology is available, but expensive. Wireless LANs are readily available and cost effective.

d. X.500 E-mail Standard: Directory services for electronic mail that allows for automatic routing of e-mail among differing systems, and automatic updating of directories.

e. Palmtop Computers: Also called Personal Digital Assistants (PDAs) are small computers fitting in the palm of a hand. The PDA can be connected to other computers using wireless technologies.

3. Need Further Review:

a. Artificial Intelligence
b. Distributed Relational Database
c. Language Translation
d. Multimedia
e. Voice recognition

3.

STAGES OF TEAM DEVELOPMENT

Following are the **four stages** of team development:

1. Getting started
2. Going in circles
3. Getting on course
4. Full speed ahead

These stages are outlined in the figure below:

Stages of Team Development

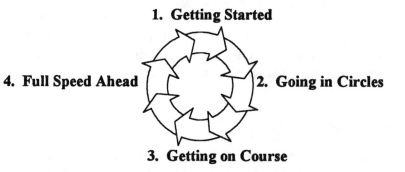

1. Getting Started

4. Full Speed Ahead

2. Going in Circles

3. Getting on Course

Getting Started

In the first stage, **getting started**, the team is getting to know the task and team members, learning each other's skills and expectations, testing each other's commitment and attitude, beginning to define tasks and roles, focusing on symptoms and problems not related to the task. Team members in this stage feel excited about being part of something new, anxious about the goals and what it takes to achieve them, suspicious about what is expected of them, unsure about how their contributions will fit in with the team's mission and goals.

Going in Circles

In the second stage, **going in circles**, the team may be setting unrealistic goals, relying on only one person's experience and ideas, resisting working together, not making much progress, competing for control, focusing on the task or goal, not on how to get it done. As a team member in this stage, you might feel frustrated that progress is not being made as fast as expected, angry that ideas are criticized or ignored, impatient with members who are slow or who don't pull their weight, jealous of others who might have more rewarding or easier responsibilities.

Getting on Course

In the third stage, **getting on course**, the team may be having some difficulty, but making progress toward reaching the goal, using each other's ideas, giving and receiving constructive feedback, setting and usually following team ground rules and norms, valuing individual differences. As a team member in this stage, you feel respect for other members' needs and capabilities, relief that the team is making progress, a growing sense of trust because everyone is committed, increasingly comfortable working together.

Full Speed Ahead

In the fourth stage, **full speed ahead**, the team is making progress toward the goal with speed and efficiency, working together to diagnose and overcome obstacles, using feedback to make changes, and finding ways to continuously improve how the members work together. As a team member in this stage, you feel pride in your work, excited about being part of the team, enjoyment in working together and meeting goals, fully committed to the team, and secure in relying on other members. As a team leader, strive to have your team in this fourth stage as much of the time as possible. However, teams typically go through the various stages several times during a project.

Team Temperature

A high-performance team is one in which the members meet their goals, trust each other, actively listen, create realistic and challenging objectives, work out conflicts in a healthy manner, use performance standards, give positive feedback, create a positive, candid, and relaxed team environment, define clear roles and goals, and make decisions through consensus. Take the **team temperature** at various stages in the project so that you can correct areas that are weak. An example of a team temperature survey is shown below.

Rating our Project Team

Please complete this survey as honestly as possible so that we can see where our team is strong and where we need to improve it.

	No, not at all	Yes, very much so
1. **Purpose:** clearly state team goals and objectives.		
▪ My team has clear direction, goals, and objectives.	1 .. 2 .. 3 .. 4 .. 5	
▪ The project goals are consistent with company goals.	1 .. 2 .. 3 .. 4 .. 5	
▪ We have the support of upper management.	1 .. 2 .. 3 .. 4 .. 5	
▪ The project is popular and wanted.	1 .. 2 .. 3 .. 4 .. 5	
▪ Users and management agree on objectives.	1 .. 2 .. 3 .. 4 .. 5	
2. **Process:** using well-defined procedures for making decisions, solving problems, and accomplishing work assignments.		
▪ My team has well-defined procedures and uses them consistently.	1 .. 2 .. 3 .. 4 .. 5	
▪ Meetings start on time and are worthwhile.	1 .. 2 .. 3 .. 4 .. 5	
▪ I have an adequate budget (or ability to spend if needed).	1 .. 2 .. 3 .. 4 .. 5	
3. **Communication:** expressing oneself openly, honestly, and clearly with others.		
▪ My team's members always express themselves openly, honestly, and clearly.	1 .. 2 .. 3 .. 4 .. 5	
▪ We resolve conflicts in a healthy manner.	1 .. 2 .. 3 .. 4 .. 5	
▪ The team environment is positive, candid, and relaxed.	1 .. 2 .. 3 .. 4 .. 5	
▪ We encourage new ideas.	1 .. 2 .. 3 .. 4 .. 5	
▪ We make decisions timely with enough discussion and consensus.	1 .. 2 .. 3 .. 4 .. 5	

Rating our Project Team (continued)

	No, not at all	Yes, very much so

4. **Involvement:** using individual skills and talents to help the team succeed.
   - My team's members actively volunteer skills and ideas. — 1 .. 2 .. 3 .. 4 .. 5
   - I am enthusiastic about this project. — 1 .. 2 .. 3 .. 4 .. 5
   - I have adequate time to spend on the project. — 1 .. 2 .. 3 .. 4 .. 5
   - I have adequate skills to complete this project. — 1 .. 2 .. 3 .. 4 .. 5
   - I have sufficient authority to complete this project. — 1 .. 2 .. 3 .. 4 .. 5
   - We have the right people involved. — 1 .. 2 .. 3 .. 4 .. 5
   - The team is enthusiastic about the project. — 1 .. 2 .. 3 .. 4 .. 5
   - I am able to get assistance from the right people when I need it. — 1 .. 2 .. 3 .. 4 .. 5
   - Roles and responsibilities are clear. — 1 .. 2 .. 3 .. 4 .. 5

5. **Commitment:** willingness to accept responsibilities and perform them in a timely manner.
   - My team's members always fulfill their responsibilities. — 1 .. 2 .. 3 .. 4 .. 5
   - I fully support the team's stated goals and direction. — 1 .. 2 .. 3 .. 4 .. 5

6. **Trust:** confidently relying on others to fulfill their individual responsibilities toward the team.
   - My team's members confidently rely on each other. — 1 .. 2 .. 3 .. 4 .. 5
   - We have respect for each other. — 1 .. 2 .. 3 .. 4 .. 5

Comments:

Issues, or things that are not going so well:

Things that are going well:

Team Improvement

You need to stress that it is the responsibility of each team member to help the team improve in areas where they feel the team is weak. Often, team participants will blame the leader for a less than perfect environment, rather than taking action themselves to improve the team. Following are suggestions for improvements within each area of the team temperature survey.

Purpose

If the team needs improvement in purpose, try to:

- Write a charter or mission statement. Keep it and the goals posted in a common team area.
- Relate short-term goals to your company's mission and long-term goals.
- Ensure that each team member has a clear and meaningful role.
- Revise roles and short-term goals as projects or tasks change.
- Question assignments that do not contribute to the long-term goals.
- Write clear and concise goals that everyone agrees with.

Process

If your team needs improvement in process:

- Establish procedures for solving conflicts.
- Establish a set of steps for solving problems or carrying out new ideas.
- Provide training in problem-solving methodologies.
- Follow agendas during all meetings and publish minutes with action items.
- Use flip charts, blackboards, and schedules in meetings. Come prepared with copies of information for all members.
- Make procedural suggestions.
- Listen and respond with empathy.

Communication

When your team needs improvement in communication:

- Listen and respond with empathy.
- Maintain or enhance self-esteem.
- Explore ideas instead of judging them.
- Avoid jumping from topic to topic in discussions or meetings.
- Share information with everyone.
- Include all team members in decisions, updates, and problem solving.

Involvement

When your team needs development in involvement:

- Encourage quiet team members to contribute.
- Ask for help and encourage involvement.
- Distribute action items evenly.
- Let everyone have a say before making a decision.
- Encourage and build on others' ideas and initiatives.
- Recognize others' ideas.
- Share information; avoid holding back facts and materials.

Commitment

When your team needs development in commitment:

- Ask for help in solving problems.
- Respect others' ideas.
- Use others' unique individual talents.
- Encourage the involvement of all team members.
- Meet deadlines and live up to agreements.
- Attend all scheduled meetings and events.
- Focus on team goals.
- Attend and start meetings on time.

Trust

When your team needs development in trust:

- Maintain each other's self-esteem.
- Support and praise each other.
- Keep sensitive information confidential.
- Stand up for each other.
- Avoid gossip or unfair criticism of others.
- Get the facts; do not deal with opinions.
- Appreciate each other's skills and differences.

Provide these guidelines for improvement to all team members and post them in a common team area.

4.

DETAILED

SCRIPT

General

Company Information and Overview

Information request topics

1. Annual Sales: U.S., Europe, Worldwide
2. # of customers: U.S., Europe, Worldwide
3. # of employees: U.S., Europe, Worldwide
4. Quick ratio (Cash & Accounts Receivable and Current Liabilities)
5. License and service revenue as a percentage of overall revenue
6. R&D % to revenue
7. # of programmers and developers
8. Turnover rate for programmers and developers
9. Sales and marketing expense percentage to revenue
10. Largest account dollar amount
11. Average contract size
12. Percentage of customers on current version
13. Percentage of customers on annual maintenance
14. List of major customers in our market, including our competitors
15. Is your software ISO certified?
16. Where is the nearest customer training center for personnel in the following locations? Would support at these locations be direct or through business partners?
17. What is the oldest working installation of your client/server product? How long ago did you implement it?
18. Provide a list of your last five installations in the U.S. (currently in production), including contact name and phone numbers as a reference.

19. Is there an active local user group? If not, is there any local representation on a regional or national user group? Contact name and number.
20. Provide a list of software modules offered.
21. Provide an annual report.

Demonstration and discussion topics

22. Discuss strategic direction of your company.
23. What industries do you see as your primary markets?
24. Discuss planned software enhancements, rewrites, and R&D direction.
25. Date and features of next release.
26. What are the key differentiating features of your product?
27. Discuss the amount of time required for training in each module.
28. Describe typical configuration and set-up for multinational, multi-division, multiplant.
29. Describe multilingual capabilities:
    a) Are all modules translated? Help screens and documentation?
    b) Which languages?
    c) What is the typical delay for translation of new releases?

System Implementation Management

30. What tools are available to help the implementation process?
31. Discuss implementation process; average time (and range) to implement complete integrated package.
32. Which consulting firms are most familiar with your products?

Navigation

33. Demonstrate general system navigation. Is navigation similar throughout all modules?
34. Does your product have data dictionaries for every field?
35. Demonstrate any online help feature. Is it available for all programs, screens, and fields? Is it text sensitive? Is it modified to incorporate user-defined set-up?

36. Demonstrate how users can modify the menus.
37. Can online inquiry and update screens be easily added by the user?
38. Show how you can carry over fields from screen to screen (for example, if you are in inventory status and switch to a purchasing inquiry, will the part number be automatically retained?)
39. Can field default values be established?
40. Are there pop-up menus available to list valid field codes for all codes?

Report Writer

41. Create a simple sales report by product group comparing actual to budget to prior year data, along with calculated fields such as percentage growth and variance to budget.
42. If possible, use drill down capability to see detail by product supporting product group sales in above example, then product sales by customer.
43. Using this report, demonstrate changing of report bucketing: Daily, Weekly, Monthly, Yearly, Budget, Forecast, and Actual.
44. Create a graph of the data in the report. Can graphical and report outputs be printed WYSIWYG?
45. Can the report writer do online inquiries? If so, what is the effect on system performance? Do customers typically do this?
46. Can the report writer combine more than five files easily? Show an example. Can you save queries for use by other users?
47. Can reports be set up in batch processing mode?
48. Does the report writer use summary files that need to be refreshed or realigned?
49. Can you integrate data from affiliates outside the system into the report writer system?
50. What tools are available for online report viewing and storage of print files?
51. Is there a separate data warehouse? How do you combine to obtain worldwide information?
52. Is there an integrated EIS? Demonstrate drill-down capabilities and discuss ease of establishing EIS elements. Explain flexibility of EIS data collection and consolidation rules.

Interfaces

53. Demonstrate capability to upload and download data to Microsoft Excel or Access for Financial, Sales, Manufacturing, and other data.
54. Is there a tool for easily downloading to and uploading from the network? Show us. Is the environment integrated so you can share data without duplicating?
55. What type of work or additional middle-ware is required to set up interfaces between the report writer and the application system?
56. Does your product interface with CAD/CAM?
57. Does your product interface with our document control software and Product History File (PDIS)?
58. Does your software interface to optical imaging system? Is there other imaging capability?
59. Do you have an integrated EDI system or is it a third-party "bolt-on" product?
60. Describe your interface capabilities to electronic mail.

General Software Features

61. Discuss the capabilities of the search function. Is it real time or does it depend on batch indices? Can you use wildcards to search all fields?
62. Discuss bar coding capabilities:
    a) Shop Floor
    b) Distribution
    c) Receiving
    d) Inventory Control
63. How do you handle conversion of key fields and entities between different plants (for example, feet to meters as unit of measure)?
64. How many user-defined fields are there per database?
65. How can we make certain fields mandatory?
66. Demonstrate the security provisions by module, transaction, field, and classification.
67. General discussion of process capabilities (versus discrete).
68. Demonstrate any work-flow capabilities.
69. Demonstrate any document imaging capabilities, electronic signatures, and approvals.

Manufacturing

1. Discuss the coexisting manufacturing environment of discrete and process.

Part Master

Information request topics for part master

2. How many digits can part numbers have?
3. Is there an option for item-specific shrinkage factor?

Demonstration and discussion topics

4. Demonstrate the parts search capabilities.
5. Demonstrate ability to identify duplicates and substitutes.
6. Demonstrate how a part can be both purchased and manufactured in the same plant.
7. Demonstrate obsolete parts (obsolete for manufacturing, still available for sales) and interaction with order entry.
8. Show the implementation and flow of revision levels and effective dates.
9. Demonstrate audit trail for the part master.
10. Add two parts (purchased and manufactured) to the part master file.
11. Enter a valid but incorrect part number, and show the results and how to correct the error to demonstrate the editing and error correction capabilities.
12. Is there Engineering Change Order (ECO) control of the part master?
13. Discuss required fields and equivalent system locations (for example, usage control codes).

Routings

14. Demonstrate the following routing features:
    a) Effective dates of Engineering Change Order (ECO).
    b) Discussion of ties between Bill of Materials (BOM) and routing.

    c) Capacity unit of measures and definition of workstation.

    d) Demonstrate yield's route and operation (for example, parent and component).

    e) Ability to access manufacturing documentation (procedures, drawings, specs).

15. Demonstrate the ability to change units of measure between operations.

Bill of Materials (BOM)

16. Can BOM quantities be less than 1, or be equal to zero (0)?
17. Does the system allow for a circular bill?
18. Can you support alternate parts? Phantom parts?
19. Demonstrate Lot Potency in BOM.
20. Show a one-level BOM. Show an indented BOM.
21. Demonstrate the "where used" feature.
22. Demonstrate material tied to operations and a BOM with the same item used at different steps.
23. Demonstrate and discuss the ability to import and export BOM information (for example, transferring to and from CAD systems).
24. Demonstrate revision control in a multiple plant environment
    a) For example, different effective dates by plants
    b) Tracking and reporting of effective date changes
25. Demonstrate an Engineering Change Order (ECO)
    a) Effective dates
    b) Approval process
    c) Interaction with MRP and work orders
26. Demonstrate a mass replacement.

Lot Master File

27. Can there be multiple products per lot?
28. Do you have a lot status feature?
29. Demonstrate lot number assignment (manual and auto). Where is lot number assignment defined?
30. Demonstrate serialization (manual and auto).

31. Demonstrate expiration assignment
    a) Auto-calculate ship dates both domestic and international and define how ship dates are calculated. Can you define by customer?
    b) Dynamic user-definable expiration date calculations
    c) Manual expiration maintenance on shop floor
    d) Ability to automatically move expired material to a non-useable inventory status
    e) Options for transactions that trigger expiration date assignment
32. Demonstrate lot tracing capabilities
    a) Tie to vendor lot.
    b) Tie to revision of specification used for purchase and inspection of raw materials.
    c) Ability to access lot master information for all materials on an indented Bill of Materials (BOM) of a specific parent lot.
    d) Lot history, including how made and how used.
    e) Forward and backward lot tracing.
    f) Demonstrate lot-split and lot-combine capabilities.
33. Discuss and show QC status tracing capabilities plant to plant
    a) Ability to indicate quality release status.
    b) Ability to indicate manufacturing deviations with disposition (for example, "use as is," "rework," "scrap").
    c) Trace quality attributes.
    d) Link to Quality Control records and data.
34. Discuss and show material technical information capabilities, such as titer and other attributes.
35. Show regulatory information capabilities, including:
    a) Country of origin (ability to access this information for indented Bill of Materials).
    b) U.S. Department of Agriculture.
    c) Usage control capabilities by lot.

Production and Resource Plan

36. Demonstrate any software to state production levels by family by units.
37. Demonstrate a bill of resource.

Forecasting

38. Review the Forecasting workbench
    a) Set up a Geographical Forecast.
    b) Demand history file and sales transaction flow. In order to forecast by geographic area, do you need geographic warehouse sales transactions?
    c) Demonstrate bottom-up and top-down product/group relationship.
    d) Generate a performance and variance report: budget, forecast, actual.

Distribution Requirements Planning (DRP)

39. Discuss the features of DRP, including the DRP workbench and the processing options.
40. Discuss the ability to transfer a sales order from one location to another.

Master Production Schedule (MPS)

41. Review the MPS workbench
42. Demonstrate Available to Promise (ATP) capabilities, including the ATP calculation and how you handle reservations.
43. Is there a Customer Service Report?

Rough Cut Capacity Plan (RCCP)

44. Review RCCP set-up.
45. Define a "bill." Is it sensitive to space and suppliers?

Material Requirements Planning (MRP)

Information request topics for MRP

46. How does the system handle dependent demand between plants?

Demonstration and discussion topics

47. Discuss MRP options
    a) Regenerative versus Regenerative in batch, versus continuous versus net change (system performance impacts).
    b) Future view of expired material.
    c) Non-netting lots, non-netting warehouse.

Manufacturing Execution System (MES) and Capacity Planning Capabilities

48. Can you schedule decimal transit days?
49. Do you have shop calendar by work center?
50. Review scheduler's workbench
    a) Constraint screen and report
    b) Materials and labor

Purchasing and Receiving

Information request topics for Purchasing

51. Is there a preferred parts and supplier list?
52. Is there the ability to track material revision levels from Purchase Order (PO), to specifications, to incoming inspection, to specific material lots?
53. Can you link a purchase order to a work order?
54. Do you have a credit card interface?
55. Do you have drop ship option?
56. Is there in-bound transportation functionality?

Demonstration and discussion topics

57. Review the vendor master file.
58. Show a Purchase order.
59. Show a Purchase requisition.
60. Demonstrate online approval system capabilities.
61. Show a receipt.

62. Demonstrate the return mechanism. Does it cue PO adjustment? Can you return parts to the vendor after closing the purchase order?
63. Discuss paperless receiving.

Shop Floor Control

Information request topics for Shop Floor Control

64. Are there Research & Development work order capabilities? Are there work orders charged to other departments?
65. What are paperless capabilities for online documentation and records, electronic signatures?
66. Can you schedule the plant without work orders?

Demonstration and discussion topics

67. Demonstrate the work order flow
    a) Create then maintain work order types: discrete, process, re-work work order, firm planned order
    b) Review job packet elements
    c) Multiple releases on one work order
    d) Material available check screen
    e) Lot allocation procedure, auto and manual
    f) Lot split, lot combine
    g) Demonstrate back-flushing, pre-flushing, and pay points
    h) Back-flushing with lot numbers?
    i) Labor reporting
    j) Close the job
    k) Variance report
68. Show Manufacturing Metrics.

Inventory Management

Information request topics for Inventory Management

69. Are raw material pick lists automatically generated?

70. Can the shortest expiring material become the expiration date for parent product?
71. Are there transaction warnings to indicate that an inventory balance will go negative? Is there a negative balance report?
72. Is there an inventory accuracy report?
73. Is there an electronic import capability for outside inventory samples?

Demonstration and discussion topics

74. Demonstrate planned and unplanned cycle count, and physical inventory capabilities.
75. Demonstrate how to manage R&D inventory:
    a) Archived inventory, not available for regular production, no cost
    b) Demonstrate how non-stock items can be viewed and accessed without part numbers
76. Demonstrate warehouse and location masters.
77. Demonstrate inter-plant and intra-plant transfers.
78. Demonstrate FIFO, LIFO, FEFO, and shelf life capabilities.
79. Review the inventory availability screens.
80. Demonstrate inventory transactions and audit trail.
81. Show Inventory Management tools:
    a) Forward looking excess and obsolete
    b) Forecast inventory dollar report
    c) Inventory turnover measurements
    d) Models, model variances
    e) Dynamic safety stock?
    f) User-defined excess
82. Show automatic conversion for units of measure.
83. Show capability for inventory capacity planning and space utilization reporting.

Quality

84. Is there an inspection priority list?
85. Are there attachments for documents?
86. Is there a Quality module? Explain the capabilities.

87. Demonstrate supplier performance measures:
    a) Explain calculations and criteria
    b) Quality and delivery measures
    c) Purchase price variances
88. Demonstrate Quality Control capabilities:
    a) Show vendor sample evaluation prior to bulk receipt. Show how this is handled with and without a work order tie.
    b) Demonstrate ability to handle refurbished instrument history information.
    c) Does the system handle skip lot testing?
    d) Is there "Positive recall" capability (for untested material needed for urgent manufacturing or long lead times)?
    e) What are capabilities for maintaining Quality Control data?
    f) Is the system able to prevent product from being put into useable inventory location before review and approval of History Record?
89. Demonstrate Product Quality Assurance and Regulatory control capabilities:
    a) Explain and demonstrate Device Master Record capabilities including linkage to Standard Operating Procedures, equipment with status of validation, calibration, and maintenance, process validation, training, facilities.
    b) Demonstrate capability to link shipping requirements and records to the Device Master and Device History records when shipping controls necessary to maintain product quality.
    c) Demonstrate ability to retain records, data, lot information and transaction history for extended time, capable of flagging records for retention times.
    d) Does the system support medical device reporting such as multiple site document input, capability to include complaints?
    e) Is there capability for handling Regulatory and Clinical data?
    f) Is the system capable of Certificate of Analysis auto-generation when a product is sent out (international by language, by specific information required by country)?
    g) How flexible are the usage control options (control of product shipments)? Does the system support item master-level usage control with lot specific override?
    h) What are systems information trending capabilities by product and lot? Does it have the ability to link to manufacturing deviations, corrective and preventative action, and customer complaints?

90. Discuss and demonstrate safety reporting and control capabilities:
    a) Online Material Safety Data Sheets (MSDS).
    b) MSDS auto print with shipment including language and format options by country.
    c) MSDS online for internal use.
    d) Demonstrate MSDS link to Bill of Materials (BOM) for automatic update or update flag.
    e) Demonstrate ability to auto generate and print (hazardous) shipping stickers required on shipments by product.

91. Demonstrate Document Control and Record Control:
    a) Demonstrate system set-up, editing, and maintenance (Bill of Materials, routings, item masters, including copy and copy excerpt).
    b) Demonstrate effective date control (Bill of Materials, routings, documents).
    c) Show revision control capabilities — automatic update and flagging options (links between product master, BOM, specifications, work orders).
    d) Does the system support paperless documentation system? Online design change order (DCO)? Electronic records, data, documents ability? Does the system support electronic signatures?
    e) Is there capability to retain and retrieve design change order (DCO) historic information by item and access information by indented BOM?
    f) Is the system able to auto-assign part numbers, lot numbers?
    g) Is system able to handle auto-label request system?

Cost and Manufacturing Accounting

Costing Methods

Information request topics

1. What types of costing does the system support? (For example, Standard, Activity Based Costing, Actual Cost, Average Actual Cost, Theory of Constraints.) Are multiple costs supported for the same item (for example, same product is produced at two locations but will have different costs because of local differences in costs).

2. How would you maintain multiple cost methods? (For example, ABC for management reporting, standard costing for financial reporting.)
3. What types of cost drivers are available for absorbing overhead into product cost? (For example, machine hours, direct labor hours, completed units, etc.)

Demonstration and discussion topics

4. Job and Process Costing.
5. Activity Based Costing.
6. Actual Costing.
7. Standard Costing.
   a) How are yield issues handled?
   b) Demonstrate cost roll-up and inquiries available.
   c) Can standard costs be selectively changed (rolled)? (For example, all products, specific item, specific indented Bill of Materials, by general ledger, product class, other.)
   d) Demonstrate inquiries and reports that track effective date, revision, and ECO changes.

Inventory

8. Categories and accounts (Raw Materials, Work-in-Process, Finished Goods, In Transit, Demo)
   a) How does the system cost and track Research & Development and other restricted usage inventories?
   b) How does the system handle demo and loaner inventory? How does the system handle the return of demos and loaners to regular inventory?
   c) How are these returns handled if you must refurbish the equipment before being returned to inventory?
9. Show available inventory reports.
10. Cycle counting.
    a) Does the system allow posting of the cycle count expense to more than one general ledger account based on product or product class?

Shop Floor

11. Demonstrate a "rework" work order.
12. Demonstrate a work order with an outside operation.
13. Is shop floor a closed loop system?
14. Does it generate one report that shows inventory movement, labor and overhead absorption, outside operations receipts, variances?
15. What are assumptions in shop floor module regarding "over issues" and yields?
16. Can shop floor and work-in-process inventories be segregated by locations, product groups, or is all work-in-process recorded in one "bucket"?
17. Demonstrate types of variances and how variances are calculated.
18. Can shop floor variances be project accounted (for example, charged to an internal department, coded to a refurbishment account)? Can pilot lots be identified?
19. Capture and report labor information at the operation level.

Product Master

Information request topics

20. How many user-defined Product Master fields are available to accommodate product classifications by family, marketing class, product line?

Demonstration and discussion topics

21. How are product types switched (for example, Make to Buys, Phantom to Make, Obsolete items)?
22. Demonstrate product maintenance tools such as copy and paste and mass maintenance.

Cost of Sales

23. How does the system handle shipping items to customers at no charge (for example, warranty replacements, leased equipment)?

24. How does the system account for equipment placed at customers under lease arrangements?
25. Can the system accommodate builds and transfers of inventory to internal customers at less than standard cost (for example, at material cost only)?

Other

26. Demonstrate Performance Measures.
27. Demonstrate transaction history inquiries and reports. Are reports and inquiries available by product, product line, work order?
28. Demonstrate costing simulation capabilities based on current and future Bill of Materials and routings.
29. Demonstrate how the system stores, accesses, and compares historical cost information with current information.
30. What query and reporting tools are available?
31. What audit reports are available (for example, Work Order Aging, Obsolete Product with On-Hand Balances, Items with Zero Cost)?

Financial

General Ledger

1. General
   a) Demonstrate integration of modules (inventory, Accounts Receivable, Accounts Payable, Sales) into the General Ledger system including the ability to "drill down" from General Ledger to Accounts Payable and online account number validation.
   b) Demonstrate capabilities to extract General Ledger data to Excel.
   c) Demonstrate online inquiry capabilities including ability to view both sides of journal entry on screen.
   d) Demonstrate number of data storage years for actual and budgets.
2. Account Numbering
   a) Demonstrate ability to create new account numbers, both (1) manually and (2) automatically based on journal entry or interface from other modules such as Accounts Payable.

b) Demonstrate ability to perform mass creation and changes to certain account number blocks (for example, setting up a new department).

c) Demonstrate ability to change roll-up structure (for example, department rolls up to a new parent department).

3. Demonstrate the journal entry process including:
    a) Entries to invalid accounts.
    b) Viewing of entries prior to posting (including the interfaces from subsystems).
    c) Ability to change journal entries prior to posting.
    d) Posting Approval.
    e) Tagging of journal entries by user.
    f) Upload or "paste" from Excel.
    g) Entering notes with the journal entry.
    h) Account number "masking."
    i) Reversing, Recurring and Statistical entries.
    j) Discuss ability to bring in data from outside source such as ADP payroll and travel reimbursement.

4. Allocations
    a) Demonstrate multiple allocation capability including number of allocation types and the ability to perform mass maintenance of the allocations.

Reporting

5. Demonstrate user capabilities to write reports including the ability to "drag and drop" blocks of the chart of accounts (companies, departments, natural accounts, and product lines) and data types (budget, actual, and year).

6. Demonstrate the incorporation of Excel for reporting.
    a) Demonstrate dynamic access to the ledger directly from Excel.
    b) Demonstrate the pulling of data without running predefined queries.
    c) Demonstrate multidimensional capabilities from within Excel.

7. Demonstrate ability to "drill down" to underlying data from reports viewed online.

Foreign Currency

8. Demonstrate foreign currency capabilities.
9. Demonstrate translation from local currency to reporting currency.
10. Demonstrate calculation of realized and unrealized transaction gains and losses.

Budgeting

11. Demonstrate budgeting capabilities.
12. Demonstrate ability to upload data from Excel or other external source.

Accounts Receivable

13. Demonstrate identifying and maintaining non-paying customers (credit holds).
    a) Before an order is received.
    b) After order is processed but before it is shipped.
14. Demonstrate the ability to grant different customers different credit terms.
    a) Demonstrate the proper aging buckets on reports, including statements (for example, an invoice with 90-day terms would remain in the current bucket for 90 days).
    b) Demonstrate tracking and printing special terms on invoices.
15. Demonstrate how returns and credit memos work through the system.
16. Demonstrate ability to handle payments by credit and other electronic means (for example, Electronic Data Interchange).
17. Demonstrate system calculation of Freight and Sales Tax.
18. Demonstrate ability to send copies of invoices electronically to customers.
19. Demonstrate cash application capabilities and non Accounts Receivable cash application.
20. Demonstrate online inquiry capabilities.
21. Demonstrate the ability to handle leases and rentals (automatic recurring transactions).

22. Demonstrate ability to adjust invoice and statement formats including preparing invoices in foreign languages.
23. Demonstrate ability to generate current statements any day of the month, not just month end.
24. Demonstrate ability to enter notes by customer (for example, collection efforts).
25. Demonstrate how the system handles billing in foreign currencies including the granting on debit and credit memos. At issue is whether the debit and credit are at the current rate or can the system perform the transaction at the original rate.
26. Demonstrate ability to calculate average payment days.
27. Demonstrate how system handles individual accounts within a corporate customer group.
28. Demonstrate imaging capabilities including the link to our optical imaging.
29. Demonstrate standard and user-defined reporting.

Accounts Payable

30. Demonstrate Electronic Data Interchange (EDI) to Vendor invoices.
31. Demonstrate integration with Purchase Order and receiving system.
32. Demonstrate how you set up new vendors.
33. Demonstrate typical batch processing (for example, cover sheets, transaction reports).
34. Demonstrate tracking of discounts.
35. Demonstrate ability to pay vendors by credit card.
36. Demonstrate tracking of Debit memos and the Return to Vendor process.
37. Demonstrate logging and approval of invoices requiring management approval.
38. Demonstrate ability to enter an invoice without generating a journal entry pending inventory receipt or approval.
39. Demonstrate calculation and reporting of Purchase Price Variance (PPV) and booking to General Ledger.
40. Demonstrate how system handles "Received but not Invoiced" (including detailed reporting).
41. Demonstrate the ability to process manual checks through the system including automatic printing.

42. Demonstrate imaging capabilities including the link to our optical imaging.
43. Demonstrate 1099 capabilities.
44. Demonstrate how system handles voids.
45. Demonstrate reporting capabilities, both standard and user defined.

Fixed Assets

46. Demonstrate asset tagging system.
47. Demonstrate ability to track multiple depreciation methods
    a) Book
    b) Tax
    c) Other
    d) Suspension of depreciation for a number of months
48. Demonstrate ability to sort assets
    a) By location
    b) By General Ledger account
    c) By department
49. Demonstrate standard and user-defined reporting.
50. Demonstrate ability to project depreciation by department or General Ledger account.
51. Demonstrate automatic updating of fixed assets from Accounts Payable.
52. Demonstrate mass and partial transfers of assets between companies.
53. Demonstrate physical inventory capabilities.

Project Accounting

54. Demonstrate overall functionality.
55. Demonstrate integration into the General Ledger and Accounts Payable.

Order Entry

Customer Information

Information request topics

1. Capability to automatically check Federal Government Table of Denials
   a) Interface with other government agencies (from other countries).
   b) Interactive at order entry.

Demonstration and discussion topics

2. Create both a domestic and an international customer bill to, ship to, sold to, and intermediate consignee. Include demonstration of customer master and customer search capabilities.
3. Demonstrate customer hierarchy and classification capabilities.
   a) Corporate or group buying accounts.
   b) Multiple classifications (groups) for sales reporting.
   c) Separate and common information by customer group.
   d) Capability to have customer history follow customer number in the event of change of status.
   e) History by bill to and/or ship to.
4. Demonstrate customer tax and tax exemption capability:
   a) Exemption certificates.
   b) Tax by county, state, zip code.
   c) Demonstrate ability to tax or not tax by: service, capital equipment, product, freight, duty, VAT (by specific tax set-ups).
   d) Calculate and validate sales tax from automatically updated tables with effective dates.
   e) Interface with tax packages.
5. Show extensive note capability:
   a) By customer
   b) Ability to direct printing on (export and shipping) documents
   c) Interface with word program or Windows mailing programs

Freight Charges

6. Demonstrate the different methodologies available to charge freight.

Pricing Capabilities

7. Demonstrate pricing methodologies available:
   a) Is there one pricing module for the entire system?
   b) Cost per reportable and meter contracts.
   c) Display options for pricing in foreign currencies.
   d) Price effective dates, protection and history.
   e) Demonstrate ability to track source of pricing (for example, bid, quote, inter-company).

8. Demonstrate promotional pricing capabilities.
9. Demonstrate price increase capabilities, list and contract
   a) Are "what if" parameters available?
   b) Price and profitability analysis.
   c) Ability to easily download to Excel.

Order Entry

10. Order Header information, demonstrate:
    a) Ability to add ship to from order entry.
    b) Data and documentation requirements.
    c) Specific order text (ability to print on different documents).
    d) Order type: billing, inter- and intra-company, repair, replacement, warranty (also this ability to be available by line item).
    e) Shipping codes, including: specific carrier codes to be interfaced with carrier systems (for example, FedEx, Airborne, UPS).
11. Demonstrate credit and other "hold" abilities, including:
    a) Regulatory holds: by product, customer, country, and lot number.
    b) Credit check and hold at order entry and prior to shipment.
    c) NRC (Nuclear Regulatory Commission) holds: by product type and customer.
    d) Other user-defined hold options available.
12. Demonstrate display of critical account status capabilities.
13. Demonstrate order entry to display:
    a) Source of pricing.
    b) Demonstrate interaction between allocation and order entry program including warehouse, availability of product, and manual allocation.
14. Demonstrate generation of standing orders; multiple delivery dates.
15. Demonstrate generation of multiple (hundreds) of orders for specific product(s), including one change to multiple orders.
16. Demonstrate ability to generate online:
    a) Accept orders via Electronic Data Interchange (EDI).
    b) Order acknowledgments via fax or EDI to customer.
    c) Invoice via fax or EDI to customer.
17. Demonstrate ability to handle advanced replacements and returned goods.
18. Demonstrate ability to track no charge reason codes by line item.

19. Demonstrate features and options capabilities.
20. Demonstrate ability to keep track of movement of systems and product, including inter- and intra-company.
21. Demonstrate ability to check customer buying and secrecy agreements (block certain customers and customer groups from specific products and product lines).
22. Demonstrate online capabilities to cross reference customer part numbers, including OEM part number, internal part number conversions, and alternate part numbers.
23. Demonstrate ability to:
    a) Generate a shopping list for a particular customer.
    b) Generate warning if customer has never purchased specific item or item in that quantity level.
24. How does system handle unit of measure and alternate unit of measure?
    a) Order and invoice unit of measure = each and ship measure = case.
25. Demonstrate drop shipment capabilities.
26. Demonstrate online order inquiry.
27. Demonstrate ability to process credit card orders. Is authorization process through Electronic Data Interchange (EDI) possible?

Invoices

Information request topics

28. Review invoice processing options. Is the processing online or in batch?

Demonstration and discussion topics

29. Does the system have the ability to handle progress payments (multiple payment terms) by line item? Down payment (or progress billing without shipment) must only create an Accounts Receivable transaction, the final invoice will create the sales transaction.
30. Demonstrate ability to invoice in U.S. dollars and foreign currencies. Include the ability to change the local or default currency.

31. Demonstrate ability to handle credit and re-invoicing; adjustments to Accounts Receivable, inventory or sales.
    a) Possible interface required with service system.
32. Does the system have the ability to invoice for freight, taxes, legalization, non-standard (non-inventoried) parts and other miscellaneous charges?
    a) Billings only.
33. Provide the following documents:
    a) Invoice
    b) Proforma invoice

Contract Compliance, Quotations, and Bid Process

34. Demonstrate the ability to generate a quotation at a generic level, not as a specific order.
    a) Convert quotation to an order.
    b) Convert quotation to a contract.
35. Demonstrate the ability to track quotations and how quotes interface to the contract compliance system.
    a) Lost bids (with reasons).
    b) Bid awards.
    c) Bid via Electronic Data Interchange (EDI).
36. Does the system have immediate margin visibility? Do financial statements include depreciation and service charges? Are there any ties to field automation?
37. Demonstrate the ability to establish and record contracts.
    a) Show generation of contract paperwork and ability to online fax or Electronic Data Interchange (EDI) to customers.
    b) Purchase commitments.
    c) Effective dates for products and pricing (multiple terms per contract).
    d) Validation time periods for evaluation.
    e) Audit trails for changes.
38. Demonstrate ability to record OEM sales against contracts. Can the system handle multiple vendors on one contract?
39. Demonstrate how sales history interfaces with contract commitment compliance based on:

a) Product number, number of tests.
b) Group purchasing organizations.
c) What user-defined fields are available?
40. Demonstrate online inquiry capabilities.
41. Demonstrate how the pricing module interfaces with contract compliance system.
42. Demonstrate report capabilities in the contract module.

Shipping

Information request topics

1. Illustrate steps involved in picking, packing, and shipping.
2. Picking orders:
   a) Is there batch allocation and print process?
   b) Does it print only items to be picked?
   c) Do pick lists show location of items?
   d) Will pick slip's reference customer part numbers?
3. Can the system generate export and shipping documents, including:
   a) Document requirements by country or state or product?
   b) Certificates of origin, printed in regional format and language?
   c) North American Free Trade Agreement (NAFTA) certificates?
   d) Shipper's Export Documentation (in U.S. dollars for invoices in foreign currencies, in foreign currencies for shipment from other plants)?
   e) Dangerous goods documents; International Air Traffic Association (IATA)? Department of Transportation (DOT), European community?
   f) Language conversion, including invoice, products, multiple currencies?
   g) Any other International documents available (worldwide)?
4. Can the system cross reference license information (General Destination License)?
   a) Final destination clearance and embargoed destinations.
5. Does the system interface with:
   a) Freight forwarder (manifest)?
   b) Electronic transfer of invoice and shipping documents to forwarders and customers?

Demonstration and discussion topics

6. Demonstrate logic to fill forward pick locations
   a) Wave picking.
7. Demonstrate pick list, pack list, and load list
   a) Show the ability to display pick list on scanner instead of paper (paperless approach).
   b) Demonstrate bar code verification of pick list.
   c) Demonstrate ability for special packaging and labeling requirements
      i)   By product
      ii) By customer
      iii) By product destination
      iv) By carrier
   d) Automatically calculate anticipated shipping containers; weights and dimensions. Include weight of special packaging materials.
8. Picking orders:
   a) Is there a user-defined picking template?
9. Demonstrate shipment consolidation across sales orders, pack by sales order or destination.
10. Demonstrate shipment consolidation across plants.
11. Demonstrate the ability to generate an invoice at any time through the order management process, including after original printing.
12. Demonstrate the ability to edit an invoice.
13. Demonstrate the ability to track and generate product-specific documents andcustomer and product (lot)-specific documents.
14. Demonstrate multiple modes of transportation by sales order or by line item.
15. Demonstrate Cash on Delivery (COD) capabilities; calculations and display of costs, include the ability to handle CODs with multiple modes of transportation.
16. Demonstrate cross docking capabilities.
17. Demonstrate drop shipment capabilities. For drop shipment from a vendor, is the interface to purchasing automatic?
18. Demonstrate kit ordering and shipping.
19. How is ship complete supported?
20. How does the system handle back orders?

Allocations

21. What allocation protocols are available?
    a) Can there be user-defined order allocation?
    b) Will system allow for multiple expiration dates per product (by country)?
    c) Are there user-defined time fence and impact rules?
    d) Can future order allocation time fence be established and can it be order dependent?
    e) Is there hard assignments of allocations, from order entry?
22. How does system handle fair share allocation of limited inventory?
    a) Are there user-defined reports to determine value of inventory allocated but not shipped?
23. Demonstrate how the system will handle multiple expiration dates for specific products in the allocation program.

Import

24. Demonstrate ability to store and utilize (with effective dates).
    a) Harmonized tariff codes by country.
    b) FDA codes and device listing numbers.
    c) USDA (U.S. Department of Agriculture) import permit numbers.
    d) FCC, CSA, CE mark, UL listing.
25. Country of Origin: Demonstrate how it interfaces with:
    a) Purchasing.
    b) Costing (Duties).
    c) Receiving.
    d) Export.

Sales Reporting

1. Demonstrate the flexibility and set-up. Show hierarchy levels, elements, and data types.
2. Demonstrate the capability to view data in previous (historical) groupings and in current groupings.
3. Online flexibility to define in which groups data with no realignments.

4. Interfaces to other systems:
   a) Territory alignment.
   b) Commissions.
   c) Sales Force Automation.
      i) Profit and loss models.
      ii) Mailings.
      iii) Contacts — remote capability to update customer information.
      iv) Remote printing of sales reports.
   d) Forecasting.
   e) Planning.
   f) Budgeting with ability to upload to sales analysis system.
   g) Trending.
5. Demonstrate Customer Lead Database — remote capability to update customer information.
6. Demonstrate simulation capability with territory alignments and realignments (manipulation of data).
7. Demonstrate ability to have contract information and profit and loss statement by customer.
8. Demonstrate the ability to capture individual products, classes of products, or manufacturer of products for which royalties must be paid and manipulate this data.
9. Demonstrate worldwide sales reporting:
   a) How different profit centers on the same software system view third-party sales and gross margins worldwide.
   b) OEM and drop shipment sales reporting.
   c) Customer Grouping: Identify the number of groups available (for example, corporate accounts, World Health Organization).
   d) Key customers, key products, trending with graphing, Average Unit Price calculations, margin calculations.
   e) Individual prices on each sale — not just Average Unit Price which includes no charge goods in calculation.
   f) Open order query availability.

Technical

Software

1. In what language is the software written? In what year was your software originally written?

2. How often do you have major releases?
3. What databases does it use?
4. Is the entire system Graphical User Interface and Client/Server, or just portions? Do you also have "green screen" versions available to those not having PCs? Are screens graphical, full windows, or menu driven?
5. How much of the system is object oriented? Show us what that means in your system.
6. Do you get source code when you buy the system?
7. We would like to see a copy of your programming standards. We would like to see a program listing of the order entry screen and the MRP generation.
8. Is the system truly integrated? Show it.
9. Are all aspects of your system truly online? Show it.
10. How many batch jobs are there? Provide a list of the batch jobs. How are nightly, month-end, year-end processing controlled? Can this processing be done unattended?
11. Is there an integrated job scheduler for easy automation of routine functions such as report generation, Uploads, Downloads, Job Processes, etc.? If so, demonstrate the steps required to add a new schedule and to change an existing schedule. If not, do you have a partner organization that can provide this?
12. Is your system year 2000 compliant? How is it done, is there one date module? Can this module be easily integrated into other applications?
13. Discuss disaster recovery.
14. Discuss planned software improvements with timeline.
15. Is SQL part of your programming methods?
16. Is the file structure dynamic or does it require rebuilding to add, change, or delete a field or file?
17. Electronic Data Interface (EDI):
    a) Is your EDI module another vendor's package or customized to your system?
    b) Demonstrate the interfaces used to handle and correct problem transactions.
    c) Demonstrate the trading-partner set-up and document mapping processes.
    d) Discuss the intervention required in normal day-to-day processing.
    e) Must have EDI capabilities for the following: Order Entry, Bid Process, Shipping, Receiving, Purchasing, Invoicing, Credit Card

Approval, Acknowledgments, EDI to Fax and vice versa, Automated Communications Processing.

f) Do you have any Value Added Networks business relationships?
g) Demonstrate the management and auditing tools and reports available.

Hardware

18. On what hardware does the software run?
19. On what operating systems will your software run?
20. How long after general availability of operating system upgrades can we expect before your application has been tested and certified for use with this upgrade? If changes are required to your code as a result of an operating system change, how long can we expect this to take?
21. How many different packages do you have available (for example, UNIX version, AS/400 version)? What is your revenue breakdown by platform? Do the packages contain identical business functionality? Do the packages have separate sets of code to maintain, or is the code generated?
22. Is your company involved in any early experience testing with the operating system vendor such that your application is proven to function with the proposed operating system changes prior to general availability of the operating system update?
23. Are there any particular network requirements?
24. Are there any proprietary routers or drivers required on the host system to facilitate client server architecture?
25. Is your application accessible from remote sites via dial-up capabilities? If so, what are the bandwidth requirements for this connection methodology? What emulation do you suggest or require? Does the emulated screen closely resemble the host-attached screen? Are function keys and keyboard maps identical between dial-up and host-attached systems?
26. What are the PC requirements?
27. Do you provide an ODBC DLL for your database? If not, is one available? Is a 32-bit ODBC DLL available?

System Maintenance

28. How often do you release upgrades? How do you handle fixes? Are there monthly tapes distributed with cumulative patches for problems?
29. How do you make modifications?
30. How do you apply upgrades or releases and carry forth modifications?
31. If I asked your average customer, how long does it take to install an upgrade?
32. What is the average number of file changes per upgrade such as new fields or redefining old fields or splitting files?
33. Show how to change a screen. For example, suppose the users wanted to change "item number" to be called "company number" on every screen, how would you do it? Can a user do it, or is it an Information Systems function?
34. Are there debugging and testing tools available?
35. What systems documentation do you have available?
36. Is there a program code generator?
37. Was the software written with CASE? Are there CASE tools available?
38. How many flex fields or user-defined fields do you have? How many fields for order header and order detail? Can the user define a flex field, or is it an Information Systems function? Show how to set up the use of a user-defined flex field.
39. Do upgrades generally require more hardware?
40. Is there an additional charge to increase the number of users or the CPU platform?
41. How do you size the hardware that we will need? What is your track record on accuracy of sizing?
42. Do you have a change management system?
43. How do you handle record locking?

Security

44. What levels of security do you have (for example, screen, field)? Is it every field, or just some? Show how to maintain security for a screen or a field. Is it an Information Systems or a user function?
45. Demo your menu system.
46. Is encryption available for files electronically transferred?

Miscellaneous

47. Do you have any conversion aids or current software packages? Is there an import file structure for converting existing MRPII systems? How do you get the data there? Do you have to use IBM tapes? Will it accept Excel spreadsheets and if so, can a file be broken down into multiple sheets? Is there any communication hooks like SNA or X.25?

48. How do you handle distributed processing (for example, combining to produce worldwide information)? Do you need an entire copy of the data at the consolidated site? Can a transaction go out and get data from multiple CPUs and present the information consolidated?

49. Discuss any capabilities you have with workflow management. Can you visualize workflows graphically? Can you modify them without programming? Can workflow generate multiple messages for multiple users based on a single event? Can a user approval automatically trigger action in the system?

50. What is your turnover rate for programmers and developers? What is your turnover rate for customer support staff?

51. What kind of call tracking do you do in your customer support area? Show statistics from your customer support center. What is average length of time to close a call?

52. How many employees do you have for customer support? If I talk to one person today and my problem is not resolved, will I have to talk to a different person tomorrow and relay the story again?

53. Do you do Dial Up Support?

54. What about custom modifications? Where do you draw the line between a custom fix and a new feature to be incorporated in the next release.

55. What efforts have you made to move toward a paperless system? What tools are available for online report viewing and storage of print files?

56. Discuss the amount of training necessary for a technical person who will support your system.

5.

KEY REQUIREMENTS

Key Requirements — General

1. Vendor vision and direction are in alignment with our company vision and direction.
2. Vendor has strong international organization.
3. Vendor has quality support record in U.S. and Europe.
4. Vendor is financially stable.
5. Vendor focus is in similar markets as our business.
6. Stable vendor customer base
   - Growing market presence
   - Low rate of customers lost
   - Active user groups
7. Executive Information Systems: worldwide, real-time financial and manufacturing information for measuring past and projecting future, including Profit and Loss by business unit, product line.
8. Easy-to-use system (ease of navigation, intuitive, user documentation and help, consistency throughout the system, systems integration, GUI, client/server)
9. Drill down help menus.
10. Easy to us *ad hoc* reporting and queries (user report writer at different levels, EIS).
11. Flexible system with the ability to modify system without programming changes (table drive, object oriented, ability to change process flows).
12. Automated functionality such as EDI, bar coding, paperless, online report viewing.

13. Reporting capabilities throughout all modules:
    - Easy to write reports including the ability to "drag and drop" blocks of the chart of accounts (companies, departments, natural accounts and product lines) and data types (budget/actual/year).
    - Ability to construct reports using data from up to five sources.
    - Ability to drill down to underlying data from reports viewed online.
    - Easy export/link to Excel for reporting.

Key Requirements — Manufacturing

1. Lot control, including lot tracking, lot allocations, lot visibility in MRP, lot potency, expiration, and USDA.
2. Worldwide control and management for sales orders, purchase orders, work orders, MRP, inventory visibility and transfers.
3. ECO links to MRP, shop floor, Bill of Materials, routings, including revision control, enhanced effective date system.
4. Manufacturing Execution System, finite scheduling, rule-based scheduling.
5. System-wide item control fields, such as:
    - Shelf life
    - Hazard control
    - Shipping conditions
    - Storage conditions
    - Domestic and international ship intervals
6. Capability to incorporate set-up and run-time in costing calculations.
7. Worldwide Distribution Requirements Planning capability.
8. Resource planning, including rough-cut, CRP with labor forecasting ability.
9. Engineering and R&D playpen for Bill of Materials, cost builds. Includes automated transfer to and from live structure.
10. Supply chain management functionality (logistics, EDI, exports, vendor/customer interfaces).
11. Quality tracking systems, for non-conformance, vendor quality, preventive action controls.
12. Simulation options and graphics.
13. Inventory Management System (forecast excess, models, model variances).

14. Worldwide forecasting (24 months, geographical, performance, and variance).
15. Workbench concept for key functions (forecasting, planning, buying, scheduling).
16. Multi-mode manufacturing environment (discrete, process).
17. Functionality to restrict usage and shipment of product by lot, product, customer, country, status.
18. CIM.

Key Requirements — Technical

1. Ability to easily and quickly obtain worldwide information without duplicating the data. This implies distributed processing capability and open systems.
2. Ability to easily interface to outside systems (for example, document control, CAD/CAM, bar coding). This implies open, non-proprietary database architecture, ODBC compliant.
3. Ease of maintenance and support (how modifications are done and carried forward, number of new releases and methods to install, systems documentation, customer support, automation of routine reports and processes, availability of source code and de-bugging aids, ease of modifying screens and reports, number of user-defined fields available and ease of implementing them).
4. Availability (7 days, 24 hours).
5. Secure (field, screen, person, group level security, disaster recovery, record locking).
6. Ease of implementation (conversion aids, support, implementation plan, training).
7. Year 2000 compliant (one date module).

Key Requirements — Distribution

1. Meet multi-national import and export statutory and regulatory requirements. Includes possible interface to governmental databases.
2. Domestic and International tax capabilities.
3. Domestic and International freight capabilities.

4. Regulatory and other "hold" capabilities at order entry (customer, product and lot levels).
5. Ease of order entry:
   - Availability of information.
   - Ability to order kits and cases under the same part number.
   - Standing orders.
   - Multiple orders.
   - Customer shopping lists (with warnings, suggestions at order entry) refreshed from recent history.
6. EDI:
   - Order entry/acknowledgments.
   - Invoicing.
   - Advanced shipping notices.
   - Credit card authorization and payment.
   - Bids, bid awards.
7. Product features and options capability at order entry screen.
8. OEM and drop shipment capabilities.
9. Multiple invoicing types (online, batch, proforma).
10. Convenient, efficient, and easy credit/debit processing.
11. Non-labor intensive contract system
    - Contract pricing (effective dates, documentation of pricing history metered [cost per test] contracts).
    - Bids and quotes.
    - Contract compliance.
    - Analysis of profitability by customer.
    - Pricing analysis with "what if" profitability analysis capabilities.
    - Automated price increase (list and contract) capabilities.
12. Automated shipping and warehousing:
    - Bar coding.
    - Forward pick locations.
    - Wave picking.
    - Picking templates.
    - Interface with forwarders and airlines.
    - Cross docking.
13. Automatically generated shipping documents (country, state, carrier, and/or product specific), including dangerous goods documentation.
14. Shipment consolidation across warehouses and plants; shipment separation for optimal use of cost-effective carriers.

15. Allocations:
    - Time fences.
    - Online.
    - Batch processing.
    - Fair share.
16. Need ability to attach country of origin at product level and lot level.
17. Extremely user-friendly Sales Analysis system with "what if" capabilities
    - Many (>30) available reporting hierarchy levels (company, territory, product families and classes, etc.)
    - Multiple classes and families.
    - Group Purchasing Organizations.
    - Capability to have customer history follow customer number in the event of change of status.
    - History by bill-to and ship-to.
    - Can quickly define reporting periods and data types (actual, budget, prior year, etc.)
    - Integrated graphics capability.
    - Ability to perform price/volume analysis.
    - "What if" analysis for territory realignments.

Key Requirements — Cost Accounting

1. Availability and functionality of alternative costing methodologies (Theory of Constraints, Activity Based Costing, Actual Cost, Average Actual Cost).
2. Ability to create alternative measurements of manufacturing performance (for example, reporting tools able to draw information from various sources).
3. Multiple costs supported for the same item (for example, same product is produced at two locations, but will have different costs because of local differences in costs).
4. What types of cost drivers are available for absorbing overhead into product cost (for example, machine hours, direct labor hours, completed units)?
5. Can standard costs be selectively changed (rolled) (for example, all products, specific item, specific indented Bill of Materials, by general ledger, product class, other)?

6. Is shop floor a closed loop system?
7. Can the system generate one shop floor report that shows inventory movement, labor and overhead absorption, outside operations receipts, variances?

Key Requirements — Finance

1. Integrated modules (Inventory, Accounts Receivable, Accounts Payable, Sales) into the General Ledger system including the ability to drill down from General Ledger to Accounts Payable, and online account number validation in sub-ledger modules.
2. Account numbering:
   - Ability to create new account numbers, both manually and automatically based on journal entry or interface from other modules such as Accounts Payable.
   - Ability to perform mass creation/changes to certain account number blocks (for example, setting up a new department).
   - Ability to change roll-up structure (for example, department rolls up to a new parent department).
3. Advanced reporting features.
4. Credit hold functionality both before an order is received and after the order is processed, but before it is shipped.
5. Ability to grant different customers different credit terms.
   - Account aging buckets on reports (including statements) based on due date, not invoice date.
   - Demonstrate how special terms are tracked and printed on invoices.
6. Demonstrate cash application capabilities and non AR cash application.
7. Integration of Accounts Payable with Purchase Order and Receiving system.
8. Ability to track debit memos and the return to vendor process.
9. Imaging capabilities including the link to our optical imaging system.
10. Functional project accounting capability with integration into the General Ledger and Accounts Payable modules.

Index

A

Accounts payable, 224, 257–258
Accounts receivable, 224–225, 256–257
Acid tests, 31
Annual objectives, 23–24, 26, 28, 132–135
Application architecture, 6
Asset, information systems as an, 3–4

B

Backlog, 23–24, 26, 28, 81–86
Bar coding, 227
Benchmark information, 172
Bill of material script, 244
Billing, 222
Boundaries, 5, 40
Budgeting, 225, 256
Business
    Analysts, 77
    Application assessment, 24–26, 29,
        146–150
    Application description, 215–226
    Application environment, 65–68
    Charter, 36–37
    Detailed level direction, 21
    Direction, 21, 28–29, 34–36
    Drivers, 5–6, 40
    Environmental factors, 38
    Environmental requirements, 21, 26, 28,
        41–42
    Environmental requirements assessment,
        24–26, 144–145
    External requirements, 21, 26, 28, 41, 43
    External requirements assessment, 24–26
    Goals, 21, 26, 28, 35–37
    Goals, and information systems, 110–120
    High level direction, 21
    Information, 21, 26, 26, 28, 37
    Information needs assessment, 24–26,
        47–51
    Mission, 21, 26,35–37
    Objectives, 21, 26, 28, 35–37
    Operating vision, 18–19, 22, 26, 28, 44–47
    Operating vision assessment, 24–26,
        143–144
    Plan, 6, 19, 26, 36
    Priorities, 21, 26, 28, 37
    Processes, 23, 26, 28, 52–58
    Requirements, 23, 26, 28–29, 57–59
    Requirements assessment, 24–26, 150–151
    Strengths, 38
    Unit strategy, 33–34
    Values, 21, 26, 28, 35–37
    Vision, 21, 26, 28
    Weaknesses, 38

C

Capacity requirements planning (CRP), 219
CASE tools, 228
CD-ROM, 228

Client, 64, 125
Client/server, 121–125, 228
Conceptual
  Business level phase, 20–22, 27–46
  IS plan and vision phase, 20, 23–24,
    61–141
Contents, 25–27
Corporate strategy, 33–34
Cost and manufacturing accounting script,
    251–252
Costs, 171–172
Communication, improving, 3–4, 11
Company information script, 239–240
Competitive advantage, 7
Competitor profiles, 23–24, 26, 28–29,
    90–93
Components of a plan, 17–18
Computing architecture, 23–24, 26, 28,
    120–126
Cost accounting key requirements, 275–276
Costing, 223–224
CRUD criteria, 127
Current situation, 63
Custom software, 102–105
Customer
  Order entry, 222
  Requirements, 22, 41, 43

D

Data package, 205
Decision support, 64
Demo agenda, 206
Demonstration guidelines
  For vendor, 205–206
  For team participants, 205, 207
Desktop computing environment, 68–70
Detailed
  Business analysis phase, 20, 22–23, 46–60
  IS recommendation phase, 20, 24–25,
    143–211
  Script, 239–270
Distribution key requirements, 273–275
Distribution requirements planning (DRP)
    script, 246
Direction, 21
Disaster recovery, 121–125

Discrete and repetitive manufacturing
    execution, 220
Distribution, 222–223
Documentation, 64

E

EDI, 227
Environment, IS, 23–24, 26, 28, 63–63
Environmental
  Requirements, 22, 41–42
  Requirements assessment, 24–25, 144–145
ERP, 89
Executive committee, 11, 14–15
Executive committee presentation, 187–196
Executive management interviews, 36–39
Expectations of information systems, 7
Expenditures, 23–24, 26, 28, 79–81
External
  Requirements, 22, 41, 43
  Requirements assessment, 24–25, 146
  IS situation, 21, 86–93
Executive interviews, 21–22

F

Finance, 223–225
Finance key requirements, 276
Financial
  Script, 254–258
  Summary, 22
Fixed assets, 223, 258
Forecasting, 221, 246
Full speed ahead phase, 232
Functional automation, 64

G

Gap from current to future, 18, 21, 24–26,
    29, 143–157, 193
General software feature script, 242
General ledger, 223, 254–256
Getting
  Started phase, 231–232
  On course phase, 232

Global
   Information, 126–130
   Objectives, 46
Going in circles phase, 232

H

HELPdesk, 75–78

I

Imaging processing, 228
Implementation
   Phase summary, 195
   Team, 11, 15–16
Industry
   Trends, 23–24, 26, 87–90
   Summary, 22
Information
   Architecture, 23–24, 28, 126–130
   Flow 3,6
   Needs, 23, 47–51
   Needs assessment, 24–25, 146
Information Systems
   And the business goals, 23–24
   Annual objectives, 23–24, 26, 28
   Backlog, 23–24, 26, 28, 81–86
   Computing architecture, 23–24, 26, 28
   Current situation, 63
   Environment, 23–24, 26, 28, 63–64
   Executive committee, 11, 14–15
   Expenditures, 23–24, 26, 28, 79–81
   Industry trends, 23–24, 26, 28, 87–90
   Information architecture, 23–24, 28
   Interviews, 61–63
   Mission, 23–24, 26, 28, 96–98
   Objectives, 100–102
   Organization, 11, 15, 23–24, 26, 28, 72–79, 135–140
   Policies and responsibilities, 23–24, 26, 28
   Processes, 135–136
   Service architecture, 23–24, 26, 28, 135–140
   Steering committee, 11–14, 27, 191
   Strategies, 23–24, 26, 28, 102–110
   Strategic objectives, 23–24, 26, 28, 100–102

Vision, 23–24, 26, 28, 98–99
Infrastructure projects, 81–86
Interface script, 242
Internal information systems situation, 21
Internet, 228
Inventory control, 215–216, 248–249, 252
Involving the organization, 9–16
Iterative planning framework, 211

J

JIT, 89

K

Key
   Criteria decision table, 169–170
   Measures, 47–51
   Requirements, 205, 271–276

L

LAN, 227
   Environment, 68–70
Life cycle, 3, 7–9
   Improved steps, 8,10
   Typical steps, 8
   Time on improved steps, 8,10
   Time on typical steps, 8–9
Lines of code, 67–68
Linking to the business, 3, 4–6, 9
Lot master script, 244–245

M

Macro business processes, 52–53
Major projects, 82
Make versus buy decision, 103–105
Management
   Overview, 183–187
   Summary, 190
Manufacturing
   Control, 218–219
   Evolution, 89

Execution system (MES) script, 247
 Key requirements, 272–273
 Script, 243–254
Master production scheduling (MPS), 217, 246
Material requirements planning (MRP), 218, 246–247
Micro business processes, 53–54
Minor projects, 82
Mission, 23–24, 26, 28, 96–98
MRP, 89
MRPII, 89

N

Navigation script, 240–241
Network, 64, 70–72
 Faxing, 228
 Group, 76

O

Objectives, 23–24, 26, 28, 100–102, 132–135
Object oriented programming, 229
Office automation, 64
Open, 121–125, 227
Operating software, 64
Operating vision, 22, 44–47
Options, 24–25
Option
 Analysis, 171–177, 193
 Identification, 160–161
 Summary, 194
Order entry script, 258–263
Organization
 Information systems, 11, 15, 72–79
 Involvement, 9–16
Outsourcing, 103

P

Packaged software, 102–105
Palmtop computers, 229
Part master script, 243

PC environment, 68–70
 support group, 75
Pen based computers, 229
Phases of the planning process, 20–21
Phase
 1: Conceptual business level, 21–22, 27–46
 2: Detailed business analysis, 22–23, 46–60
 3: Conceptual information systems plan and vision, 23–24, 61–141
 4: Detailed information systems recommendation, 24–25, 143–211
Phases of information systems growth, 87–88
Plan
 Boundaries, 30–31
 Components, 17–18
 Contents, 25–27
 Process, 19–25, 26, 28–30, 32
 Purpose, 3–8, 21–22, 26, 28–30, 32
 Scope, 22, 26, 28–31, 32
Planning groups, 29
Policies, 23–24, 26, 28, 130–131
Portfolio management, 33–34
Prioritizing
 Business processes, 55–57
 By business objective, 133
 By forced ranking, 134
 By business criteria, 134–135
 Projects, 132–135
Process, 19–25, 26, 28–30, 32, 52–58
Production and resource plan script, 245
Product structure, 216–217
Programming group, 76
Projects, 81–86
Project
 Accounting script, 258
 Backlog, 81–86
 Budget, 203
 Communication, 202
 Goals, 199
 Kick-off meeting, 203
 Logo, 198
 Scope, 199
 Schedule, 203
 Roles and responsibilities, 199–201
 Team organization, 199
 Mission, 199

Name, 198
Plan, 198–199
Purchasing and receiving, 220–221, 247
Purpose
    Of the plan, 3–8, 21–22, 26, 28–30, 32
    Of planning, 1–8

Q

Quality
    Assurance compliance guidelines, 202
    Script, 249–251

R

Rapid prototyping, 228
Rating methodology, 205
Recommendation, 21, 24–25, 29, 177,
    208–209
Re-engineering, 52–57
Relational databases, 121–125, 228
Report writer script, 241
Resources, 3, 7
Resources to implement, 172
Resource hours, 84–85
Restructuring, 55
Request for quote, 162–166
    Questionnaire, 164–166
    Response review, 166–170
Risk management, 209–210
Rough cut capacity plan, 246
ROI analysis, 24–25, 29, 178–181
Routing script, 243–244

S

Sales reporting script, 265–266
SCI, 89
Scope, 22, 26, 28–31, 32
Script, 204, 239–270
Server, 64
Service architecture, 6, 23–24, 26, 28,
    135–140
Service architecture assessment, 152–153
Shipping, 222–223, 263–264

Shop floor control script, 248, 253
Situation analysis, 18
Skill set criteria, 138–140
Squeaky wheel syndrome, 95
Stages of team development, 231–237
Steering committee, 11–14, 27, 191
Strategy
    Formulation, 18
    Implementation, 18
Strategies, 23–24, 26, 28, 102–110
Strategic objectives, 23–24, 26, 28,
    100–102
Strategic projects, 103–104
Supplier requirements, 22, 41, 43
Support, 82
System implementation script, 240

T

Table of contents, 27–29
Team
    Development, 231–237
    Improvement, 235–237
    Temperature, 233–234
Technical
    Architecture, 6
    Computing architecture assessment,
        24–26, 151–152
    Key requirements, 273
    Script, 266–270
Technology
    Description, 227–229
    Evolution, 89
    Trend impact, 91–92
Time to implement, 172
TQM, 89
Training plan, 203
Transforming events, 160

V

Vendor review, 204
    Introduction to company, 207–208
    Selection, 208
    Team, 11, 15–16, 27, 197

Vendor software packages, 102–105
Video teleconferencing, 227
Vision, 23–24, 26, 28, 98–99

Wireless communications, 229
Work group software, 228
Worldwide locations, 86

W

Why now, 189
Wide area networks, 228

X

X.400 e-mail standard, 227
X.500 e-mail standard, 229